TO GOVERN IS TO SERVE

A VOLUME IN THE SERIES

Medieval Societies, Religions, and Cultures
Edited by M. Cecilia Gaposchkin and Anne E. Lester

A list of titles in this series is available at cornellpress.cornell.edu.

TO GOVERN IS TO SERVE

AN ESSAY ON MEDIEVAL DEMOCRACY

Jacques Dalarun

Translated and with an introduction
by **SEAN L. FIELD**

Foreword by M. Cecilia Gaposchkin and Anne E. Lester

CORNELL UNIVERSITY PRESS
Ithaca and London

Originally published in 2012 as *Gouverner c'est servir: Essai de démocratie médiévale* by Alma Editeur, Paris. Copyright © 2012 by Jacques Dalarun.

English-language translation and introduction by Sean L. Field and foreword by M. Cecilia Gaposchkin and Anne E. Lester copyright © 2023 by Cornell University.

Cet ouvrage a bénéficié du soutien des Programmes d'aide à la publication de l'Institut français.

The English-language edition of this book has benefited from the support of the Institut Français's publication assistance programs.

All rights reserved. Except for brief quotations in a review, this book, or parts thereof, must not be reproduced in any form without permission in writing from the publisher. For information, address Cornell University Press, Sage House, 512 East State Street, Ithaca, New York 14850. Visit our website at cornellpress.cornell.edu.

First published 2023 by Cornell University Press

Library of Congress Cataloging-in-Publication Data

Names: Dalarun, Jacques, author. | Field, Sean L. (Sean Linscott), 1970– translator.
Title: To govern is to serve : an essay on medieval democracy / Jacques Dalarun ; translated and with an introduction by Sean L. Field ; foreword by M. Cecilia Gaposchkin and Anne E. Lester.
Other titles: Gouverner c'est servir. English
Description: Ithaca [New York] : Cornell University Press, 2023. | Series: Medieval societies, religions, and cultures. | Translation of: Gouverner c'est servir : essai de démocratie médiévale. | Includes bibliographical references and index.
Identifiers: LCCN 2022014426 (print) | LCCN 2022014427 (ebook) | ISBN 9781501767852 (hardcover) | ISBN 9781501768354 (paperback) | ISBN 9781501767869 (epub) | ISBN 9781501767876 (pdf)
Subjects: LCSH: Power (Christian theology)—History of doctrines—Middle Ages, 600–1500. | Political theology—History of doctrines—Middle Ages, 600–1500.
Classification: LCC BT738.25 .D3513 2023 (print) | LCC BT738.25 (ebook) | DDC 261—dc23/eng/20220909
LC record available at https://lccn.loc.gov/2022014426
LC ebook record available at https://lccn.loc.gov/2022014427

This game of the government of some by others, of everyday government, of pastoral government, it is this that was regarded for fifteen centuries as the science par excellence, the art of all arts, the knowledge of all knowledges.
—Michel Foucault

Contents

Series Editors' Foreword ix
List of Abbreviations xiii
Translator's Introduction xv

Preface	1
PART ONE: THE SERVANT SERVED	5
1. A Shocking Story	7
2. Sisters	14
3. Assisi	23
4. Ritual	31
5. Body	39
6. Inversions	45
7. Paradox	54
PART TWO: UNWORTHINESS IN POWER	63
1. Benedictine Beginnings	65
2. Fontevraud	70
3. The Paraclete	79
4. Grandmont I: Facts	88
5. Grandmont II: Conjectures	93
6. Preachers	103
7. Lesser Brothers I: Writings by and about Francis	111
8. Lesser Brothers II: Chronicles	120
9. Lesser Brothers III: About Face	127
10. Experiments	134
PART THREE: MATERNAL GOVERNMENT	141
1. Treasure Trove	143
2. Pastorate	149

CONTENTS

3. A Note — 160
4. Mother — 167
5. Word by Word — 173
6. Resumption — 181
7. Bonds — 188

Afterword — 196

Bibliography 205

Index 225

Series Editors' Foreword

First published in French in 2012, Jacques Dalarun's *Gouverner c'est servir: Essai de démocratie médiévale* has been translated into Italian (2015), Spanish (2018), Portuguese (2021), and now—a little more than a decade after its original appearance—into English by Sean Field, himself an eminent medievalist, who has produced an elegant and updated version for English-speaking readers. In lucid prose, Dalarun offers his readers a forensic yet poetic exploration of the theme of governance as service. Through a compelling application of Michel Foucault's arguments to the specifics of religious history, Dalarun unfolds a new perspective on the history of democracy as a form of constituted governance. The book has lost none of its importance or relevance in the decade since its initial publication in French. Indeed, its central preoccupations with power, leadership, and virtue are if nothing more relevant now, both to the scholarly moment and to the contemporary world.

Jacques Dalarun is the former director of the medieval department of the École Française de Rome and of the Institut de Recherche et d'Histoire des Textes (IRHT), and a member of the Institut de France (Académie des Inscription et Belles-Lettres), as well as a corresponding fellow of the Medieval Academy of America. He is also author or coauthor of over twenty books, and director, editor, or coauthor of over twenty more editions and collections of essays dealing with religious, monastic, and particularly Franciscan history of the high Middle Ages. The texts and ideas that form the center of the present book have occupied his thought for much of his career. Here, in *To Govern Is to Serve*, Dalarun addresses cutting-edge manuscript discoveries and situates them within the framework of decades of scholarship, theory, and questioning focused on religious governance and pastoral authority. The book's animating provocation is Dalarun's identification of the central paradox of Christianity: how it was that a religion of the margins became the dominant ideology and thus locus of power in the medieval West and what that meant for the conceptions of governance to take institutional forms. To address this paradox, Dalarun offers an extended essay on governance as service. Here we meet an ideology of governance that has its roots in the religious sphere, in a specific notion of pastoral care and motherly consolation. What, he asks, does it mean—in practice, in communities, and in the political sphere—for a leader to be a servant to the servant? How is it that the medieval West came to offer up an example of governance built upon an inversion of power as a form of power?

There are many reasons to read this book, particularly at this moment. To delight in the sheer virtuosity of Dalarun's extended exposition of a single episode from the life of St. Clare as we see in part 1. Or to follow the careful historical analysis of governing and the dynamics of power within the monastic and mendicant reform movements of the High Middle Ages. And there is the innovative and provocative new reading of St. Francis's own articulations of governance as "mothering"—although not so much with its traditional association with nurturing as with a more powerful compulsion toward consolation. And in the end, there is Dalarun's use of history as a vehicle of political philosophy. Among the many reasons to read this book, however, we want to highlight three that make *To Govern Is to Serve* especially compelling for inclusion in this series dedicated to exploring and redefining Medieval Societies, Religions, and Cultures.

First, the present book is quite simply an exquisite demonstration of the practice of close reading as a technique, that is, a *techne*, a way of doing something, and a methodology, a commitment to a scholarly practice that opens a source or set of sources to deeper meaning and interpretation. Dalarun's close attention in part 1 to a single episode toward the end of Clare of Assisi's life is a deft demonstration of how to read medieval sources, how to interpret hagiography, and how an exploration of the smallest actions can invite myriad meanings. This practice of working over and working within a text was familiar to medieval people as the act of *ruminatio*, rumination, the four-fold digestion of word, sense, meaning, and parable or allegory. But Dalarun moves masterfully one step further to show what the intimacies of history afford us: a closeness to our subjects, to their actions, to their character and their context. In the case of Clare and Francis, this intimacy yields a greater understanding of the very special kind of authority created through inversion, by making the lesser great, by serving the servant. Some close readings lay bare the paradox.

Second, by turning, or indeed returning, to the nature of governance, Dalarun invites the reader into a much longer and broader intellectual dialogue on the history and philosophy of governmentality, one that take us explicitly to Foucault in the late 1970s. In reading *To Govern Is to Serve* one is witness to an on-going conversation between Foucault the political philosopher and Dalarun the historian and scholar of medieval religious life and practice. Together they find common ground in articulating the place of religion in society and the role social dynamics play in shaping religion, meeting in a discussion of pastoral authority that identifies the pastor as leader and servant. In our present age when Foucault and his arguments have permeated the terms of analysis and have become so much a part of contemporary ways of reading and thinking as to be unrecognizable (as in unnoticed, itself a certain trait of ideology), Dalarun's explicit application of Foucault's ideas as *method* demonstrates what a revelation Foucault's thinking was for an earlier generation of historians. In this way, the book serves as a historiographical explanation and methodological guide to much of the previous half century of scholarship that addressed questions of power and governance; self and society; body and regulation; legitimacy and authority; ideology and its functions. In this exchange, Dalarun offers a powerful conclusion: "Medieval historians thus have much to contribute to the history of governmentality." This contribution is not in the realm of coercive power from the top down as is so often portrayed in popular culture and the media, but in the careful working out over generations of what it meant to keep peace, to trust and put faith in others, and to care for communities within communities. We still have much to learn from this medieval example, especially in reaffirming our own practices of democracy.

Finally, Dalarun engages with governance as a core subject of the Middle Ages by linking its evolution within monastic circles to its forms and cadences in the political sphere as exemplified in cultures of lordship and obligation and in the development of the medieval state. This intervention, reinforced by his reading of both Foucault and monastic normative texts, is perhaps the boldest and most definitive for shaping our understanding of medieval political ideology. In this reading, Dalarun traces a genealogy of governance and locates its roots in the monastic impulse to embrace obedience and humility as the highest form of self-regulation and communal leadership. *To Govern Is to Serve* must now be read alongside earlier studies of the medieval state and political theology such as the works of Joseph Strayer and Ernst Kantorowicz, to name but two prominent examples. Yet, whereas an earlier generation of scholars built their conclusions from legal codes, political treatises, texts of royal liturgies, and the steady accretion of bureaucratic documents in order to generate a picture of government both as it was idealized and put into practice, Dalarun offers another perspective altogether. Starting with those who esteemed renunciation, who attempted to codify through *regula* (monastic rules) and letters, and to adjudicate in *consilia* (careful counsel) and short clarifications, Dalarun extends to the reader an entirely new articulation of the origins of medieval governmental thinking and its evolution. He demonstrates that the religious, and in particular the monastic, context lends the history of governance an ideological vector that must be read alongside the political narrative.

This insight promises to change the scholarly landscape, to shift the terms of our teaching, and to reshape our questions yet again. With this book the conversation is made considerably richer and its readers will be left humbled by its revelations.

M. Cecilia Gaposchkin and Anne E. Lester

List of Abbreviations

XIIIth Cent. Chronicles	*XIIIth Century Chronicles*, trans. Placid Hermann O. F. M., introduction and notes by Marie-Therese Laureilhe (Chicago, 1961).
AA	*Tractatus fr. Thomae vulgo dicti de Eccleston de adventu fratrum minorum in Angliam*, ed. A. G. Little (Paris, 1909).
ACSD	*Acta canonizationis sancti Dominici*, in *Monumenta historica sancti patris nostri Dominici*, ed. Angelo Walz. Monumenta ordinis fratrum praedicatorum historica 16 (Rome, 1935), vol. 2, 89–194.
BF	*Bullarium franciscanum*, ed. J.-H. Sbaralea, 4 vols. (Rome, 1759–1768).
CAED	*The Lady. Clare of Assisi: Early Documents*, trans. Regis J. Armstrong (New York, 2006).
CFJ	*Chronica fratris Jordani*, ed. Heinrich Boehmer (Paris, 1908).
Chronicle of Salimbene	*The Chronicle of Salimbene de Adam*, trans. Joseph L. Baird, Giuseppe Baglivi, and John Robert Kane (Binghamton, NY, 1986).
CP	*Constitutiones primaevae s. ordinis Praedicatorum* (Fiesole, 1962).
Deux Vies	*Les Deux Vies de Robert d'Arbrissel. Légendes, écrits et témoignages—The Two Lives of Robert of Arbrissel: Legends, Writings, and Testimonies*, ed. Jacques Dalarun, Geneviève Giordanengo, Armelle Le Huërou, Jean Longère, Dominique Poirel, and Bruce L. Venarde (Turnhout, 2006).
Ep. VIII	Peter Abelard, *Institutio seu Regula Sanctimonialium*, ed. T. P. McLaughlin, in "Abelard's Rule for Religious Women," *Mediaeval Studies* 18 (1956): 242–92.
Escritos	*Escritos de Santa Clara y documentos complementarios*, ed. Ignacio Omaechevarría (Madrid, 1970; new ed., 1999).

LIST OF ABBREVIATIONS

FAED	*Francis of Assisi: Early Documents*, trans. Regis J. Armstrong, J. A. Wayne Hellmann, and William J. Short, 4 vols. (New York, 1999–2020).
FF	*Fontes Franciscani*, ed. Enrico Menestò and Stefano Brufani (Assisi, 1995).
Fonti legislative	Federazione S. Chiara di Assisi delle Clarisse di Umbria-Sardegna, *Chiara di Assisi e le sue fonti legislative. Sinossi cromatica* (Padua, 2003).
LD	*Liber de doctrina*, in *Scriptores ordinis Grandimontensis*, ed. Jean Bequet (Turnhout, 1968), 1–62.
Legenda S. Clarae	*Legenda Latina sanctae Clarae virginis Assisiensis*, ed. Giovanni Boccali (Assisi, 2001).
Legende minores	*Legende minores latine sancte Clare virginis Assisiensis*, ed. Giovanni Boccali (Assisi, 2008).
Lettere ad Agnese	Clare of Assisi, *Lettere ad Agnese. La visione dello specchio*, ed. Giovanni Pozzi and Beatrice Rima (Milan, 1999).
Letters of A and H	*The Letters of Abelard and Heloise*, trans. with an introduction and notes by Betty Radice, rev. by Michael T. Clanchy (London, 2003).
LP	Jordan of Saxony, *Libellus de principiis ordinis praedicatorum*, in *Monumenta historica sancti patris nostri Dominici*, ed. D. H. C. Scheeben. Monumenta ordinis fratrum praedicatorum historica 16 (Rome, 1935), vol. 2, 25–86.
PL	*Patrologiae latinae cursus completus*, ed. Jean-Paul Migne (Paris, 1844–1864).
Primi documenti	*Santa Chiara di Assisi, I primi documenti ufficiali: Lettera di annunzio della sua morte Processo e Bolla di canonizzazione*, ed. Giovanni Boccali (Assisi, 2002).
RS	*Regula venerabilis Stephani Muretensis* in *Scriptores ordinis Grandimontensis*, ed. Jean Bequet (Turnhout, 1968), 63–99.
RSB	*The Rule of Saint Benedict, in Latin and English*, ed. and trans. by Justin McCann (London, 1952).
Salimbene, Cronica	Salimbene de Adam, *Cronica*, ed. Giuseppe Scalia, 2 vols. (Turnhout, 1999).
Scripta	*Francesco d'Assisi, Scritti/ Francisci Assisiensis, Scripta*, ed. Carlo Paolazzi (Grottaferrata [Rome], 2009).

Translator's Introduction

Jacques Dalarun would doubtless insist that his 2012 study *Gouverner c'est servir* was not written to offer lessons to anyone. Unassumingly subtitled an *essai* in the original French sense of the word (an "attempt" that might or might not succeed), the work takes the tone of an exploration and maintains the humility of a hypothesis. And yet this intriguing book, so rich and so unique, surely has a great deal to teach us, in its original form, in its translations into Italian (2015), Spanish (2018), and Portuguese (2021), and now in this English version.

A decade after its original appearance, this three-part study, a master class in scholarship produced by a historian at the height of his career, continues to offer lessons in historical method.[1] The approach on display here has characterized all of Jacques Dalarun's work and epitomizes scholarship associated with the Institut de Recherche et d'Histoire des Textes, of which he was the director from 1998 to 2004.[2] It is rooted in the minute examination of individual manuscripts, each with its own story to tell but all related to larger textual patterns. Here this methodology may be appreciated most immediately in Dalarun's examination, in part 3, of a single scrap of parchment on which Francis of Assisi wrote a short note to his companion, Leo. The analysis of this manuscript-note is not only word by word, but letter by letter, and at times even quill-stroke by quill-stroke. Jacques Dalarun leads his readers, with infinite care, through each step of his investigation as he painstakingly establishes a new reading of a scribbled message from one of the most influential men of the entire Middle Ages. It is no accident that in these expert hands, the most meticulous of methodologies sheds new light on one of the most challenging subjects in medieval historiography.

The quest to interpret Francis of Assisi is as old as the order of *fratres minores* itself and has given rise to a mountain of modern scholarship since Paul

---

1. A complete list of Jacques Dalarun's publications through April 2021 (over 500 in all) can be found in Sean L. Field, Marco Guida, and Dominique Poirel, eds., *L'épaisseur du temps. Mélanges offerts à Jacques Dalarun* (Turnhout, 2021), 21–66.
2. See the IRHT's website at https://www.irht.cnrs.fr/.

xv

Sabatier's 1893 *Vie de S. François d'Assise*.[3] There will never be an all-encompassing answer to the question of who Francis "really" was, in light of Francis's own internal contradictions and the tangled mass of competing interpretations given by the early sources.[4] The only way to make progress, to inch closer to Francis in his own world, is a relentless insistence on making the manuscripts speak. Indeed, in 2015 Jacques Dalarun announced the discovery of an extraordinary manuscript from the 1230s, containing not only a previously unknown life of Francis by Thomas of Celano (the *Vita brevior*), but a wealth of other Franciscan texts, including early copies of the *Regula bullata*, Francis's *Admonitions*, and a commentary on the *Pater Noster* that may be (as Dominique Poirel has suggested) by Francis himself.[5] The manuscript as a physical object testifies to the earliest stages of the friars' remembrance of Francis, of their need to place him in a larger framework and to interpret his legacy.[6] The "rediscovery" of this life has produced new debates and a new phase of textual scholarship on Francis,[7] and the publication of an interdisci-

---

3. The best point of entry into the sources and the scholarship is Jacques Dalarun, ed., *François d'Assise. Écrits, Vies, témoignages*, preface by André Vauchez, 2 vols. (Paris, 2010). In English, see Regis J. Armstrong, J. A. Wayne Hellmann, and William J. Short, eds. and trans., *Francis of Assisi: Early Documents*, 4 vols. (New York, 1999–2020).

4. For Jacques Dalarun's own "questioning," see *François d'Assise en questions* (Paris, 2016). For his previous interventions in the "Franciscan question" see *The Misadventure of Francis of Assisi: Toward a Historical Use of the Franciscan Legends*, trans. Edward Hagman (St. Bonaventure, NY, 2002), and *Vers une résolution de la question franciscaine. La Légende ombrienne de Thomas de Celano* (Paris, 2007).

5. Jacques Dalarun, "Une *Vie* inédite de François d'Assise par Thomas de Celano," *Académie des Inscriptions & Belles-Lettres. Comptes rendus des séances de l'année 2015, janvier-février* (2016): 57–69; Jacques Dalarun, "Thome Celanensis Vita beati patris nostri Francisci (*Vita brevior*). Présentation et édition critique," *Analecta Bollandiana* 133 (2015): 23–86; Jacques Dalarun, ed., *The Rediscovered Life of St. Francis of Assisi, by Thomas of Celano*, trans. Timothy J. Johnson (St. Bonaventure, NY, 2016); Dominique Poirel, "Un écrit inédit de François d'Assise? L'homélie sur le *Pater* de Paris, Bibl. nat. de France, nal 3245," *Académie des Inscriptions & Belles-Lettres. Comptes rendus des séances de l'année 2016, janvier-mars* (2017): 415–85. See also Amandine Postec, "Un nouveau témoin des sermons d'Antoine de Padue," *Il Santo* 56 (2016): 231–42.

6. Sean L. Field, "La *Vita beati patris nostri Francisci* au cœur d'un triptyque franciscain," in *Le manuscrit franciscain retrouvé*, ed. Nicole Bériou, Jacques Dalarun, and Dominique Poirel (Paris, 2021), 297–313. The manuscript is now Paris, Bibliothèque nationale de France, ms. NAL 3245.

7. The scholarly literature is already almost too voluminous to cite. Debates and reactions in the wake of Jacques Dalarun's announcement include the essays in Emil Kumka, ed., *Tommaso da Celano, agiografo di san Francesco. Atti del Convegno internazionale, Roma, 29 gennaio 2016* (Rome, 2016); Jacques Dalarun, "The Rediscovered Manuscript: A Story of Friendship," *Franciscan Studies* 74 (2016): 231–38 and 259–62; Sean L. Field, "New Light on the 1230s: History, Hagiography, and Thomas of Celano's *The Life of Our Blessed Father Francis*," ibid., 239–47; Timothy J. Johnson, "In the Workshop of a Theologian: The *Life of Our Blessed Father Francis* by Thomas of Celano," ibid., 249–58; Aleksander Horowski, "Intorno alla *Vita ritrovata di san Francesco* edita da Jacques Dalarun," *Collectanea franciscana* 86 (2016): 269–89; Jacques Dalarun, "Pour poursuivre le dialogue sur la *Vie retrouvée* de Thomas de Celano," ibid., 759–63; Giovanni Paolo Maggioni, "L'edizione critica della *Vita beati patris nostri Francisci* di Tommaso da Celano," *Frate Francesco* 83 (2017): 181–90; Marco Guida, "Dalla *Vita beati Francisci* alla *Vita brevior* di Tommaso da Celano: per un confronto sinottico," ibid., 191–220; Filippo Sedda, "*Vita brevior* o *breviatio liturgica*?" ibid., 221–28;

TRANSLATOR'S INTRODUCTION   xvii

plinary volume analyzing the manuscript promises to open up even more productive avenues of future research.[8] Every manuscript in the Franciscan tradition is like a piece of an infinitely complex and endlessly absorbing puzzle, and this new discovery has forced a return to all the earlier pieces, to holding them up anew and seeing what they might look like in a fresh light. Study of Francis and the earliest development of his order is thus experiencing an exciting moment, making it all the more crucial to ask what the manuscripts can, and cannot, clarify for us.

And so if we want to understand Francis and his model of government, we cannot do better than to return, with Jacques Dalarun, to that autograph letter to Leo. Who was Francis as a leader or governor? The paradox of a founder who renounces formal leadership while remaining the unquestioned reference point for a rapidly growing order has been addressed before.[9] Here Dalarun adopts the radical tactic of taking Francis's own words seriously when the Poverello counsels Leo "as mother." From Dalarun's line-by-line analysis emerges a new picture of a "maternal" mode of government, of legislation through renunciation, of commanding each brother to find his own way to what he himself knows to be right. The singular figure of Francis stands at the center of a wider argument, grounded in fifty-four words written in a shaky

---

Felice Accrocca, "Da Tommaso a Tommaso. La *Vita beati patris nostri Francisci* nel panorama dell'agiografia francescana," ibid., 229–49; Jacques Dalarun, "La *Vie retrouvée* en questions," ibid., 250–90; Jacques Dalarun, "La ritrovata *Vita beatissimi patris nostri Francisci* (*Vita brevior*) di Tommaso da Celano," Fogli. Rivista dell'Associazione Biblioteca Salita dei Frati di Lugano 38 (2017): 1–12; Luigi Pellegrini, "Considerazzioni sulla *Vita brevior* ritrovata," ibid., 13–16; Jacques Dalarun, "Risposte a quattro domande di Luigi Pellegrini," ibid., 17–18; Jacques Dalarun, "The New Francis in the *Rediscovered Life* (*Vita brevior*) of Thomas of Celano," in *Ordo et sanctitas: The Franciscan Spiritual Journey in Theology and Hagiography. Essays in Honor of J. A. Wayne Hellmann, O. F. M. Conv.*, ed. Michael F. Cusato, Timothy J. Johnson, and Steven J. McMichael (Leiden, 2017), 32–46; Gustavo Da Silva Gonçalves, "Uma nova história de Francisco de Assis? Possibilidades de pesquisas a partir de uma recente descoberta (*Vita beati patris nostri Francisci*, de Tomás de Celano)," Ars historica 15 (2017): 43–61; Paul Bösch, "Die *Vita brevior* und drei Verslegenden als Spiegel verschollener Franziskus-viten," Archivum franciscanum historicum 110 (2017): 125–94; Paul Bösch, "Die *Vita brevior* des Franziskus von Assisi und ihre entfernten verwandten," Archivum franciscanum historicum 111 (2018): 3–32; Nunzio Bianchi, "Sulla *Vita beati patris nostri Francisci* di Tommaso da Celano," Quaderni di storia 87 (2018): 307–32; Sylvain Piron, "François d'Assise et les créatures: Le témoignage de la *Vita brevior*," in *La restauration de la création. Quelle place pour les animaux?*, ed. Michele Cutino, Isabel Iribarren, and Françoise Vinel (Leiden, 2018), 231–41; Jacques Dalarun, "Une nouvelle source pour la Légende des trois compagnons de François d'Assise," in *Fleur de clergie. Mélanges en l'honneur de Jean-Yves Tilliette*, ed. Olivier Collet, Yasmina Foehr-Janssens, and Jean-Claude Mühlethaler (Geneva, 2019), 849–70; Jacques Dalarun, "Codicologie et histoire des textes. La *Vita beati patris nostri Francisci* et ses miracles," Archivum franciscanum historicum 114 (2021): 557–84.

8. Bériou, Dalarun, and Poirel, eds., *Le manuscrit franciscain retrouvé*.

9. Jacques Dalarun, *Francis of Assisi and Power* (St. Bonaventure, NY, 2007). Augustine Thompson, *Francis of Assisi: A New Biography* (Ithaca, NY, 2012), offered perceptive analysis in a book published the same year as *Gouverner c'est servir*. Jacques Dalarun's interpretations on this subject continue to generate commentary, most recently Felice Accrocca, "*Nolo carnifex fieri*. Ancora su Francesco d'Assisi et il governo," in *L'épaisseur du temps*, ed. Field, Guida, and Poirel, 147–58.

hand on a unique bit of parchment, but really, in the end, rooted in the two words *sicut mater*. To transcribe and translate these two words, to excavate, explicate, and extricate their meaning, is to open up a whole world of reversal, of inversion, of paradox, of humble power and powerful submission. No medieval figure more vividly embodies these reversals of status, inversions of hierarchy, and paradoxes of power than Francis. No figure, that is, except Clare.

It is again no accident that Jacques Dalarun's analysis of gendered inversion intersects with the pioneering work of American medievalists such as Caroline Walker Bynum (whose *Jesus as Mother* he acknowledges). *To Govern Is to Serve* models two complementary kinds of gender studies. One is in the realm of the conceptual, symbolic, and metaphoric, highlighting Francis's own use of gendered imagery and exploiting it to peel back layers of meaning. In this area, Dalarun has been ahead of most French scholars in engaging with American scholarship on gender as an analytic framework. Indeed, Robert E. Lerner once praised Dalarun's *Francis of Assisi and the Feminine* as "one of the most important, stimulating, and engaging books . . . on medieval gender studies that I know."[10] The other kind of analysis is more simple, more direct, and perhaps even more meaningful in its insistence that serious historical study cannot afford to relegate real medieval women to the analytic margins.[11] Indeed, *To Govern Is to Serve* actually begins not with Francis but with Clare of Assisi, focusing on a single story told by several sisters during her canonization process,[12] and rewritten a few years later by her hagiographer, Thomas of Celano.[13] The story is short, seemingly simple, and easily overlooked. Why

---

10. Jacques Dalarun, *Francis of Assisi and the Feminine* (St. Bonaventure, NY, 2006). The review (*Speculum* 73 [1998]: 1129–30) was actually of the 1996 French version of the book, itself a revision of the 1994 Italian original.

11. In fact, an attention to gender characterizes Jacques Dalarun's very earliest published work; see, for instance, "Robert d'Arbrissel et les femmes," *Annales. Économies, sociétés, civilisations* 29 (1984): 1140–60. Likewise, Jacques Dalarun's turn to "Franciscan" subjects in the 1990s began not with Francis but with lesser known female figures. See his *La sainte et la cité. Micheline de Pesaro († 1356), tertiaire franciscaine* (Rome, 1992); "Lapsus linguae." *La légende de Claire de Rimini* (Spoleto, 1994); and *Claire de Rimini. Entre sainteté et hérésie* (Paris, 1999). See also his collection *"Dieu changea de sexe, pour ainsi dire." La religion faite femme XIᵉ-XVᵉ siècle* (Paris, 2008); and (with Sean L. Field and Valerio Cappozzo) *A Female Apostle in Medieval Italy: The Life of Clare of Rimini* (Philadelphia: University of Pennsylvania Press, 2023).

12. Clare's canonization process (the evidence for which is preserved only in a later Italian translation) continues to be an important field for new research. See Marco Guida, "Da Bartolomeo da Spoleto a Battista da Perugia: I processi di canonizzazione di Chiara d'Assisi," in *L'épaisseur du temps*, ed. Field, Guida, and Poirel, 213–34; Jacques Dalarun, "Du procès de canonisation à la Légende latine de Claire d'Assise," *Memini. Travaux et documents* 24 (2018), https://journals.openedition.org/memini/1044; Jacques Dalarun, "Résilience de la mémoire. Le procès de canonisation de Claire d'Assise et ses marges," *Frate Francesco* 78 (2012): 317–36, updated in Dalarun, *François d'Assise en questions*, 245–56.

13. Thomas's authorship is established in Marco Guida, *Una leggenda in cerca d'autore. La "Vita di santa Chiara d'Assisi." Studio delle fonti e sinossi intertestuale*, preface by Jacques Dalarun (Brussels, 2010). It is unfortunate that Regis J. Armstrong, ed. and trans., *The Lady. Clare of Assisi: Early Documents* (New

TRANSLATOR'S INTRODUCTION   xix

were Clare's sisters so insistent on its importance? What was the significance of the abbess of San Damiano kissing the feet of a serving sister and receiving a kick in the mouth as thanks for her trouble? Dalarun takes the tale apart, examines it from every angle, and reassembles it to show what it meant for Clare to serve others as abbess, to serve servants, to govern as a form of service. Beginning the book with a study of an abbess and her sisters is no mere nod to inclusivity. Clare's example is even more powerful than Francis's precisely because Clare—so fond of describing herself as the "little plant" of father Francis—had to accept the unwanted burdens of government out of humble obedience to Francis's wishes. The very heart of the dynamic contained in the title *To Govern Is to Serve* resides in Clare's experience. In recent decades scholars have made great progress in contextualizing Clare's career,[14] with American scholarship (following the lead of Maria Pia Alberzoni) emphasizing her determined battles with the papacy in particular.[15] Perhaps the challenge now is to reconcile Clare's warrior spirit (as Dalarun puts it) with her paradoxical refusal to dominate.[16]

An insistence on considering men and women together continues to characterize the early chapters of part 2. After an initial chapter on the Benedictine Rule (and we should not overlook the importance accorded to these Benedictine foundations), we enter the unsettling world of Fontevraud, where Dalarun began his career and which he has done so much to illuminate.[17] Here

---

York, 2006), which is otherwise so useful for anglophone readers, dismisses the likelihood of Thomas's authorship.

14. Jacques Dalarun and Armelle Le Huërou, eds., *Claire d'Assise. Écrits, Vies, documents*, preface by André Vauchez, introductions by Maria Pia Alberzoni, Marco Bartoli, and Alfonso Marina (Paris, 2013), is the best starting point for sources and scholarship.

15. Maria Pia Alberzoni, *Chiara e il papato* (Milan, 1995); Maria Pia Alberzoni, *Clare of Assisi and the Poor Sisters in the Thirteenth Century* (St. Bonaventure, NY, 2004); Joan Mueller, *The Privilege of Poverty: Clare of Assisi, Agnes of Prague, and the Struggle for a Franciscan Rule for Women* (University Park, PA, 2006); Lezlie S. Knox, *Creating Clare of Assisi: Female Franciscan Identities in Later Medieval Italy* (Leiden, 2008); Joan Mueller, ed., *A Companion to Clare of Assisi: Life, Writings, and Spirituality* (Leiden, 2010); Catherine M. Mooney, *Clare of Assisi and the Thirteenth-Century Church: Religious Women, Rules, and Resistance* (Philadelphia, 2016). For wider approaches to Franciscan women, see Bert Roest, *Order and Disorder: The Poor Clares between Foundation and Reform* (Leiden, 2013); Lezlie Knox and David B. Couturier, eds., *Franciscan Women: Female Identities and Religious Culture. Medieval and Beyond* (St. Bonaventure, NY, 2020).

16. An appealing portrayal, written for a wide Catholic audience, is Margaret Carney, *Light of Assisi: The Story of Saint Clare* (Cincinnati, 2021). See also Michael W. Blastic, Jay M. Hammond, and J. A. Wayne Hellmann, eds., *The Writings of Clare of Assisi: Letters, Form of Life, Testament and Blessing* (St. Bonaventure, NY, 2011).

17. Jacques Dalarun's 1984 thesis (directed by Pierre Toubert) was published as *L'impossible sainteté. La vie retrouvée de Robert d'Arbrissel (v. 1045–1116), fondateur de Fontevraud* (Paris, 1985). See also Jacques Dalarun, *Robert d'Arbrissel, fondateur de Fontevraud* (Paris, 1986; 2nd ed. 2007); translated by Bruce L. Venarde as *Robert of Arbrissel: Sex, Sin, and Salvation in the Middle Ages* (Washington, DC, 2006). The best entry point to sources (including English translations) and scholarship is Jacques Dalarun, Geneviève Giordanengo, Armelle Le Huërou, Jean Longère, Dominique Poirel, and Bruce L. Venarde, eds., *Les Deux Vies de Robert d'Arbrissel. Légendes, écrits et témoignages—The Two Lives of Robert of Arbrissel: Legends,*

not only do women rule over men, but less "worthy" women "converted" from the world rule over virgins raised in the community. It is this idea of "unworthiness" that part 2 adds to "service" (part 1) and to "maternal" government (part 3). Building on a brilliant 2005 study that has not received as much attention as it deserves,[18] Dalarun here reveals that in the "least read letter of the most celebrated letter collection of the Middle Ages," Peter Abelard engages directly with Robert of Arbrissel's ideas for Fontevraud. Abelard only indirectly suggests that men should be subordinated to women as at Fontevraud, but clearly proposes that experienced women should lead his imagined female community, in preference to virgins who might seem more worthy in terms of spiritual purity. The fascinating and little-known example of Grandmont, where converts held parity with clerical brothers in a complex system of elections, sets the stage for analysis of the Dominican and Franciscan cases, centered on this same question of the relationship between illiterate lay brothers and educated clerical brothers. The Dominican order has often been cited as a model of religious government,[19] with a multi-level system of elections that offered a "well-balanced synthesis of centralized authority and individual responsibility."[20] But Dalarun leads us down a less traveled path, to show that Dominic, the founder himself, proposed to give power to the illiterate lay brothers and that the ensuing revolt by the educated clerics—who feared precisely the situation that held sway at Grandmont—led to his attempted resignation at the general chapter meeting of Bologna in 1220.[21] This episode has been largely overlooked by scholarship on Dominic and the early Order of Preachers,[22] but it takes on its full significance when paired with Francis of Assisi's own resignation from formal leadership of the *fratres*

Writings, and Testimonies (Turnhout, 2006). See also Bruce L. Vernarde, trans. *Robert of Arbrissel: A Medieval Religious Life* (Washington, DC, 2003), and the fascinating on-line project directed by Jacques Dalarun, *La lettre volée. Le manuscrit 193 de la Bibliothèque municipale de Vendôme* (Ædilis, publications scientifiques, 1) (2003), http://lettrevolee.irht.cnrs.fr.

18. Jacques Dalarun, "Nouveaux aperçus sur Abélard, Héloïse, et le Paraclet," *Francia. Forschungen zur westeuropäischen Geschichte* 32 (2005): 19–66; updated in Jacques Dalarun, *Modèle monastique. Un laboratoire de la modernité* (Paris, 2019), 129–56.

19. Jacques Dalarun himself refers to "perfection dominicaine" in *Modèle monastique*, 171–72.

20. Dennis E. Showalter, "The Business of Salvation: Authority and Representation in the Thirteenth-Century Dominican Order," *Catholic Historical Review* 58 (1973): 564.

21. See also Jacques Dalarun, "Le premier chapitre général. Bologna, 1220," in *Domenico e Bologna. Genesi e sviluppo dell'Ordine dei Frati Predicatori*, forthcoming.

22. For an up-to-date entry point to the sources and scholarship on Dominic, see Nicole Bériou and Bernard Hodel, eds., *Saint Dominique de l'ordre des frères prêcheurs. Témoignages écrits fin XIIe–XIVe siècle* (Paris, 2019). On Dominican lay brothers generally see Augustine Thompson, *Dominican Brothers. Conversi, Lay, and Cooperator Friars* (Chicago, 2017). A good starting point on Dominican government is Gert Melville, "The Dominican *Constitutiones*," in *A Companion to Medieval Rules and Customaries*, ed. Krijn Pansters (Leiden, 2020), 253–81. For Dominican sanctity, see Viliam Štefan Dóci and Gianni Festa, eds., *Fra trionfi et sconfitte: La "Politica della santità" dell'Ordine dei Predicatori* (Rome, 2021).

minores that very same year. In both cases, the charismatic founders reached a point where their early brotherhoods, rooted in radical equality, ran up against institutional imperatives for hierarchical governance. In Francis's own order, the status of the less-educated brothers (the "holy lay brothers," as Brother Leo put it) was eroded by the institutionalizing power of the educated clerics.[23] As the *fratres minores* became an order heavily invested in preaching,[24] they needed education,[25] literacy, and priestly status to hear confessions. Success has a way of making equality obsolete.[26]

And so we arrive back at the central example of Francis. Or not quite, because the move from part 2 to part 3, from Francis's order to his autograph note, first "climbs aboard" the thought of Michel Foucault. The move would be entirely unexpected, if it were not announced in the author's preface. But it is this theoretical "truncated tangent" that lends a profound coherence to the book. The minute study of Clare and the "served servant," the meticulous march through twelfth- and thirteenth-century experiments in democratic "unworthiness," the model of "maternal" government revealed in Francis's note to Leo—the three parts cohere in the ideal of the pastorate, as borrowed from Foucault. The unifying image of the shepherd and his (her?) flock is a windfall from his Collège de France lectures of 1978, not published until some three decades later. Dalarun leads the reader through the historical implications of Foucault's analysis, not in order to test or even clarify the philosopher's claims, but to use them to new ends—that is, to focus on the founding moment when a shepherd acquires government of his flock as a whole and the responsibility for each and every individual soul, in a moment of transgression that implies always having already renounced that same pastoral power.

It might perhaps be easy to miss a further theme that runs throughout the book, in which Dalarun insists on the inseparable intertwining of religious and secular structures in medieval society. Citing classic studies by Marc Bloch, Georges Duby, and Jacques Le Goff, the concluding sections of the book return to the idea that these monastic and mendicant examples must be located in the larger society of the High Middle Ages. The paradox that Dalarun highlights in

---

23. See Michael F. Cusato's extended essay on "The Minorite Vocation of the *Fratres laici* in the Franciscan Order (13th–Early 14th Centuries)," *Archivum franciscanum historicum* 112 (2019): 21–124.

24. Nicole Bériou, *Religion et communication. Un autre regard sur la prédication au Moyen Âge* (Geneva, 2018).

25. Neslihan Şenocak, *The Poor and the Perfect: The Rise of Learning in the Franciscan Order, 1209–1310* (Ithaca, NY, 2012); Bert Roest, "The Franciscan School System: Re-Assessing the Early Evidence (ca. 1220–1260)," in *Franciscan Organisation in the Mendicant Context: Formal and Informal Structures of the Friars' Lives and Ministry in the Middle Ages*, ed. Michael Robson and Jens Röhrkasten (Berlin, 2010), 269–96.

26. For updates to approaching the wide swath of twelfth and thirteenth-century monastic experience studied in part 2, see Jacques Dalarun's 2019 collection *Modèle monastique*.

both the preface and the afterword makes sense only in this light. Christianity, seen as an ideology, always sat uneasily with medieval power structures. The endlessly unsettling effect of the Gospel message that "the last shall be first" can only be measured against a society built on a very different ethos of domination; conversely the tendency of that very society to embrace inversions and reversals of status can only be understood when it is firmly rooted in that unstable ideological soil.

Begin with the manuscripts, build carefully, bring in a wide range of historical actors including women and men, break down artificial boundaries between religion and society, be receptive to the most profound insights of scholars from other disciplines—these lessons (*omnes et singulatim*) are not, of course, unique to Jacques Dalarun or to this book, but they are on display here with an openness and intellectual honesty that might inspire any scholar studying the Middle Ages.

And indeed this study suggests lessons that extend beyond scholarship. *To Govern Is to Serve* does not argue that medieval Europe invented democracy, or even that medieval Europe is the best place to investigate the roots of modern political thought, which are nourished by many sources in a multicultural world. But, as Sylvain Piron has recently remarked, medieval Europe can offer a privileged vantage point for comparison, precisely because it constitutes the "nearest alterity to the modern world."[27] That is, medieval Europe is different enough from our world to offer new perspectives, while not so alien as to make those perspectives seem irrelevant. *To Govern Is to Serve* is a work of scholarship, not a political manifesto, but its investigations offer powerful material for reflection on our own politics. To be clear, Dalarun does not suggest that modern democracy should be infused with Christian values or that it should return to some kind of medieval purity. Instead, the ideas gathered here imply that uncovering unexpected aspects of embryonic democracy in unexplored corners of the medieval world may allow us to perceive new possibilities for the many forms renewed modern democracies might take. Like an interconnected web of potential patterns, the themes that emerge from this study can be woven into new configurations. They are not blueprints but rather "invitations to a reflection on power and obedience," hence on democracy itself. They remind us of recurring tensions between democratic processes and democratic openness. If they suggest any overarching lesson, it is the necessity for vigilance, as the afterword stresses. The reciprocal bonds between governor and governed in a democracy must be based on shared humility and shared responsibility. The "danger," Dalarun wrote with a certain prescience

---

27. Sylvain Piron, *Généalogie de la morale économique* (Brussels, 2020), 13.

in 2012, is "charisma which refuses to relinquish its hold on power." Combating that danger depends on all of us together and each one individually finding our way forward. Yet that path forward cannot be forced. Democracy "is created not by imposing constraints, even those overflowing with good intentions, but by removing them; by releasing pressure, not by applying it: If you believe something is good for you and for others, do it!"

Jacques Dalarun titled a recent essay "L'avis des autres" ("Other People's Perspectives"), with a gallic wink, knowing that the phrase could be heard also as "La vie des autres" ("Other People's Lives").[28] In the end, what else should we ask of our democracies, but that government and governors value each life, respect all perspectives, think about others, and serve all while serving each one?

Several points about the present translation may be useful for readers to know in advance. First, it is slightly shorter than the French original, because much of what had been the third chapter of part 3 is omitted, with the remainder of that chapter integrated into chapter 2. This change was made at Jacques Dalarun's suggestion, as a result of thinking about what might work best for anglophone audiences. In a very few other places, a sentence or two has been cut, where we similarly agreed that an example or phrase was superfluous. In an even fewer number of cases, a new sentence or two has been added. Thus while this English translation is not a systematic revision of the original text, a reader who compares it to the French version will perceive a few small differences and should be aware that they result from the author's preferences and his consultation with the translator.

Second, the original French text was published without notes, with a chapter-by-chapter reference list pointing the reader to primary and secondary sources. For the present volume, I have followed American academic conventions by footnoting all quotations from and direct references to primary and secondary sources. For secondary sources, where English translations exist I have cited those translations. For primary sources, I have cited original language (Latin, French, or Italian) editions and also, where possible, pointed to standard English translations. However, because this book presents extensive and often minute analysis of its sources, it is essential that the English translations of those primary sources match closely with the vocabulary and syntax used in Dalarun's French treatment. Thus although I have consulted and benefited from English translations of these primary sources where they exist, in all cases the translations that appear here have been phrased to harmonize with

---

28. Jacques Dalarun, "L'avis des autres," *Critique, Giorgio Agamben* 836–837 (2017): 109–21, revised in *Modèle monastique*, 177–89.

the author's analysis. Biblical passages are given in slightly modernized translation based on the Douay-Rheims version, while references to the Psalms follow Vulgate numbering.

I would like to thank Mahinder Kingra, Cecilia Gaposchkin, and Anne Lester for welcoming this translation to Cornell University Press and its Medieval Societies, Religions, and Cultures series. I am also grateful to Miri Rubin, who improved the penultimate draft with a detailed reading and many wise suggestions. Most importantly, my thanks go to Jacques Dalarun, who commented on each chapter as the translation progressed and turned this project into a true collaboration. Any weaknesses in the translation lie entirely with me, but its strengths should be credited equally to these generous souls who sought not to dominate but to serve the governing ideals of the work.

TO GOVERN IS TO SERVE

Preface

I have devoted almost forty years to reading medieval sources—printed or in manuscript, well-known or unpublished, usually in Latin but sometimes in medieval French or Italian. After all this time, I have an idea of how they work.

Or at least some idea. The sheer volume of published sources thwarts any attempt at exhaustive reading. For unpublished sources, the difficulty of deciphering old handwriting inevitably slows down the process. No matter how hard we try, the meaning of the text is never entirely freed from the veil of old languages. In the end, we really only sift through what remains of these sources.

The filter of our interests combines with the chance nature of what has been preserved. I don't know which of these two kinds of selection is the more random. The rigor of our research results from the methods we employ, not from the themes we choose to study. Critical reading of the sources, gone over with the fine-tooth comb of scholarly erudition, is our only guarantee. To quote Paul Ricoeur, "We have nothing better than testimony, and criticism of testimony, to substantiate the historian's representation of the past."[1]

In my generation, anyone studying the humanities—and, indeed, a cultivated and curious public well beyond that—read Michel Foucault. Those lacking a

---

1. Paul Ricoeur, *Memory, History, Forgetting*, trans. Kathleen Blamey and David Pellauer (Chicago, 2004), 278.

flair for philosophy read him with a hint of terror, but everyone read him with a sustained sense of intense excitement. We used Foucault then more than we cite him now. We filed away our youthful enthusiasms out of modesty, out of disciplinary rigidity, sometimes out of an inability to face the complexity of his thought.

I have retained only a simple conception of Michel Foucault's work. In his *History of Madness, Discipline and Punish,* and *I, Pierre Rivière*, I was infinitely intrigued, as were so many others, by the paradoxical proposition that a society's core can be read in its exclusions and at its margins.[2]

Perhaps it was for this reason that my reading of medieval sources began with the lives of holy hermits. These little bands of forest-dwellers, inhabitants of green "deserts," displayed their marginality in the very location of their lives, opening a gap between themselves and the world, which was often at the same time a gap between their behavior and what was considered acceptable.

But the Middle Ages seemed to me to introduce a paradox into the paradox. The modern madman, prisoner, or murderer really is banished from society (*Saint Genet, Actor and Martyr* remains an exception due to the double subversion of Jean Genet and Jean-Paul Sartre).[3] Medieval saints—the real ones, those whose real lives play out in the written "lives," not those for whom unsubstantiated legends are made up out of whole cloth—repeatedly break the rules of social conduct. But it is this very gap that creates their aura, consecrates them, and in the end lifts them up to the heavens.

Here is a society with a sharp divide between the powerful and the lowly, eternally symbolized by the solid mass of the castle tower looming over the peasant's hut. Here is a society based on domination, still visibly linked to physical force, to the art of killing or at least striking down an adversary, a domination that justifies all kinds of extortions. Here is an age when knowledge opens up another seemingly unbridgeable chasm between the learned and the simple. Here is a world of emperors, kings, princes, counts, and knights along with its clerical branch, descended from the same stock, with its popes, cardinals, bishops, abbots, and canons, who need not envy their secular relations in terms of luxury and riches.

But all of them—the powerful and the humble, the learned and the simple, clerics and laypeople—can suddenly join in shared devotion to a barefoot wanderer who denounces violence as an insult to creation, power as blindness,

---

2. Michel Foucault, *History of Madness*, trans. Jonathan Murphy, ed. Jean Khalfa (New York, 2006); Michel Foucault, *Discipline and Punish: The Birth of the Prison*, trans. Alan Sheridan (New York, 1977); Michel Foucault, ed., *I, Pierre Riviere, Having Slaughtered My Mother, My Sister, and My Brother . . . : A Case of Parricide in the 19th Century*, trans. Frank Jellinek (New York, 1975).

3. Jean-Paul Sartre, *Saint Genet. Actor and Martyr*, trans. Bernard Frechtman (1952; repr. Minneapolis, 2012).

money as leprosy, knowledge as vanity, and who is a saint not in spite of this denunciation, but because of it.

This plot of inverted values might seem merely anecdotal and selective, while at the same time all too predictable. A feast of fools, fools for Christ; a parenthetical pause, a release before the return of worldly order. But in fact this plot is intrinsic to the structure of medieval society. It spans the thousand years of the Middle Ages, playing itself out over and over again, following the winds of reform, the waves of return to stricter observance within religious life, and the details of these holy lives, unique yet resembling each other, in bursts always based on an ascent to the sources, to the Source: scripture in general and the Gospel in particular. The wood of the cross is both guiding structure and goading splinter for medieval societies.

In other words, the European Middle Ages unfolded in the shadow of a dominant religion ill-suited to being a dominant ideology, at least within its own specific political circumstances. This is what I call the Christian paradox of the medieval West.

The Gospel's promise that "the last shall be first and the first shall be last" is not, on the face of it, very conducive to social stability. Neither is it really threatening, since it places this reversal in hopes for the hereafter. But it does sow the seeds of doubt.

During the medieval millennium and right up to the Protestant Reformation, which marks the end of the epoch, it was religious reforms, rather than social revolts or political revolutions, that took place in the name of the Gospel. Yet during the Middle Ages the inversion of the first and the last decisively influenced modes of government, particularly the government of religious communities, insofar as such communities claimed to submit themselves completely to the precepts and counsels of the Gospel, through constant supervision of every aspect of each member's life, from dress to thought and including the most minute details of behavior.

My hypothesis is that medieval religious communities served as a testing ground for the development of modern "governmentality"—and here I pick up the thread of my Foucauldian reading: not a sovereignty exercised over a territory, but an art of governing that enfolds people more than it dominates them.

This book takes its point of departure less from a question than from the deep sense of wonder and awe that I have always felt in the face of the Middle Ages' tendency to inversion: How could a society of order(s)—in the singular and the plural, in the multiple meanings of the Latin term *ordo*—base itself on a morality of reversal and from there invent a new art of governing?

I make no pretension to a work of synthesis on a theme so vast, so fluid, so omnipresent, and so difficult to trace with clear ideas and precise terms.

Renouncing this reasonable path, my purpose instead oscillates between a reading of sources and an essay. In the three parts that make up the book—the first centering on a single episode in the life of Clare of Assisi, the second examining a collection of institutional religious experiences from the twelfth and thirteenth centuries, the third deciphering a short autograph note by Francis of Assisi—I allow myself an insistent investigation of the sources in order to arrange the ideas they inspire in me, from time to time, into a bouquet that takes the form of an essay.

If the essay does not succeed, the sources will remain. Their bloom has lost none of its brilliance.

Part One

The Servant Served

He rises from supper and lays aside his garments and, taking a towel, wraps himself. After that, he pours water into a basin and begins to wash the feet of the disciples and to dry them with the towel with which he was wrapped. . . .

Then after he had washed their feet and taken his garments, he sat down again and said to them: Do you know what I have done to you? You call me Master and Lord. And rightly you say so, for so I am. If then I, being your Lord and Master, have washed your feet, you also ought to wash one another's feet. For I have given you an example, that as I have done to you, so you do also.

—John 13:4–5, 12–15

1. A Shocking Story

Thomas of Celano recounted Clare of Assisi's saintly life. In composing his *Legend of Saint Clare, Virgin*, he described her birth, her family, her exemplary behavior in her father's home, her meeting with Francis, her entry into religious life, her enclosure at San Damiano (the little church restored by Francis, which would become the monastery of the community of "Poor Ladies"), and her renown. Then, abandoning chronological order, he set about sketching her moral portrait, virtue by virtue, beginning with the most important, essential, and fundamental of them all: humility. The chapter dedicated to this virtue concludes with a well-chosen anecdote:

> She frequently and reverently washed the feet of the servants who returned from outside. And after washing their feet, she kissed them. Once, when she was washing the feet of one of these servants, while she was bending to kiss them, that sister, not able to stand such humility, withdrew her foot, and with that foot she kicked the lady in her mouth. Yet she gently took the servant's foot again and planted a firm kiss on its sole.[1]

Thomas of Celano wrote because he had been asked to do so. The commission came from Alexander IV, pope since 12 December 1254, to whom Thomas respectfully addressed his work:

> To the most holy father in Christ by divine providence sovereign pontiff of the sacrosanct Roman Church, my lord Alexander IV, brother Thomas of Celano commends himself with devoted submission while devoutly kissing his blessed feet.[2]

In writing his *Legend of Saint Clare, Virgin*, the hagiographer had exceptionally valuable material at his disposal: the depositions of twenty-one witnesses who had testified between 24 and 29 November 1253, during the information-gathering phase of Clare of Assisi's canonization process. Clare had been born in 1193, entered religious life in 1211, and died on 11 August 1253. Two months later, on 18 October, the pope at the time, Innocent IV, decided to open her canonization process. The inquiry was entrusted to Bishop Bartholomew of Spoleto. The first sixteen witnesses were Clare's sisters in religion, some of whom had known her since childhood.

---

1. *Legenda S. Clarae*, 120 (chap. 8); *CAED*, 292.
2. Battista Alfani, *Vita et leggenda della seraphica vergine sancta Chiara distinta in capitoli*, ed. Giovanni Boccali (Assisi, 2004), 75. This address from Thomas to Alexander IV is preserved only in Sister Battista Alfani's Italian adaptation.

I. THE SERVANT SERVED

The very first witness, Sister Pacifica, daughter of Guelfuccio of Assisi, made only a general reference to Clare's washing of the sisters' feet. Like all the other depositions in the canonization process, her testimony must have been given in Umbrian, the mother tongue of both Francis and Clare, then written down in Latin by the notary Martino. Finally, it was inserted into the records of these sessions, where the witnesses' statements were changed to the third person:

> She [Pacifica] also said that the blessed mother [Clare] was humble, kind, and loving to her sisters, and had compassion for the sick. While she was in good health, she served them and washed their feet and gave them water with her own hands.[3]

Sister Benvenuta of Perugia, the second to testify, was more precise:

> This witness says that from the moment when this mother St. Clare entered religious life, she was so humble that she washed the feet of the sisters herself. Once, while washing the feet of a servant, she bent over, wishing to kiss her feet. This servant, pulling her foot away, recklessly hit the mouth of the blessed mother with her foot.[4]

The third witness, Sister Filippa, daughter of the late Leonardo of Ghislerio, went one step further:

> She also said that the blessed mother's humility was so great that she held herself in complete disdain. She abased herself before the other sisters, making herself less than all others, serving them, giving them water for their hands, washing the commodes of the sick sisters with her own hands, and even washing the feet of the servants. Once, while washing the feet of one of the monastery's servants, she wanted to kiss her feet. The servant carelessly withdrew her foot and thus, while pulling it away, she hit the holy mother in the mouth with her foot. Nevertheless, due to her humility, Clare did not desist, but kissed the sole of the foot of the servant. Asked how she knew these things, she replied that she saw them because she had been present.[5]

The scene must have made an impression on the sisters, because the tenth witness, Sister Agnes, daughter of the late Oportulo, son of Bernardo of Assisi, retold it:

---

3. *Primi documenti*, 12; CAED, 147. The depositions from Clare's canonization process survive only in a fifteenth-century Italian translation.
4. *Primi documenti*, 96–97; CAED, 150.
5. *Primi documenti*, 112; CAED, 157.

She also spoke of the lady's humility, which was such that she washed the feet of the sisters and the servants, so much so that once, while washing the feet of one of these servants, and wanting to kiss them as she usually did, that servant unintentionally hit her in the mouth with her foot. The lady rejoiced at this and kissed the sole of that foot. Asked how she knew this, she replied that she had seen it. Asked when, she replied "during Lent." Asked what day, she replied "a Thursday."[6]

So we have here a fact attested under oath, before an ecclesiastical tribunal, by four people, two of whom said that they had been eye witnesses. Comparing these accounts with each other, we find the details of the scene becoming clear: It took place after Clare of Assisi's entry into religious life (1211) and after the arrival of Agnes of Oportulo at San Damiano (1220), but before Clare fell ill (1224). It was a Thursday during Lent: Should we deduce from this that is was on Holy Thursday, the commemoration of the Last Supper, Christ's last meal, when he washed the feet of his disciples? The four witnesses agree on the central fact that Clare washed the feet of others; of the sick—probably sick sisters—according to Pacifica; of the sisters in general according to Benvenuta; of the servants according to Filippa; and of the sisters and the servants according to Agnes, which seems the most likely interpretation.

Against this background, the same shocking story bursts forth from the last three testimonies: once, while washing the feet of a servant, Clare wanted to kiss the foot she was holding; but the servant, by pulling her foot away, kicked Clare in the mouth. Agnes adds that Clare was in the habit of kissing the feet that she washed, and Benvenuta specifies that Clare bent down to do this. Perhaps the servant was clumsy, abrupt, ill-mannered: she pulled her foot away "recklessly" or "carelessly," according to Benvenuta and Filippa. Agnes shows herself less judgmental: the kick was "unintentional." Only Filippa and Agnes go further and testify that Clare nevertheless followed through with her desire to plant a kiss on the wayward foot. She carried out her gesture in all humility, says the former; not without rejoicing in the kick, adds the latter.

Agnes is also the most sensitive to distinctions of status and social standing within the female community. Clare's humble practice seems to include all the women of the monastery. But in describing this community, Agnes divides it up. That is, even while linking them together, she clearly distinguishes two categories: Clare "washed the feet of the sisters and the servants." And here Clare is no longer "the blessed mother" referred to by Pacifica, Benvenuta, and Filippa; for Agnes, faced with the clumsy servant, Clare is the "lady." Is it not

---

6. *Primi documenti*, 171–72; *CAED*, 178.

this very condition that allows her humility to be exalted? A servant who washes a lady's feet is not practicing a virtue, but merely fulfilling a duty. When Filippa informs us that Clare "held herself in complete disdain" and "abased herself before the other sisters, making herself less than all others," she is perfectly aware of the reversal involved, at least the spiritual reversal, because she is giving her deposition in order to demonstrate that the deceased woman was the most saintly of all and in order to praise her deeds: "washing the commodes of the sick sisters with her own hands, and *even* washing the feet of the servants." To put it as an oxymoron: Clare achieved the height of abasement.

Thomas of Celano was a Franciscan—that is, a "minor" or "lesser" brother. In joining this order, he embraced the Franciscan spirit. More specifically, by recounting the life of Francis of Assisi in several different versions, he made a powerful contribution to shaping the contours of the founder's sanctity. Two years after Francis's death on 4 October 1226, in the days following the proclamation of his sanctity by Gregory IX on 16 July 1228, and at the pope's order, Thomas prepared the first biography of Francis, the *Life of the Blessed Francis*, which was approved on 25 February 1229. Between 1232 and 1239, he then produced a shortened version of the *Life of the Blessed Francis* on the order of Brother Elias, minister general of the Franciscans or Lesser Brothers (*fratres minores*). Finally, in 1246–1247, based on accounts gathered from Francis's closest companions, he composed a new *Memorial* and completed it over the next few years with a collection of some two hundred miracles.[7]

Thomas of Celano is Francis's hagiographer par excellence, the one who painted and fixed the image of Francis's dissolute youth, his conversion, his stripping of all his clothes in front of the bishop of Assisi, his kiss of the leper, his voyage to Rome, his vision of the fiery chariot, his meeting with the sultan, his preaching to the birds, his Christmas at Greccio, his reception of the stigmata on Mount La Verna, his holy death, his canonization, his translation, and so many other deeply moving scenes that make up the memory of Francis. Thomas exalted Francis's prayer, obedience, purity, gift of seeing into others' consciences, self-disdain, humility, desire for martyrdom, charity, compassion for the poor, love of animals; his spirit of prophecy, his poverty, hatred for money, evangelical spirit, simplicity . . .

But unlike Francis, Thomas was of noble birth and elite culture, perhaps from the family of the counts of Celano in the Abruzzi, with a biblical knowledge and a stylistic virtuosity as deep as they were dazzling. It was also

---

7. For Thomas's hagiographies of Francis see *FAED*, vol. 1, and Jacques Dalarun, ed., *The Rediscovered Life of St. Francis of Assisi, by Thomas of Celano*, trans. Timothy J. Johnson (St. Bonaventure, NY, 2016).

Thomas—Marco Guida has recently established this beyond doubt—whom Alexander IV ordered to take the accounts that had accumulated during Clare's canonization process and form them into a proper legend.[8] From the outset, Thomas was careful to situate her within the social context of Assisi:

> An admirable woman, Clare, clear in name and in virtue, was originally from the city of Assisi, from a lineage of shining clarity; at first a fellow citizen with the blessed Francis on earth, afterward she reigned with him in heaven. Her father was a knight, and on both sides of her family through her parents she was of knightly lineage; her home was rich and abundant in its means, according to local fashion.[9]

Still, the first virtue that Thomas lauded in the young aristocratic woman from Assisi was of course "her holy humility." It is worth citing the rest of the chapter:

> As the cornerstone and noble foundation of her order, she sought from the beginning to place the building of all virtues on the foundation of holy humility. Thus she promised holy obedience to the blessed Francis and never deviated from her promise. Three years after her conversion, declining the name and office of abbess, she wanted humbly to obey rather than to command, and, among the servants of Christ, to serve more willingly than to be served. But, compelled by the blessed Francis, she accepted the government of the ladies; hence fear rather than arrogance was born in her heart; and her liberty did not increase, but rather her service. Because the higher she seemed to be elevated by the appearance of superiority, the more worthless she became in her own judgment, the more ready to serve, the more unworthy of veneration she considered herself. She never shirked any of the servants' chores, so much so that she often poured water on the hands of the sisters, assisted them when they were seated, served them when they ate. Only most unwillingly would she order anything, but she acted spontaneously, preferring to do things herself rather than to order the sisters. She herself washed the commodes of the sick, cleaned them herself with her noble spirit, without fleeing their filth nor recoiling from their stench.[10]

The hagiographer's role is to reconcile: to reconcile disciples around the founding memory; to reconcile intuition with institution, the initial project with

---

8. Marco Guida, *Una leggenda in cerca d'autore. La "Vita di santa Chiara d'Assisi." Studio delle fonti e sinossi intertestuale*, preface by Jacques Dalarun (Brussels, 2010).
9. *Legenda S. Clarae*, 92 (chap. 1); CAED, 280.
10. *Legenda S. Clarae*, 120 (chap. 8); CAED, 291–92.

the reality to which it gave birth; to reconcile the past time of origins with the present time of writing, death with life, God with humans. But he also has to absorb the shock of sanctity, to muffle it in the fabric of the text. Sanctity sometimes causes scandal. It always emerges from a gap, from an excess, and so provokes trauma. Across the Christian era, its variations were endless, its inflexions infinite. For in order to show itself, sanctity must be out of tune with the times, oppose conventions, thwart expectations. It must be the unanticipated note within the expected chord, the touch of impropriety at the heart of convention. It is the constant reversal of a well-known theme, a change of mode, of tone, of register, of timbre, of rhythm and tempo.

Franciscan sanctity is written in a minor key, in a complete reversal of normal perspective. Here is the difficulty Thomas of Celano faced: Clare had in fact agreed to be abbess (she is given this label in all the sources that refer to her). She had certainly wanted neither the title nor the function; she wanted only "humbly to obey." But precisely for this reason, she finally had to agree to force herself to do it, in the name of the obedience she had promised Francis. The striking fact is that Francis had never wanted the title of abbot either; in his case, he would accept only the name of "minister," which is to say "servant," of the brothers. And even then, in the last years of his life he resigned this inverted authority to once again become the last of the brothers, the "lesser" brother par excellence: the "smallest" or "least" of the "lesser brothers." His two disciples knew this, Clare just as well as Thomas. She had to force herself, because Francis forced her into it, within the system of inverted values she had absorbed from him. And Thomas had to force himself to recount this use of force.

The hagiographer invents nothing, or almost nothing. At most Thomas embroiders things a bit, very discreetly. Concerning the matter of the "government of the ladies," he sticks very closely to the only sister who testified about it, the first to give a deposition, Pacifica:

> This witness also said that three years after Lady Clare had entered religious life, at the prayers and insistence of St. Francis, who forced her, so to speak, she accepted the direction and government of the sisters. Asked how she knew this, she said she had been present there.[11]

Thomas's work consists of sewing together the patchwork of testimonies to form a legend. To deal with the title of abbess, he starts by exalting Clare's humility, then the obedience to Francis that flows from it and in turn forces her to accept the unacceptable. Thomas has to quickly weave his text around this tear in the fabric. The semantics of service offer the guiding principle: "servants of

---

11. *Primi documenti*, 85–86; CAED, 146.

Christ," "to serve more willingly than to be served," "service," "more ready to serve," "servants," "she served." And Thomas adorns these terms with certain well-chosen expressions that allow a slippage from humility to humiliation: "more worthless in her own judgement," "more unworthy of veneration," "without fleeing their filth nor recoiling from their stench." The abbess makes herself the "servant," thus conforming to the model of the "minister" in the Order of Lesser Brothers. It only remains for Thomas to select and include two crowning anecdotes: "She washed the commodes of the sick herself"; "she frequently and reverently washed the feet of the servants who returned from outside and, after washing them, kissed them." Lower than a servant, servant of servants, and, as thanks, a kick in the very mouth that was about to plant a kiss.

Thomas adroitly employs the depositions of Benvenuta, Filippa, and Agnes. He takes a great deal from Filippa, including the fact that Clare washed the feet of servants specifically. From Filippa and Agnes, he draws the fact that the gesture continued all the way to its conclusion. He imbues it with tenderness—the caress of the hand, the intensity of the kiss. At the same time, he abandons any sense of chronology. He adds a realistic and plausible detail with explanative power: the feet of the servants needed washing more than the others because they were the only ones to leave the monastery. Discarding the idea of unintentional clumsiness, he imagines the servant's motivation for abruptly withdrawing her foot—she could not stand "such great humility." In so doing, Thomas invents a new witness to Clare's humility: the servant who is served.

2. Sisters

So there were ladies and servants in the Order of Poor Sisters.

In 1211, when Clare of Assisi converted to religious life, there was no question of a new order or even of a monastery for her, just of an eighteen-year-old girl running away from home. During the canonization process, the story was recalled by Clare's youngest biological sister, Beatrice:

> She said that, having heard of the fame of her holiness, St. Francis went many times to preach to her, so effectively that the virgin Clare complied with his preaching, renounced the world and all earthly things, and went to serve God as soon as she could. For she sold her entire inheritance, and part of the inheritance of the witness [Beatrice] too, and gave it all to the poor. Then St. Francis tonsured her in front of the altar in the church of the Virgin Mary called the Portiuncula. Then he sent her to the church of San Paolo delle Abbadesse. When her relatives wanted to drag her out, Lady Clare grabbed the altar cloth and uncovered her head, showing them that she was tonsured. In no way did she acquiesce, neither letting them take her away from there, nor going away with them. Then St. Francis, Brother Filippo, and Brother Bernardo took her to the church of Sant'Angelo di Panzo. After staying there for a short while, she was led to the church of San Damiano, where the Lord gave her several sisters for her direction. Asked how she knew these things, [the witness] responded that being her sister, she saw some things herself and heard some from Lady Clare and from others. Asked how long ago this was, she replied "about forty-two years."[12]

San Damiano sits outside the walls of Assisi, below the city, toward the plain. At the time of his conversion, Francis had taken refuge in this small, half-ruined church and then restored it with his own hands even before the arrival of his first companions. In 1211 it became the fledgling female community's shelter. Very quickly several companions gathered around Clare. Agnes, her biological sister, had already joined her at Sant'Angelo di Panzo. Pacifica and Benvenuta came to San Damiano in 1211; Cecilia in 1213–1214; Filippa in 1215. In its first years, San Damiano was more like a hermitage than a monastery, a place withdrawn from the world, sheltering a few solitary women; or like a beguinage (a house of beguines; that is, women living an informal existence in religious micro-communities).

But in 1214 Francis imposed on Clare "the direction and the government of the sisters," which translated into the title of abbess, the female equivalent

---

12. *Primi documenti*, 185–87; CAED, 183–84.

of the abbot at the head of a monastery. Even if this title was a bit comical for such a small number of inhabitants, it nevertheless calmed fears. Endowed with a superior, the upstart little community could now take its place within the monastic tradition inherited from St. Benedict. And most importantly, Clare's promotion would free Francis from institutional responsibility for the embryonic female community. Naming an autonomous superior would clear him of the suspicions that always surrounded a religious endeavor that brought together men and women. Now he could devote himself freely to his brothers and to the multitude of believers. At most, he provided Clare and her companions with a kind of spiritual direction, promising his protection and that of his brothers. As though it were the most precious of gems, Clare preserved the basic "form of living" that Francis had written for her and her sisters, at the beginning of the experiment that was San Damiano:

> Since by divine inspiration you have made yourselves daughters and servants of the most high and sovereign King, the heavenly Father, and have taken the Holy Spirit as your spouse, choosing to live according to the perfection of the Holy Gospel, I resolve and promise for myself and for my brothers always to have a loving care and special solicitude for you as I do for them.[13]

They were all servants, but of the heavenly Father. In 1217, and again in 1218–1219, Hugolino, cardinal-bishop of Ostia, the future Pope Gregory IX, was sent to central Italy as a papal legate, acting there in the name of Pope Honorius III. Hugolino then composed a "formula of life" for the monastery in Assisi and for a myriad of small female foundations closely tied to it, in Spello, Foligno, Perugia, Arezzo, Siena, Florence, Lucca, Tortona. He addressed it to them around 1219. These Constitutions, the original version of which has recently been discovered and edited, were intended to complement the Rule of St. Benedict. In them we find the first trace of a division within these female communities between the "ladies" (*domine*) and "those who serve" (*servientes*).

> When they die, both the ladies as well as the servants who will have been professed, should be buried within the cloister.[14]

Indeed, it is expected that the servants (or serving sisters) will make their profession in the same manner as the ladies: "This should also be firmly observed as far as the servants are concerned."[15]

---

13. *Fonti legislative*, 68; CAED, 118.
14. Giovanni Boccali, "La *Cum omnis vera religio* del cardinale Ugolino," *Frate Francesco* 78 (2008): 458; CAED, 77.
15. Boccali, "La *Cum omnis vera religio*," 460; CAED, 77.

I. THE SERVANT SERVED

In 1238, the community of San Damiano reached fifty members. A document in which the sisters named as their procurator the former *podestà* Oportulo demonstrates this by providing the names of fifty signatories. But in two places the document adopts an ambiguous formulation when referring to these women: "the ladies or the sisters."[16] Are the two terms placed side by side as synonyms, one explaining the other, meaning "the ladies, that is to say, the sisters"? Or do they rather indicate two distinct categories, meaning "on the one hand the ladies, on the other hand the sisters"? What is at stake is our understanding of whether the names of the servants are included in the fifty names given.

In 1247, Innocent IV prepared a new "form of living" for the monasteries of the "Order of San Damiano." He repeated the prescriptions from Cardinal Hugolino's Constitutions on the burial place for "both the ladies as well as the servants" and on the common procedure for profession. The required fasts are the same for the two categories of religious women. The sisters were to wear a cord as a belt; the servants a belt of wool. The sisters were to wear a black veil, the novices a white veil, and the servants a piece of white linen long enough and large enough to hide their shoulders and their chest, especially when they went outside. The most precise prescriptions for the servants, logically enough, concerned behavior when outside the monastery:

> Concerning the servants who are not bound to remain always enclosed like the others, we wish it to be strictly observed that no one may leave the cloister without permission and that those who are sent out be upright and of appropriate age. Let them embark with decent footwear, both they and the sisters who must at times be sent out, as in the cases described above. The same may also be permitted for those who remain within, if they wish. Let a certain time for returning be fixed for those who go out. Let it not be permitted for any of them to eat, drink, or sleep outside the monastery without special permission, or to be separated from one another, or to talk to someone in private, or to enter the dwelling-place of the chaplain of the monastery or of convents or of the brothers staying there. If one of them does something contrary to this, let her be severely punished. Let them zealously take care that they not turn aside to suspicious places or become familiar with persons of a bad reputation. Upon their return let them not recount to the sisters worldly and useless things through which they can be disturbed or

---

16. Luke Wadding, *Annales Minorum seu trium Ordinum a S. Francisco institutorum*, vol. 3 (Quaracchi [Florence], 1931), 14–15 (*anno 1238*); *CAED*, 429.

weakened. And while they are out, let them so conduct themselves that they are able to edify those who see them, by their upright manner. Whatever is given or promised them, let them bring it and report it to the abbess or another who takes her place in this regard.[17]

Clare of Assisi also worked on the composition of a normative text. In and of itself, it was a defiant challenge for a woman to write a form of life for her sisters. Up to now this task had been reserved for male authority, such as in the sixth century when Caesarius of Arles wrote a rule for his sister Caesaria, or Leander of Seville for his sister Florentina.[18] The female community of San Damiano had carried on its combat under the teachings of Francis, a charismatic authority, then under the norms of a cardinal-legate, Hugolino of Ostia; the "Order of San Damiano" had received a form of living from a pope, Innocent IV. In an absolute sense, Clare was the first woman to have had the audacity to make herself the legislator of her order. Yet the text that she had composed was not approved by Cardinal Rainaldo, the future Pope Alexander IV, until 16 September 1252, and by Innocent IV on 9 August 1253, just two days before Clare's death.

Nevertheless, it interests us in the highest degree, because even if it held sway at San Damiano only for the briefest moment during Clare's lifetime, it surely conveys her spirit:

> The Form of Life of the Order of Poor Sisters that the blessed Francis established is this: to observe the Holy Gospel of our Lord Jesus Christ, by living in obedience, without anything of one's own, and in chastity.[19]

Chapter 2 explains in detail the reception of new recruits. The following clause is inserted at the end of the process:

> Let the form described above be observed in the examination and reception of the sisters who serve outside the monastery [*sorores servientes extra monasterium*], and let them be able to wear shoes.[20]

The sisters *servientes extra monasterium* return in the chapter on fasting:

> The younger sisters, those who are weak, and those who are serving outside the monastery may be mercifully dispensed as the abbess sees fit.[21]

---

17. *Escritos*, 259–60; CAED, 101–102.
18. Caesarius of Arles, *Œuvres monastiques. Œuvres pour les moniales*, ed. Joël Courreau and Adalbert de Vogüe (Paris, 1988); Leander of Seville, "Regula," in *PL*, vol. 72, cols. 873–94.
19. *Fonti legislative*, 68; CAED, 109.
20. *Fonti legislative*, 34–36; CAED, 112.
21. *Fonti legislative*, 42; CAED, 113.

I. THE SERVANT SERVED

The same softening appears concerning silence:

> Let the sisters keep silence from the hour of Compline until Terce, except those who are serving outside the monastery.[22]

But in the chapter on discipline, Clare's Form of Life becomes more expansive about the *sorores servientes extra monasterium*:

> Let the sisters serving outside the monastery not delay for long unless some manifest necessity requires it. Let them conduct themselves virtuously and say little, so that those who see them may always be edified. And let them strictly beware of having suspicious meetings or dealings with others. And let them not be co-mothers to men or women, lest gossip or trouble arise because of this.[23]

"Co-mothers" and "co-fathers" are those who are joint god-mothers and god-fathers at an infant's baptism. A strong link is forged between them, that of "co-motherhood." But, as the term's double meaning in French suggests,[24] what could lend itself more to gossip or to disorder than co-motherhood? The servants need to remain untouched by the world through which they walk. The Form of Life continues:

> And let them not presume to repeat the gossip of the world inside the monastery. And let them be strictly bound not to repeat outside the monastery anything that is said or done within which could cause scandal. If anyone should innocently offend in these two matters, let it be left to the prudence of the abbess mercifully to impose a penance on her. But if she does this through a vicious habit, the abbess, with the advice of her discreet sisters, may impose a penance on her according to the nature of the fault.[25]

All the layers of the normative sources converge here. At San Damiano, almost from the beginning, at least from as early as 1220 (if indeed the regulations reflect lived reality, which seems likely in this case), there were two categories of religious women: the "ladies" or "sisters," on one hand, and the "servants" or "serving sisters," on the other. To deny this fact would be to deny a reality proved by documentary evidence. Yet to present this division as an expression of raw class warfare or as the exploitation of women by other women would be to descend to the level of caricature and bad faith.

---

22. *Fonti legislative*, 58; CAED, 116.
23. *Fonti legislative*, 88–90; CAED, 122.
24. *Commérage* means both "godmother-hood" and "gossip" in French.
25. *Fonti legislative*, 90–92; CAED, 122.

In fact, the status of the servants of San Damiano is similar to that of male or female "converts." Before the eleventh century, in the traditional monasticism inspired by St. Benedict, the label "convert" applied to people who had not entered the monastery in childhood or adolescence, but rather had joined the cloister as adults. These people had thus known a worldly existence and had "converted" from the world to religious life.

With the monastic reforms of the eleventh century, a new type of convert appeared. Alongside the "choir" monks—the most prestigious members of the community, who sang the divine office in the choir and were usually of aristocratic origin and clerics or priests as well as monks—the "converts" from this time on formed a lesser category. They were of more modest social background, notably less educated, and charged primarily with manual labor, while the choir monks devoted themselves to study and the liturgy.

This division might seem harsh. In reality, the emergence of these new converts allowed more people access to a "regular" religious life (the communal religious life "regulated" by a rule); and this larger number was drawn from a wider segment of society. Specifically, sons or daughters of peasants could now take an active part in religious life within the framework of a regular community, whereas previously their parents and ancestors had been mere serfs or tenants of the monastic lordship, the domain where the monks accumulated the rights of landholders and the powers of a lord possessing a share of public authority. Doubtless this was a second-class advancement—but it was an advancement all the same. And with the spiritual benefit came a material guarantee: to be a member of a religious community sheltered one from need or want, and above all from hunger.

The "new style" converts appeared, it seems, in the eleventh century at Vallombrosa, in the monastery founded by John Gualbert near Florence. They are then found at Camaldoli, the foundation of Romuald of Ravenna close to Arezzo; at Hirsau, a Benedictine monastery in the German Black Forest reformed by its abbot, William; at the Grande Chartreuse, a congregation of hermits founded by Bruno of Cologne in the alpine Chartreuse mountains; at Cîteaux, the "new monastery" created by Robert of Molesmes between Dijon and Beaune to reform the tradition of St. Benedict; at Fontevraud, the community of men and women planted in the Loire Valley by Robert of Arbrissel; at Prémontré, a community of regular canons (priests living in the manner of monks) established near Laon by Norbert of Xanten; at Sempringham, a double monastery (for men and women) begun by Gilbert in Lincolnshire; and in many other places.

The dates prove beyond doubt that these religious establishments, founded or reformed between the eleventh and the twelfth centuries, were all part of the same movement. They all emerged from the same burst of renewal of the monastic life, as is made evident either by the reform of existing communities or rules, or by the creation of entirely new communities and norms. Both cases involved a return to the sources: a return to the intermediary sources of the rules of Augustine (for canons) or Benedict (for monks) in the first case; a return to the source of sources, the Gospel, in the second.

Male and female converts were also present in reformed female communities. At the Paraclete, the mixed monastery whose existence and idealized statutes had been delineated by Peter Abelard, the Institutions that actually regulated the life of the nuns (the customs, something less than a rule) were written between 1142 and 1147 by "the very wise Heloise." She was perfectly aware of the emergence of male and female converts:

> It was part of our religious way of life to live from the cultivation of the earth and from our labor, if we were able to do so. But since, due to our weakness, we cannot do that, we admit male and female converts, so that what the rigor of a religious life does not allow us to do ourselves, others may accomplish for us. We also receive all possible alms from the faithful, just as other churches do.[26]

If we place the servants of San Damiano in the context of this wider development, it must be said that this second category of religious women enjoyed a more favorable status than most. At the beginning of their religious lives they made the same profession as their sisters, and at the end they had the same place of burial. They were truly members of the community. Fasts, the habit, and silence were mitigated in their favor or modified for their status, but primarily for functional reasons due to the fact that these women, in contrast to the "ladies," were in contact with the outside world.

"The sisters serving outside the monastery": Thomas of Celano is perfectly in accord with Clare of Assisi's Form of Life when, in connection to the washing of feet, he evokes the "servants who return from outside." This is what defines them and what burdens them. The entire monastic life, even more so for women than for men, is thought of as a withdrawal, a retreat, a cloistering, a move apart from the world and a shelter from its defilements, as a safeguard of consecrated purity, above all virginity. For this reason, contact with the world, a burden borne exclusively by the servants, represents a permanent risk of pollution. This risk is clearly expressed in the precautions contained in Clare's Form of Life, which transform (but also confirm) a likely social inferiority into a moral danger.

---

26. Chrysogonus Waddell, ed., *The Paraclete Statutes "Institutiones nostrae."* Troyes, Bibliothèque Municipale Ms 802, ff. 89r–90v: Introduction, Edition, Commentary (Trappist, KY, 1987), 11.

Fifteen of Clare's sisters were interviewed individually during her canonization process. All were presented as "nuns of the monastery of San Damiano." On 28 November 1253 the collective questioning of "Lady Sister Benedetta, then abbess, with the other nuns of the said monastery of San Damiano" took place. Since nothing specifically signals their participation, I am inclined to think that the servants were not called on to testify. Yet they were still present in the depositions, not only in the triple retelling of the washing of the servant's feet (*servitiale* is the term used in the surviving fifteenth-century Italian translation of the process), but also in two other places. One is in the testimony of sister Cecilia, daughter of Gualterio Cacciaguerra of Spello:

> But God chose her [Clare] as mother of the virgins, as the first and principal abbess of the Order, so that by her example and in harmony with the holy purpose of religious life, she might watch over the flock and strengthen the other sisters of the monastery of this Order. She was certainly most diligent about encouraging the sisters and watching over them, showing compassion toward the sick sisters. She was solicitous about serving them, humbly submitting herself to even the least of the servants, always looking down upon herself.[27]

The emphasis on "even" and "the least" is notable: submission to "the least" of the servants (*alle mimime servitiale*) is the ultimate self-humbling. The other is in testimony from a nun, Angeluccia, daughter of Angelico of Spoleto:

> She also says that when the most holy mother used to send the servants outside the monastery, she would remind them to praise God when they saw beautiful trees, flowering and leafy; and likewise, always to praise God for and in all things when they saw other people and creatures.[28]

The Italian term employed is not quite the same: *servitrice* rather than *servitiale*. But most importantly, it is joined to the term "sisters" (*sore servitrice*) and includes the mention "outside the monastery" (*de fora del monasterio*), just like the "sisters serving outside the monastery" in Clare's Form of Life. It is striking that the association of terms that finally expresses the "sisterhood" of the servants would suddenly appear at this point, in the only passage where the "most holy mother" addresses them with an admonition that takes into account and superbly values their specific roles in the community. Here, to go outside the monastery is not to be exposed to the defilement of the world, but to see creation and creatures, to see them and to contemplate them in order to praise the

---

27. *Primi documenti*, 142; CAED, 168.
28. *Primi documenti*, 201; CAED, 189.

Creator. Clare's exhortation echoes and amplifies a verse from the *Canticle of Brother Sun*:

> Praised be you, my Lord, through our Sister Mother Earth,
> who sustains and governs us,
> and who produces various fruit with colored flowers and herbs.[29]

Francis composed this *Canticle*, let's recall, at San Damiano.

---

29. Jacques Dalarun, *The Canticle of Brother Sun: Francis of Assisi Reconciled*, trans. Philippe Yates (St. Bonaventure, NY, 2016), 2–3.

3. Assisi[30]

Clare was the daughter of Lord Favarone and Lady Ortolana. The nineteenth witness at her canonization process, a layman, described in his deposition the social position of the family:

> Pietro of Damiano of the city of Assisi, under oath, said that he, the witness, lived near—he and his father—the house of St. Clare, her family, and other members of her family. He knew Lady Clare when she was in the world and knew her father, Lord Favarone, who was noble, great, and powerful in the city—he and the others of his household. Lady Clare was noble, of a noble family, and of an upright manner of life. Seven knights were part of her household, all noble and powerful. Asked how he knew these things, he answered that he had seen them, because he was her neighbor.[31]

In fact, Clare of Assisi's entire canonization process is the expression of a network of family, friends, and neighbors; they were the group of aristocrats whose daughters made up the little militia of San Damiano. Sister Pacifica, daughter of Guelfuccio of Assisi, the first witness, "knew St. Clare while that holy woman was in the world in her father's house." And for good reason:

> Asked how she knew these things, she answered that when she was in the world she was her neighbor and distant relative, and that only the square [*piazza*] was between her house and that of the virgin Clare, and that she was in her company on many occasions.[32]

Oddly, Pacifica had never met Favarone, Clare's father. But she was well acquainted with her mother, Ortolana, her neighbor on the *piazza* in front of the cathedral of San Rufino in Assisi. Pacifica had accompanied Clare's mother on pilgrimage to the Holy Land, to San Michele of Monte Gargano in Apulia, and to Rome. Very early on, Pacifica had rejoined Clare at San Damiano, and eventually Ortolana had joined them there, too. In 1211 Agnes, daughter of Favarone and Ortolana, had been the first to come to her biological sister Clare; Agnes's death in 1253 followed Clare's by only a few days. Beatrice, their youngest sister

---

30. The French title of this chapter, "Assise," is the French form of "Assisi." But *assise* is also a French noun meaning "seat" or "base," as well as the feminine form of an adjective meaning "seated." Thus the chapter title in French makes a triple, untranslatable, play on words, with Clare settled (or "seated") in Assisi, the base (or "seat") of her family's power.
31. *Primi documenti*, 219; *CAED*, 194.
32. *Primi documenti*, 84; *CAED*, 144.

and the twelfth witness, came to San Damiano in 1229. Thus for several years the mother and her three daughters shared the same experience of religious life.

Bona, the seventeenth witness, was Pacifica's biological sister and lived in Clare's family home. She had accompanied Clare as a faithful chaperone during her secret meetings with Francis. She too had made the pilgrimage to Rome, but had not entered religious life. Her sister Pacifica declared that after having joined Clare at San Damiano, "she had served her, so to speak, for the most part almost day and night."[33] The two sisters were thus part of Clare's "family" in the wider—ancient and medieval—sense; they were close neighbors and also distant relatives, though doubtless of lower standing, serving the women in Ortolana's house. In contrast to the fathers of the other nuns, theirs, Guelfuccio, is never called "lord." Pacifica transferred and thus perpetuated within the heart of the cloister the dependent tie that had been established at the *piazza* San Rufino.

Benvenuta of Perugia, the second witness, entered San Damiano some six months after Clare. She had known Clare as a child between 1202 and 1204, when the family of Favarone and Ortolana had taken refuge in Perugia, driven out by the "popular" party of Assisi, the faction opposed to the nobles during the city's internal political battles. The noble Leonardo of Ghislerio, lord of Sassorosso, had also lived in exile in Perugia with Clare's family; the friendship between Clare and Filippa, Leonardo's daughter and the third witness, dated from this period. Cecilia, the sixth witness, was the daughter of Lord Gualterio of Spello. Gualterio's family, the Cacciaguerra, may have been related to the consuls of Perugia who had sought to subdue Assisi's popular commune in 1200–1202.

Amata, daughter of Lord Martino of Coccorano, the fourth witness, was the younger sister of Balvina, the seventh witness. Their father was Clare's first cousin; the acts of the canonization process present Amata and Balvina as Clare's nieces. Cristiana, the fifth witness, was the daughter of Lord Cristiano of Parisse, one of the consuls of Assisi's commune. Francesca, the ninth witness, was the daughter of Lord Capitaneo, master of the castle of Collemedio until 1200, when he came to establish himself in Assisi.

Bearing the same name as Clare's sister Agnes, the tenth witness was the daughter of the late Lord Oportulo of Bernardo of Assisi, the *podestà* who had been excommunicated by Bishop Guido II in 1225. It was to reconcile this *podestà* (the leading magistrate of the commune) with the bishop that Francis had composed the second-to-last stanza of the *Canticle of Brother Son*. In 1238, Oportulo had been made procurator of the sisters of San Damiano, empow-

---

33. *Primi documenti*, 85; CAED, 145.

ered by them to manage temporal affairs in their name. It is possible that the eleventh witness, Benvenuta of Lady Diambra of Assisi, was his illegitimate daughter, and thus the half-sister of the previous witness, Agnes. Lord Rainiero of Bernardo of Assisi, the eighteenth witness, may have been the brother of Oportulo and uncle to the half-sisters Agnes of Oportulo and Benvenuta of Diambra. Since Rainiero testifies just after Bona of Guelfuccio and shares all her opinions about Clare, he may have been her husband, and thus the brother-in-law of Sister Pacifica. Rainiero specifies that he was frequently at Favarone's house and that his wife was related to Clare, which was "to some slight degree" the case for Pacifica, and thus for Bona, her sister.[34]

Clare's successor at the head of San Damiano, the abbess Benedetta, had in the world borne the lovely name of Ginevra, the Italian version of Guinevere, a name inspired by Arthurian romances and highly prized at aristocratic courts. She was in fact the daughter of Giorgio of Ugone of Tebalduccio, and her family was one of the most powerful in Assisi. Her cousin Angelo, a knight before becoming one of Francis's closest companions, was present at both Clare's death and her canonization process. The noble Rufino, another companion of Francis, was himself Clare's first cousin.

The sixteenth witness, Lord Hugolino of Pietro Girardone, a knight and several times city magistrate (he carried the title of "rector of the commune of Assisi" in 1237 and that of "captain of the war and of the gates of Assisi" in 1240), also lived in the noble neighborhood of San Rufino. He knew Favarone's family very well; he could cite the names of Favarone's father, Offreduccio, and his grandfather, Bernardino. Pietro of Damiano of Assisi, the nineteenth witness, was a neighbor of Clare's family. The twentieth witness, Giovanni of Ventura of Assisi, was a servant in Favarone's house and perhaps one of his men-at-arms. He too knew the names of three generations of Clare's male ancestors.

San Damiano was thus the female religious manifestation of an identifiable group of Assisi's citizens, united by family ties, marriage alliances, neighborhood proximity, patronage, and a shared culture and ideology; they were the noble families of the upper town, gathered around the cathedral of San Rufino. "Family" or "house" here has a wider meaning, encompassing everyone from the powerful householding couple down to the servants and including men-at-arms, the ladies' companions, poor relatives, clients, and dependents. The men bore knightly titles. The most powerful lineages held castles in the surrounding countryside, the *contado*. Within the city, they occupied the highest political offices at the heart of the commune.

---

34. *Primi documenti*, 84; CAED, 144.

I. THE SERVANT SERVED

André Vauchez has perfectly contextualized the evolutions that Italian cities, Assisi in particular, experienced in Francis's day.[35] Over the course of the twelfth century, communal regimes spread across all of north-central Italy. In the space opened up by the battles between popes and emperors, the cities seized substantial de facto autonomy. At the very heart of the cities, the collective power of the commune rivaled the power of the count or bishop. The commune was definitely not a democracy in the modern sense. A communal regime lay in the hands of a small, dominant group: vassals of the count or of the bishop, legal experts, perhaps some of the wealthiest merchants in the biggest cities. Only members of this group sat on the communal council. Real power was entrusted to several magistrates, the consuls, who came from an even smaller number of families. At the end of the twelfth century, in order to escape internal battles between factions, a new type of magistrate appeared, the *podestà*. He was usually chosen from another city as a way of transcending local rivalries and was appointed for only a very short time, six months or a year.

In theory, Assisi was subject to the German Empire. In 1197, following the death of the Hohenstaufen emperor Henry VI, the people of Assisi rose up and drove out the German garrison that had been installed in the fortress overlooking the town, la Rocca, which they proceeded to dismantle. The destruction extended to the fortified towers of the noble families, who had traditionally adhered to the emperor's party against that of the pope. In 1198—late compared with many other cities—the commune of Assisi was born. We should not imagine that "the people" (*il popolo*) refers to the popular masses; rather it refers a middle class of merchants, shop-keepers, and master artisans who envied the powers and prestige of the aristocratic lineages. The family of Clare belonged to the twenty or so dominant families. That of Francis, son of the merchant Pietro of Bernardone, was of the *popolo*.

In reaction to the birth of the commune, the great families fled the city and found refuge in Perugia; hence the exile that Clare suffered there, and her opportunity to make the acquaintance of girls from the Perugian nobility. Taking the side of the exiles and only too happy to find an excuse to gain the upper hand on the neighboring city, Perugia declared war on Assisi and invaded its territory in 1202. Armed as a knight (a grandiose dream transformed into a real transgression), Francis took part in the battle of Collestrada, where the popular forces of Assisi were defeated by the troops of Perugia and the nobles of Assisi (the real warriors). There, he was taken prisoner.

---

35. André Vauchez, *Francis of Assisi: The Life and Afterlife of a Medieval Saint*, trans. Michael F. Cusato (New Haven, CT, 2013).

The nobles returned as conquerors to their city of Assisi. A delicate internal balance was found with the popular party. External balance was established between the pope and the emperor, keeping both at equal distance. In 1210, a pact sealed more concretely the coexistence of the nobles and the popular party and their joint direction of the commune. In this document, the former are called the "majors" (*maiores*, greater ones) and the latter the "minors" (*minores*, lesser ones), thus heralding the name "minor" or "lesser," which Francis, from the popular party, would choose for his brothers in 1215.[36] Moreover, this 1210 accord abolished all serfdom in the city. In its own way, the spiritual adventure of Francis and Clare is the religious manifestation of the 1210 civic pact. Clare's flight from home dates from the following year, 1211. A year later, in 1212, construction of the communal palace on the town square (*piazza*) began.

An Italian city is a theater, with the *piazza* as its stage. Each person ostentatiously plays his or her role there. Each is precisely located by everyone else within a genealogy, a family network, a social class, a political faction, within the urban topography that itself expresses gradations of position, from the upper town where Clare resided to the lower town where Francis lived. The Italian terms used in the canonization process express these gradations. Clare's nobility is constantly affirmed. "The said Lady Clare was of the most noble [families] of the city of Assisi, on both sides, her father's and her mother's," specifies Rainiero of Bernardo.[37] Favarone is a knight, like seven other "noble and powerful" members of his house and like Hugolino of Pietro Girardone, the sixteenth witness.

The label "lord" (*mesere*) is used for the heads of the dominant families; for most of the fathers of the nuns called to testify; for Clare's great-grandfather, grandfather, and father; for all the popes mentioned; for the bishop of Assisi, his archdeacon, and the archpriest of Trevi. The notary of the process, by contrast, is only "sir" (*ser*). The last two witnesses, Pietro of Damiano and Giovanni of Ventura, who must have been in the service of Clare's family, do not receive any title. Neither does Guelfuccio, the father of two women, Pacifica and Bona, who also held subordinate positions in the household of Favarone and Ortolana.

Clare is called "lady" (*madonna*); so is her mother, Ortolana; so are all the nuns who testify; Diambra, mother of the eleventh witness, sister Benvenuta; a woman from Pisa who benefited from a miracle; five women sent by Francis to San Damiano to be received there; Guiduccia, wife of the knight Hugolino of Pietro Girardone; and Bona of Guelfuccio. The latter reference indicates that

---

36. Attilio Bartoli Langeli, "La realtà sociale assisana e il patto del 1210," in *Assisi al tempo di san Francesco* (Assisi, 1978), 271–336; Attilio Bartoli Langeli, "Il patto di Assisi: Ritorno sulla *Carta Pacis* del 1210," *Franciscan Studies* 65 (2007): 1–8.

37. *Primi documenti*, 216–17; *CAED*, 194.

I. THE SERVANT SERVED

the title of "lady" was more freely given to women than was that of "lord" to men, since the daughter Bona receives a title (unless it came to her through her marriage), whereas her father does not.

The Latin acts of the process are lost (only an Italian translation survives), but the "lords" were certainly referred to there by the Latin title *dominus* and the "ladies" by *domina*. These terms are heavy with social and ideological significance. They carry within them the idea of *dominium*, the domination over others that structures all of medieval society. Let's return to the original scene narrated by Thomas of Celano:

> Once when she was washing the feet of one of these servants, while she was bending to kiss them, that sister, not able to stand such humility, withdrew her foot, and with that foot she kicked the lady in her mouth.[38]

Servientes, servitiale, servitrici: all the terms that designate the servants establish not only a hierarchy of status between them and the ladies, but a relation of dominant to dominated, of served to servant. Yet in medieval Latin, the root *servus* suggests both ancient servitude and contemporary serfdom. The pact of 1210 had made all the inhabitants of the city legally free, but in the same triumphant burst the commune of Assisi extended its domination over the villages and small towns in the surrounding countryside, the *contado*. In the *contado*, the serfs remained under the power of the feudal lords, both lay and ecclesiastical.

Where did the servants of San Damiano come from? Alas, we have almost no evidence to answer this question. Doubtless their origins were a notch down the social scale from those of Pacifica of Guelfuccio, a city-dweller whose father was not a "lord" but whose sister Bona is called "lady," even though she occupied a subordinate place in Clare's family home. Were the servants daughters of peasants from the *contado*, as though they had seamlessly slipped from one form of servitude to another, from that of their parents to their own, from feudal to monastic servitude?

The seventh witness of the canonization process, Sister Balvina, daughter of Martino of Coccorano, must have had regrets after giving her deposition to the tribunal; she had forgotten to report an episode glorifying Clare, which she had heard from a sister who had witnessed it. So Balvina had her story recorded unofficially. It survives, by chance, in a manuscript of the Sacro Convento in Assisi.

> Once, when one of the servants of the monastery [*serviciales monasterii*] was gravely ill, the blessed Clare, a mirror of virtue and of humility, served

---

38. *Legenda S. Clarae*, 120 (ch. 8); *CAED*, 292.

[*servivit*] her in person. Since this servant had totally lost her appetite due to the severity of the illness, the blessed Clare said to her: "My sister, isn't there something that you could eat, or that you would have the appetite to eat?" As though she was disgusted by all food, [the servant] answered as though in a foul mood: "I would like," she said, "some trout from Valtopina and flatbreads from Nocera," knowing and believing that it would be nearly impossible to find these products, since Nocera was at least sixteen miles from Assisi. The blessed Clare, hearing this and with great sympathy for the sick woman, gave herself to prayer on bended knees, so that the Lord would grant what she had asked for.[39]

Again a servant served by Clare! This one did not let loose with kicks, but she did express her foul mood. As though drunk on the intoxication of the unnatural service offered to her, she became hateful, ungrateful, and tyrannical, asking for what she knew to be impossible.

Some five miles apart, Valtopina and Nocera Umbra are small towns on the Via Flaminia, east and northeast of Mount Subasio, whose foothills shelter Assisi on its western side. They lie about eighteen miles from the city of Assisi, down tortuous roads. What was so special about the trout of Valtopina and the flatbread of Nocera Umbra, if not that they came from the servant's own native region? To taste the dishes of one's childhood: the desire of the sick, the dream of the dying.

A marvelous thing! Indeed barely had Clare finished her prayer, by then quite late and with a torrential rain pouring down, when a very handsome young man—charming and with a pleasant face, carrying a cloth or a towel with the corners tied together two by two—came to the door and knocked urgently. The blessed Clare, hearing the noise, sent one of the servants to the door, thinking that it was one of the brothers. But when the servant arrived at the door, she received from the said young man the knotted cloth to take to Clare, with the provision that she would bring him back the cloth once the present had been put aside. The blessed Clare, untying the knots with her hands and returning the cloth to the young man, miraculously found the trout and flatbread—that is little cakes made of bread dough—that the sick woman had requested and that Clare had asked of the Lord; and this by the Lord's doing. The said young man, although invited by the brothers to stay due to the late hour and the bad weather, departed right away and no one saw him afterward. The blessed

---

39. *Legende minores*, 560–62 (from Assisi, Biblioteca conv. Comunale, ms. 442, fol. 167r-v).

I. THE SERVANT SERVED

Clare thus thanked God for the divine kindness which he had shown to her and she offered to the sick woman what she had desired.[40]

A manuscript held by the Bavarian State Library in Munich contains the same story. It adds this ending:

The blessed Clare, giving thanks for what had been granted to her by God, gave it to the sick woman. This sick woman was seized by a very delectable sweetness, and that very night, leaving behind this valley of misery, she returned happily to the Lord.[41]

---

40. *Legende minores*, 562.
41. *Legende minores*, 554 (from Munich, Bayerische Staatsbibliothek, ms Clm 23846, fols. 236va–239ra).

4. Ritual

The *Legend of Saint Clare, Virgin* was translated into French several times. Sometime in the fifteenth century, a new adaptation of Thomas of Celano's life was inserted into a legendary (a collection of saints' lives). The only known manuscript of this collection is preserved in Paris, in the library of the Institut de France. The episode of the washing of feet had not been forgotten:

> And here [San Damiano] Clare initiated the religious way of life that is called the "religion of the Poor Sisters," and she accomplished so much through her good works that her church was soon filled with a great number of sisters. She was their lady and their governess, but still she remembered well what is read in the Gospel of Saint—; because the more she was raised up in the government of others, the more she humbled herself and served them in all their needs. And if it happened that some of her sisters came back from being outside for the needs of the church, she would be the first to wash their feet and to dry them, then she would kiss them, following the example of Jesus Christ.[42]

The name of the Evangelist is scratched out. Perhaps the copyist had trouble identifying him. For the next phrase, however, the translator was surely thinking of Matthew 20:28: "Thus is the Son of man come, not to be served, but to serve." Behind the practice of washing the sisters' feet, the translator evidently recognized the model of Christ washing the apostles' feet during the Last Supper, as in John 13:1–15:

> He rises from supper and lays aside his garments and, taking a towel, wraps himself. After that, he puts water into a basin and begins to wash the feet of the disciples and to dry them with the towel with which he was wrapped. He comes therefore to Simon Peter. And Peter says to him: "Lord, you wash my feet!" Jesus answered, and said to him: "What I do you do not now know; but you will know hereafter." Peter says to him: "You shall never wash my feet!" Jesus answered him: "If I do not wash you, you will have no part with me." Simon Peter says to him: "Lord, not only my feet, but also my hands and my head!" Jesus says to him: "He who is washed, needs only wash his feet, but is clean wholly. And you are clean, but not all." For he knew who he was that would betray him; therefore he said: "You are not all clean."

---

42. Martine Pagan, "Les Légendes françaises de Claire d'Assise (XIIIᵉ–XVIᵉ siècle) III. Édition et commentaire du manuscrit 663 de la bibliothèque de l'Institut de France," *Études franciscaines* n. s. 8 (2015): 8.

I. THE SERVANT SERVED

Jesus put back on his clothes, returned to the table, and explained:

> Know you what I have done to you? You call me Master and Lord. And rightly you say so, for so I am. If then I being your Lord and Master, have washed your feet, you also ought to wash one another's feet. For I have given you an example, that as I have done to you, so you do also. Amen, amen I say to you: The servant is not greater than his lord; neither is the apostle greater than he who sent him. If you know these things, you shall be blessed if you do them. I speak not of you all: I know whom I have chosen. But that the scripture may be fulfilled: "He that eats bread with me, shall lift up his heel against me."

Medieval texts are palimpsests. One text hides another, which hides yet another, which hides, in the end, a relic of scripture. But the actions and gestures of medieval men and women are also themselves dictated by pericopes. These episodes from scripture, forming units of narrative and meaning, affected the innermost depths of the spirit, particularly through readings for the Mass, as the ultimate and most fundamental of texts: living words. It is all the more evident that Clare of Assisi had Christ's gesture in mind, especially since monastic tradition required that the abbot should ritually wash the feet of his monks on Thursday evening during Holy Week, and since at San Damiano, on the same day, the abbess did indeed wash the feet of her sisters. The witness Agnes, daughter of Oportulo, understood perfectly what the translator of the Institut de France manuscript emphasized, what Clare herself wanted, because she carefully preserved the liturgical dimensions of the event: "during Lent," "a Thursday."[43]

In the Rule of St. Benedict, washing the feet of guests is a simple act of hospitality:

> Let the abbot pour water on the hands of the guests; let the abbot as well as all the community wash the feet of all the guests.[44]

But a much more complex ceremony, tied to the celebration of Holy Thursday, developed in the monastic world during the Carolingian period. This was the *mandatum* (the "commandment"). The best known example is the one practiced in the great Benedictine abbey of Cluny, as attested in various layers of its customaries (books recording the monks' daily practices, including liturgical ones). Let's follow the oldest one, recorded during the time of Abbot Odilon (994–1049). The poor were gathered. Away from the monks, they heard mass. Once mass had been celebrated for the monks, and they had eaten,

---

43. *Primi documenti*, 172; *CAED*, 178.
44. *RSB*, 120–21 (chap. 53).

Let the dean send the poor to the place established (the cloister) for this purpose, and there, their feet will be washed by the brothers. When the latter have left the refectory, let the prior sound the bell. And let them walk before the poor singing the Psalm *Miserere*. Then let them prostrate themselves on the ground before the poor, and following that let them wash the feet of each one. Let the chanter intone the antiphon *The Lord Jesus, after he had dined with the disciples, washed their feet and said to them:* "Do you know what I have done for you? I, the Lord and master, have given you the example so that you also can do the same." [Let them further sing] the antiphon *I give you a new commandment* [mandatum], *that you may love one another as I have loved you, says the Lord.*[45]

The antiphons and the verses to be sung, of which only the initial words (the *incipits*) are given here, are based first and foremost on the story of the washing of the disciples' feet during the Last Supper and secondly on two episodes concerning the anointing the Christ's feet, one by the female sinner at the home of Simon, the other by Mary, sister of Martha and Lazarus. The ceremony continues: "Let each one wash only the feet of one poor person, then dry them and kiss them." The abbot goes first, then the brothers take their turn, two by two: one washes, the other dries, then they switch roles. At the close of the ceremony, each poor person receives some wine and two pennies. In the evening, the abbot washes, dries, and kisses the feet of all the monks, and then the same thing is done to him by three monks, two who wash his feet and one who kisses them.

This ritual of the *mandatum* enjoyed an enormous success, so much so that in English Holy Thursday eventually became known as Maundy Thursday. From the monastic world the ritual spread to the secular (non-monastic) church and the world of laymen and laywomen. Bishops, communities of canons, popes, and even kings—all practiced it. Louis IX, the king of France, better known as St. Louis, engaged in the ritual. So did his sister, Isabelle of France (d. 1270):

She had this custom, that on Maundy Thursday she would take thirteen poor people and wash their feet and serve them with her own hands with two pairs of dishes and would give them shoes and would offer to each thirty Parisian sous in remembrance of the price for which our Lord was sold.[46]

---

45. *Consuetudines cluniacensium antiquiores cum redactionibus derivatis*, ed. Kassius Hallinger (Siegburg, Germany, 1983), 79–80.
46. Sean L. Field, ed. and trans., *The Writings of Agnes of Harcourt: The Life of Isabelle of France and the Letter on Louis IX and Longchamp* (Notre Dame, IN, 2003), 65.

I. THE SERVANT SERVED

Through the papal liturgy, the *mandatum* was introduced into the Franciscan liturgy, which the sisters followed at San Damiano:

> After the altars have been stripped, at a convenient time, at the sounding of the bell, the brothers gather to carry out the *mandatum*. The superiors [*maiores*] wash, dry, and kiss the feet [of the others] and, during this time, the chants written below are chanted, in whole or in part, according to the decision of the chanter.[47]

Among the antiphons and the verses "written below," the "new commandment"—the story of the washing of the feet during the Last Supper and the episode of the female sinner at the home of Simon—was sung, just as it was at Cluny. Francis of Assisi himself had made explicit the institutional and moral sense of this ritual, in chapter four of his *Admonitions*, which Clare certainly knew:

> "I have not come to be served but to serve" (Matthew 20:28), says the Lord. Those who have been placed over others, let them glory in that position as much as if they had been assigned the duty of washing their brothers' feet. And if they are more bothered by having their place over others taken away from them than by losing the duty of washing feet, it is as though they had amassed "a money bag" (John 12:6) to the peril of their soul.[48]

The translator of the Institut de France manuscript evidently had this body of Gospel texts and liturgical customs in mind when he wrote, "She was the first to wash their feet and to dry them, then she kissed them following the example of Jesus Christ." Yet although Christ did wash his disciples' feet, he never actually kissed them. One Gospel text can also hide another. Clare of Assisi's gesture in fact combines two passages that tradition had already intertwined, in multiple ways, well before her time, as the customary of Odilon of Cluny and the order of the Franciscan liturgy attest. Luke (7:36–50) recounts the other episode:

> And one of the Pharisees wanted him to eat with him. And he went into the house of the Pharisee, and sat down at table. And behold a woman who was in the city, a sinner, when she knew that he sat at table in the Pharisee's house, brought an alabaster box of ointment. And standing behind, at his feet, she began to wash his feet, with tears, and dried them with the hairs of her head, and kissed his feet, and anointed them with the ointment.

---

47. Stephen Joseph Peter Van Dijk, ed., *Sources of the Modern Roman Liturgy: The Ordinals by Haymo of Faversham and Related Documents (1243–1307)* (Leiden, 1963), 2:239.

48. *Scripta*, 358; *FAED*, 1:130.

Simon the Pharisee is shocked that this man–a poor prophet indeed!—lets himself be touched by a woman who is a sinner. Christ understands this and speaks to him:

> Do you see this woman? I entered into your house, you gave me no water for my feet; but she, with tears, has washed my feet, and with her hairs has dried them. You gave me no kiss; but she, since she came in, has not ceased to kiss my feet. You did not anoint my head with oil; but she has anointed my feet with oil. Wherefore I say to you: Many sins are forgiven her, because she has loved much.

This sinner strongly resembles the anonymous woman who anointed Christ's head with ointment contained in an alabaster vase, when he was at table at the home of Simon the Leper in Bethany (Matthew 26:6–13; Mark 14:3–9). She has points in common with Mary, sister of Martha and Lazarus, who also sat at Jesus's feet to listen to him while Martha busied herself (Luke 10:38–42), to beg him to bring Lazarus back to life (John 11:1–5, 32–33), to spread ointment on his feet and dry them with her hair (John 11:2, 13:3). It was tempting to associate her with "Mary, who is called Magdalene, out of whom seven demons had gone forth" (Luke 8:2), the same Mary Magdalene who was present at a certain distance (Matthew 27:55–56, Mark 15:40–41) or at the feet of the cross (John 19:25) and when Jesus' body was laid in the tomb (Matthew 27:61, Mark 15:47, Luke 23:55, 24:10), who went to his tomb at dawn on Easter Sunday (Matthew 28:1, Mark 16:1, 24:10), and whom John (20:1–18) makes the privileged witness to the Resurrection.

It fell to Pope Gregory the Great, in his Homily 32 on the Gospels, to fuse these female figures who only brushed against each other in scripture:

> She whom Luke calls the sinner, whom John calls Mary, we believe that she was the Mary from whom Mark testifies that seven demons were driven.[49]

Mary Magdalene, "the Magdalene," was born—one of Western devotion's most beautiful creations, one of the most complicated as well, and therefore one of the most fantastical. A figure of repentance and redemption; a figure of love, of love stronger than sin, stronger than the sin of love; the only woman to have so intimately touched the body of Christ; apostle to the apostles, since she had informed them of the Resurrection; a woman who taught men, who surpassed Peter in her love for Christ and in Christ's love for her.

---

49. Gregory the Great, *Homeliae in Evangelia*, ed. Raymond Étaix (Turnhout, 1999), 288.

I. THE SERVANT SERVED

The Magdalene landed in the Camargue (at the mouth of the Rhône) and so became the apostle to Provence; she lived as a hermit at Sainte-Baume and was buried at Aix or at Saint-Maximin or at Vézelay, at least according to the devout local traditions that fought over where her body lay. Eternally coiled at the feet of Christ, the Magdalene's privilege of love is consecrated by a pictorial tradition that places her, kneeling and prostrate, at the foot of the cross, in a scarlet robe, hair undone, tears streaming, arms embracing the pierced feet of the Beloved...

By washing her sisters' feet on a Thursday during Lent, in this universe of reversals opened up by the Gospel, Clare of Assisi also fulfilled her office: the liturgical office of the abbess, the office of the abbot, the office of Christ. The abbess—this title that Clare had not wanted, but that she had accepted—is not exactly the mother of her sisters. From Aramaic to Greek, the *abba* is the father. The New Testament refers to God the Father in this way, as *abba*. The abbess is the feminine version of a masculine title, thus more like a feminized father than a mother. On the night of the Last Supper, by his washing of feet, Christ had "given the example"; but he had not done away with the hierarchy that linked him to the apostles:

> Amen, amen I say to you: The servant is not greater than his lord; neither is the one sent [*apostolus*] greater than he who sent him.

If we had only Pacifica's testimony to go on, Clare of Assisi's gesture toward the sisters in general (or the sick in particular) would perfectly match the duty of the abbot toward his guests according to the Rule of St. Benedict. "She served them, washed their feet, and poured water on their hands." Benvenuta, Filippa, and Agnes of Oportulo felt compelled to specify that among the sisters she had also washed the feet of the servants. But the abbot of Cluny, head of a veritable monastic empire, and the pope himself, sovereign pontiff of the universal church, did they not wash the feet of anonymous poor people?

At San Damiano, the servants stood midway between the poor and the monks of Cluny. In washing "the feet of the sisters and of the servants," Clare compressed the two successive ceremonies of Maundy Thursday, as it was celebrated at Cluny, into the single *mandatum* of the Franciscan liturgy. This compression is heavy with significance. At Assisi, the poor are no longer kept outside, reduced to an annual appearance in the role of dazed walk-ons during an ostentatious display of magnificent humility. The servants are part of the community of San Damiano; they have made the same profession as the ladies and will lie by their sides for all eternity.

Kissing the foot changes things, because at this moment Clare no longer represents Christ, but the sinner; she no longer represents a man, but a woman. And not just any woman! A woman "in the city," says Luke, known for her faults. Socially and morally this woman was the opposite of the daughter of "Lord Favarone, who was noble, great, and powerful in the city—he and the others of his household," according to Pietro of Damiano.[50] Still according to Pietro, Lady Clare was not only "noble, of a noble family," but also "of an upright manner of life." "This Lady Clare was always considered by everyone to be a most pure virgin," assures Bona of Guelfuccio, along with more than half the witnesses in the process of canonization.[51] Yet it was firmly understood by all medieval readers and listeners that the female sinner of the Gospel of Luke had sinned by the flesh.

By returning from male to female, but to a femininity very different from her own, did the noble daughter of Favarone finally commit a transgression? One might think so, reading the depositions given by Benvenuta and Filippa: the kiss of the servant's feet appears there like a sudden, spur-of-the-moment gesture. Did Clare understand that through the act of foot-washing she was in fact embodying a figure of masculine authority? That she was likening herself to the abbot she had not wanted to be? That she risked identifying herself with Christ, and that she needed to dispel as quickly as possible the hint of pride peeking out from beneath this too brazenly signaled service? Agnes of Oportulo leaves no room for such imaginary scruples: "washing the feet of one of the servants and wanting to kiss them as she usually did."[52] And for good reason: the abbot of Cluny, or of any other monastery, already ritually joined the sinner's gesture to that of Christ, the kiss to the washing.

At the very heart of the matter, from the moment we start to dissect this scene of foot-washing at San Damiano, again and again we run headlong into the same internal contradiction: Why do the witnesses present a gesture that is literally insisted upon by ritual as though it were particularly remarkable and praiseworthy?

Of the three sisters who recall the scene, one, Filippa, gives no indication of its liturgical dimension: she sees it entirely through the lens of Clare's exceptional humility: "even washing the feet of the servants. Once, while washing the feet of one of the monastery's servants . . ."[53] Another, Benvenuta, restores the idea of an established practice, but without giving it additional significance: "From the moment when this mother St. Clare entered religious life, she was so humble that she washed the feet of the sisters herself."[54] Only Agnes has a fully liturgical understanding of the event. The washing is a ritual, like the kiss,

---

50. *Primi documenti*, 219; CAED, 194.
51. *Primi documenti*, 211; CAED, 192.
52. *Primi documenti*, 171; CAED, 178.
53. *Primi documenti*, 112; CAED, 157.
54. *Primi documenti*, 96–97; CAED, 150.

and the date she gives—a Thursday in Lent—is a thinly veiled reference to the Last Supper and the *mandatum*.

Of all those who recounted the episode, the one with the sharpest liturgical sense was surely the hagiographer, Thomas of Celano. He had read Agnes of Oportulo's deposition; he knew by heart the order of the Franciscan liturgy, specifically that of the Mass for Maundy Thursday: "The superiors wash, dry, and kiss the feet [of the others]." Yet in this case he suppressed the liturgical indications. Following only Filippa, he held up the servants as the sole beneficiaries of the abbess's care. The hagiographer's role is not to certify that the saintly man or woman placidly followed proper ritual, but to glorify his or her virtues on a heroic stage.

Underneath authorial strategies, underneath the testifying sisters' greater or lesser liturgical awareness, there is an element, intrinsic to ritual, of which we risk losing sight. Even if, by definition, liturgy consists of repetition, nevertheless it does not merely create routine. Instead, at its high points, its moments of extreme dramatization, it produces a continuously renewed sense of wonder. At each mass, at each consecration, the improbable descent of Christ onto the altar (through the transubstantiation of species, a doctrine that took shape precisely between the eleventh and the thirteenth centuries) is a radically new miracle. Each year, in the readings of the offices and Masses of Holy Week, the washing of the disciples' feet, the revelation of Judas's betrayal, the arrest of Christ, the cowardice of Peter, the judgement of Pilate, the release of Barabbas, the mocking, the condemnation, the crucifixion, the death, the piercing of the lance, the empty tomb, and the appearance of the risen Christ to the Magdalene caused spirits to exalt and hearts to beat faster. This is what Timothy Johnson calls "the performative dimension" of the liturgy.[55]

Ritual is neither a recollection nor a symbol. It is a commemoration, a living representation, a present ceaselessly renewed through the updating power of memory. By fulfilling the abbess's liturgical function, Clare of Assisi embodied anew both Christ and the sinner. Her gesture is ritualized, expected, prescribed. It is no less astonishing for that fact. And so for her sisters, it deserved to be added to the dossier of her sanctity.

---

55. Timothy J. Johnson, "Lost in Sacred Space: Textual Hermeneutics, Liturgical Worship, and Celano's *Legenda ad Usum Chori*," *Franciscan Studies* 59 (2001): 109–31; Timothy J. Johnson, "Meraviglie di pietre e spazi. La dimensione teologica delle narrazioni sui miracoli in Tommaso da Celano e Bonaventura da Bagnoregio," in *Paradoxien der Legitimation. Ergebnisse einer deutsch-italienisch-französischen Villa Vigoni-Konferenz sur Macht im Mittelalter*, ed. Annette Kehnel and Cristina Andenna, with Cécile Caby and Gert Melville (Florence, 2010), 479–96.

5. Body

The sudden eruption of the unexpected is ultimately due to the servant's reaction. It is she, after all, who pulls back her foot, as though by reflex, and in so doing kicks Clare in the mouth. Was this too not written? "He that eats bread with me, shall lift up his heel against me." Christ, after having washed the feet of his disciples, announces Judas's betrayal in this way, explaining that scripture must be fulfilled (John 13:18). The scriptural passage in question is verse 10 of Psalm 40:[56]

> For even the man of peace, in whom I trusted, who ate my bread, has raised his heel against me.

In the thirteenth century "to raise the heel" became shorthand for rebellion. The Franciscan chronicler Salimbene of Adam, for example, employed this phrase to describe the Emperor Frederick II's revolt against the church.[57]

The *Explanation of the Psalms* written by Ambrose of Milan in the fourth century held authoritative sway throughout the Middle Ages. For the holy Doctor of the church, following the principle of what is known as typological interpretation, the meaning of the Old Testament verse becomes clear through its usage in the story of the Last Supper as told by John:

> Judas also raised the heel, like an insolent and prideful fighter, to strike the Savior's head. But he could not wound the head of Christ, because *the head of Christ is God*. (I Corinthians 11:3)[58]

At San Damiano, still in accord with the Franciscan liturgy followed there, the biblical passage on the Last Supper was read every year at the Mass for Maundy Thursday. Yet it is true that the reading stopped at "For I have given you an example, that as I have done to you, so you do also"; that is, it stopped just before the raised heel. Did the sisters recognize the scriptural background to the servant's kick? If they did, it is not apparent in the testimonies of Benvenuta, Filippa, or Agnes, who note only a thoughtless, undiscerning, unintentional gesture.

As for Thomas of Celano, he had in mind not only John's Gospel text, but very likely Ambrose's commentary on the Psalms as well. In the *Legend of Saint*

---

56. Psalm numbering here follows the Vulgate (the Latin Bible used in the Middle Ages). Most modern translations would number this as Psalm 41.
57. Salimbene, *Cronica*, 2:575; *Chronicle of Salimbene de Adam*, 382.
58. Ambrose of Milan, *Explanatio psalmorum XII*, pars VI, ed. Michael Petschening and Michaela Zelzer (Vienna, 1999), 246; *Commentary of Saint Ambrose on Twelve Psalms*, trans. Ide M. Ní Riain (Dublin, 2000), 194.

I. THE SERVANT SERVED

Clare, Virgin, he described the servants as those "who return from outside."[59] For a monk, even a Franciscan, beyond the cloister lay the realm of defilement. Thus Thomas could have played with the words Christ addressed to his disciples during the episode of the washing of feet (John 13:10–11):

> "And you are clean, but not all." For he knew who he was that would betray him; therefore he said: "You are not all clean."

Due to his noble birth, Thomas grasped all the social expectations inherent in the exchange between the lady and the servant. Thanks to his education, his mastery of biblical commentary would have allowed him to show off by exposing the allegorical meaning of the episode. But if he momentarily considered the possibility, he let it pass. It is quite rare for a medieval author to permit his virtuosity to carry him beyond the purpose at hand. It was not part of Thomas's intention to fracture the ideal community of the sisters of San Damiano or to make Clare appear as another Christ. As he stresses in the legend's prologue, her role should be limited to a model for feminine behavior, itself shaped by the Virgin Mary's footprint:

> Therefore let the men follow the men, who are the new disciples of the Incarnate Word; let the women imitate Clare, footprint of the Mother of God, a new leader of women.[60]

And Clare could hardly be likened to Christ, because she was betrothed to him:

> Trembling with horror at the illusions of the flesh, she now proposed to be *ignorant of the marriage bed in sin* (Wisdom 3:13), desiring to make of her body a temple for God alone, and striving by her virtue to be worthy of marriage with the great King.[61]

She was a royal wife, but one who, in the fervor of prayer, could take on the loving caresses of the sinful woman:

> Very frequently, while she was prostrate on her face in prayer, she flooded the ground with tears and caressed it with kisses, so that she might always seem to have her Jesus in her hands, on whose feet her tears flowed and her kisses were impressed.[62]

---

59. *Legenda S. Clarae*, 120 (chap. 8); *CAED*, 292.
60. *Legenda S. Clarae*, 90 (prologue); *CAED*, 279.
61. *Legenda S. Clarae*, 102 (chap. 3); *CAED*, 284. Direct biblical citations within quotations are in italics.
62. *Legenda S. Clarae*, 136 (chap. 13); *CAED*, 298.

Perhaps because she felt sheltered by her virginity, preserved on earth, and protected by her longed-for heavenly union, St. Clare of Assisi, far from being a holier-than-thou hypocrite, had little hesitation in employing bodily language. During the canonization process, Filippa recalled:

> Lady Clare also related how once, in a vision, it seemed to her that she brought a bowl of hot water to St. Francis along with a towel for drying his hands. She was climbing a very high stairway, but was doing it very easily, almost as though she were moving on level ground. When she reached St. Francis, the saint bared his breast and said to Lady Clare: "Come, take and suck." After she had sucked from it, the saint admonished her to suck again. While she was sucking, what she sucked was so sweet and delightful she in no way could describe it. After she had sucked, that nipple or opening of the breast from which the milk flows remained between the lips of the blessed Clare. After she took in her hands what remained in her mouth, it seemed to her that it was gold so clear and bright that she saw everything there, as if in a mirror.[63]

This vision has received abundant commentary. I will deliberately refrain from adding my own. Any gloss only tones it down, sugarcoats it. To preserve its strange power, it is enough to read it out loud, in public, as I have had occasion to do. Clare told this story in public more than once, because three other sisters confirmed Filippa's testimony. Filippa recounted it, in its entirety, with its six repetitions of the word "suck," in front of a bishop, an archdeacon, an archpriest, three Franciscan brothers, and a notary. When the pope commissioned him to turn the acts of the canonization process into a legend, Thomas of Celano did not dare to repeat Filippa's unsettlingly vivid account. He decided to leave out the vision of the breast altogether. Poor Thomas!

He also preferred to leave out the testimony of Sister Balvina, daughter of Lord Martino of Coccorano:

> This witness added that one night she herself, being sick, was very troubled by a serious pain in her hip. She began to suffer and complain. The lady asked her what was the matter. The witness told her about the pain, and the mother threw herself directly on the hip at the place where the pain was. Then she placed the veil she had on her head over it and immediately the pain completely vanished. Asked how long ago this was, she replied, "more than twelve years ago." Asked who was present, she replied that she, the witness, was alone with her in a room where she usually

---

63. *Primi documenti*, 122–23; CAED, 161.

stayed in prayer. She did not remember the month or day or rather the night.[64]

The surviving Italian version of the acts of the canonization process uses a strong verb to describe Clare's movement: *se gittò deritto sopra quella ancha*. All in all this passage is certainly less shocking than the vision of St. Francis's breast. Yet because this case concerned real events, not a vision, the circumstances must have bothered the hagiographer: two women alone at night in a bedroom, contrary to all monastic precautions, one throwing herself on the other at hip-level, lifting up her veil . . . They were guilty of nothing, of course. But why recount such an intimate scene to a wider public, who might misinterpret it and find it disturbing?

Monastic rules or customs for women strictly regulated all relations with the few men who were likely to enter the cloister. Sometimes, too, reading between the lines, one perceives a distrust of contact between the nuns themselves. Thus at Fontevraud, at the beginning of the twelfth century, the founder Robert of Arbrissel took care to specify, concerning the celebration of mass: "Let them not give each other the kiss of peace, but instead kiss the marble which is passed to them through the window."[65] The usage of a substituted object, a "pax" (the Latin word for peace), spread in this era, eventually leading to the kiss of peace's disappearance from the mass for a very long time.

Clare seems to throw this caution to the wind. There is a certain physical energy in her. The virgin of Assisi radiates courage. In a sense, Favarone's daughter missed her true calling as a knight. Sister Cristiana, daughter of Lord Bernardo of Suppo of Assisi, remembered Clare's flight from her father's house:

> She added that the virgin of God, Clare, left her father's worldly house in a wonderful way. Because she did not want to leave through the usual exit, fearing her way would be blocked, she went out by the house's other exit which had been barricaded with heavy wooden beams and a stone column so that it could not be opened even by a large number of men. She alone, with the help of Jesus Christ, removed them and opened the door. On the following morning, when many people saw that door opened, they asked with great astonishment how a young girl could have done it. Asked how she knew these things, the witness replied that she was in that house at that time because she lived in Assisi and, before this, had been with her and had knowledge of her. Asked how long ago this was, she re-

---

64. *Primi documenti*, 153–54; *CAED*, 173.
65. *Deux Vies*, 394–95.

plied, "forty-two years or a little more." Asked what age St. Clare was at that time, she replied that, according to what was said, she was eighteen years old.[66]

Francis cropped Clare's hair at the Portiuncula, then led her temporarily to the church of San Paolo delle Abbadesse. Her family caught up with her there. We have already encountered the testimony of her younger sister Beatrice:

> When her relatives wanted to drag her out, Lady Clare grabbed the altar cloth and uncovered her head, showing them that she was tonsured. In no way did she acquiesce, neither letting them take her away from there, nor going away with them.[67]

As Thomas of Celano tells it, the battle was even more violent at Sant'Angelo di Panzo, when the men of the family, the warriors, intended to take back Clare's other sister, Agnes:

> The next day, hearing that Agnes had gone off to Clare, twelve men, burning with anger but hiding outwardly their evil intent, ran to the place, pretending to make a peaceful entrance. Immediately they turned to Agnes, since they had long ago lost hope of Clare, and said: "Why have you come to this place? Return immediately to the house with us!" When she responded that she did not want to leave her sister Clare, a mean-spirited knight threw himself toward her and, without sparing blows and kicks, tried to drag her away by her hair, while the others pushed her and lifted her in their arms. But the honest young girl, as if she had been captured by lions and torn from the hands of the Lord, cried out, "Dear sister, help me, and do not let me be taken from Christ the Lord!" While the violent ruffians were dragging the young girl along the slope of the mountain, ripping her clothes and strewing the path with her torn-out hair, Clare prostrated herself in prayer with tears, begged that her sister would be given constancy of mind and that the strength of humans would be overcome by divine power.[68]

Battle did not frighten these indomitable sisters. Blows and kicks mattered little to them. The whole family had the souls of warriors. Clare fought with the weapons at her disposal. She won. Facing off with Pope Gregory IX, who

---

66. *Primi documenti*, 191–92; CAED, 185.
67. *Primi documenti*, 186; CAED, 183.
68. *Legenda S. Clarae*, 152 (chap. 16); CAED, 303.

wanted to convince her to accept material possessions, "she resisted with a great force of mind and would not accept for anything in the world."[69] In the versified version of the *Legend of Saint Clare, Virgin*, the poet ventures:

> The woman verged on lofty pride, daring to oppose the master,
> The sovereign pontiff, to whom divine power
> Has given supreme authority to bind and loose.[70]

When in 1230 the same Gregory IX drastically reduced the Franciscan brothers' access to San Damiano, "at once she sent all the brothers back to the minister, refusing to have almoners for physical bread when she could not have almoners for spiritual bread."[71] The weakness of the female sex is transformed into a powerful counter attack.

In 1220, Clare would have liked to leave for Morocco and suffer martyrdom there. Twenty years later, in 1240, when the Saracen soldiers of Frederick II threatened San Damiano, she proudly declared to her sisters: "If they come, put me there in front of them!"[72] When they entered the cloister, she pushed them back with all the power of her prayer, just as the following year she saved Assisi from the troops of Vitalis of Aversa, the emperor's captain. It took more than a kick in the mouth to stop this fierce virgin.

We will never really know the thoughts of that servant whose feet Clare washed, nor why she recoiled from the kiss. The versified legend offers a hint: "The servant, stunned, would not allow it."[73] She may have suffered a double embarrassment, uniting the two levels of the Gospel: first, embarrassment at seeing her mistress in this position of inversion, since she may not have perceived as clearly as the better-educated sisters the scriptural and liturgical convention beneath the social impropriety; second, embarrassment at being touched by another woman, an instinctive aversion to physical contact whose sudden irruption bordered on aggression. Thomas, who has absorbed and omitted so much, in the end lets this sweet violence shine through:

> Yet she gently took back up the servant's foot and planted a firm kiss on its sole [*sub ipsa planta strictum osculum figit*].[74]

---

69. *Legenda S. Clarae*, 124–26 (chap. 9); *CAED*, 294.
70. *Legende minores*, 56–58; *CAED*, 216.
71. *Legenda S. Clarae*, 178–80 (chap. 24); *CAED*, 312.
72. *Legenda S. Clarae*, 142 (chap. 14); *CAED*, 300–301.
73. *Legende minores*, 54; *CAED*, 214.
74. *Legenda S. Clarae*, 120 (chap. 8); *CAED*, 292.

6. Inversions

To prostrate oneself at the feet of another, to bath those feet in tears, is to admit defeat, to beg the victor for mercy, to hope for pity. The most memorable example from antiquity is found in the *Iliad*. Led by Hermes, Priam crossed the Achaean lines and entered Achilles's tent. He offered gifts to ransom Hector's body, and kissed the hand that had killed his children:

> So he spoke, and in Achilles he roused desire to weep for his father; and he took the old man by the hand, and gently pushed him away from him. So the two remembered—the one remembered man-slaying Hector and wept loudly, collapsed at Achilles' feet; but Achilles wept for his own father, and now again for Patroclus; and the sound of their moaning went up through the house. But when noble Achilles had had his fill of weeping, immediately then he sprang from his seat, and raised the old man by his hand.[75]

In the *Odyssey*, Odysseus at last made his way back to Ithaca. Yet he did not reveal his identity to Penelope, besieged by her suitors, and she ordered her servants to wash the stranger's feet. He would only allow himself to be touched by Eurycleia, his old nurse:

> The old woman took the shining cauldron in which she was about to wash his feet, and poured in cold water in plenty, and then added the hot. Odysseus sat down at the hearth, and instantly turned toward the darkness, for he at once had a foreboding at heart that, as she took hold of him, she might notice his scar and the truth would be discovered. She drew near and began to wash her lord; at once she recognized the scar of the wound which long ago a boar had dealt him with its white tusk, when Odysseus had gone to Parnassus to hunt with Autolycus. . . . This scar the old woman, when she had taken his leg in the flat of her hands, remembered when she felt it, and she let his leg fall. Into the basin the lower leg fell, and the bronze rang. It tipped over, and the water was spilled on the ground.[76]

Foot-bathing was also part of the ritual of hospitality in the Hebrew Bible. Thus Abraham's response at the oak of Mamre, when Yahweh appeared to him in the form of three men (Genesis 18:4): "I will fetch a little water and

---

75. Homer, *The Iliad*, trans. Augustus Taber Murray, rev. William F. Wyatt (Cambridge, MA, 1999), 2:601 (book 24).
76. Homer, *The Odyssey*, trans. Augustus Taber Murray, rev. George E. Dimock (Cambridge, MA, 1995), 2:263, 269 (book 19).

46　I. THE SERVANT SERVED

wash your feet, and you rest yourself under the tree." But in the entire New Testament, only Mary the sister of Martha, and then Christ, wash others' feet. Hence Peter's stunned reaction: "Lord, you wash my feet!" As for the kissing of feet, the female sinner is the first and only one to do this.

In the Middle Ages, the kiss of a foot was sometimes performed as a sign of a vassal's homage to his lord. This kind of homage, more binding and humbling than that involving a kiss on the hand, is attested only in France, in the tenth and eleventh centuries. In general only kings received it. The most famous example is that of the Viking chief Rollo, *jarl*, or leader of the Normans. In 911, at Saint-Clair-sur-Epte, he and the Carolingian king Charles the Simple sealed the accord that gave birth to the duchy of Normandy. We know the terms and the setting of this agreement only through Dudo of Saint-Quentin's account in his *History of the Normans*, written to flatter Norman pride about a century later:

> To Rollo, who was unwilling to kiss the king's foot, the bishops said: "He who accepts a gift such as this ought to go as far as kissing the king's foot." And he replied: "I will never bend my knees at the knees of any man, and will not kiss anyone's foot!" Urged by the prayers of the Franks, he ordered a warrior to kiss the king's foot. And this man immediately grasped the king's foot, raised it to his mouth, and planted a kiss [*defixit osculum*] on it while he remained standing, and flipped the king flat on his back. This caused a great laugh and a great outcry among the people.[77]

Since he was the "vicar of Christ," the pope merited similar reverence, as William Durand, bishop of Mende and expert in canon law and liturgy, explained in his late-thirteenth-century *Rationale for the Divine Offices*. Before the Gospel reading for the mass, the deacon should kiss the right hand of the celebrant. With one exception:

> The sub-deacon or the deacon does not kiss the hand but rather the feet of the Roman Pontiff, to show supreme reverence to the supreme pontiff, and to show him to be the vicar of Him whose feet were kissed by that woman who had been a sinner in the city.[78]

Clare of Assisi was in direct contact with four popes: Innocent III, Gregory IX, Innocent IV, and Alexander IV (she knew the latter when he was still a cardinal, before his ascent to the throne of St. Peter). They did not hesitate to visit her:

---

77. Dudo of Saint-Quentin, *De moribus et actis primorum Normanniae ducum*, ed. Jules Lair (Caen, France, 1865), 169; Dudo of Saint-Quentin, *History of the Normans*, trans. Eric Christiansen (Woodbridge, England, 1998), 49.

78. William Durand, *Rationale Book Four: On the Mass and Each Action Pertaining to It*, ed. and trans. Timothy M. Thibodeau (Turnhout, 2013), 194–95.

And so to the deterioration of her sacred limbs through illness was joined a new weakness, which indicated her impending call to the Lord and prepared the way for her eternal health. Lord Innocent IV of holy memory, together with the cardinals, hurried to visit the servant of Christ. Since he considered her life to be beyond that of the women of our time, he did not hesitate to honor her death with the papal presence. After entering the monastery, he went to her bed and extended his hand so that she might kiss it. She accepted it most graciously and asked that she might also kiss, with the greatest reverence, the foot of the successor of the apostles. Mounting a wooden stool, the lord of the curia courteously offered her his foot, on which she planted kisses, above and below, and reverently inclined her face.[79]

The scene is almost comical. But it has an institutional dimension, acting out what Clare had just written in her Form of Life: that she and her sisters should be "always submissive and prostrated at the feet of this Holy Church." It is also a ritualized gesture. Brother Thomas of Celano, who recounts this episode of the pope perched on his stool, addressed and commended himself "with devout submission" to Alexander IV, Innocent's successor, the commissioner and recipient of the *Legend of Saint Clare, Virgin*, "while devotedly kissing his blessed feet."[80]

The *Dictatus papae*, a strange document that seems to record the most extreme expression of the universal ambitions of Pope Gregory VII and the eleventh-century "Gregorian" reformers of the church, asserts: "That only [the pope] may use the imperial insignia. That all princes kiss the feet of the pope alone."[81] As Clement VII apologized to Emperor Charles V in 1530 at Bologna, "It is against my will that I allow my feet to be kissed, but the law of the ceremonial commands it"; this reference did not escape the attention of Ernst Kantorowicz, the great historian of royal ritual.[82]

The feet of the abbess of San Damiano also attracted devotion, but spontaneously and much to her annoyance. The same witness in the canonization process, Agnes of Oportuno, recalls two opposing scenes:

> She also said that once when, at the great insistence of the witness, the feet of the holy mother Clare were being washed, the witness drank some of [the water that] had washed her feet, which seemed to her so

---

79. *Legenda S. Clarae*, 188 (chap. 27); CAED, 314–15.
80. Battista Alfani, *Vita et leggenda della seraphica vergine sancta Chiara*, 75.
81. "Dictatus papae," in *Das Register Gregors VII*, ed. Erich Caspar (MGH, Epistolae selectae, II/2) (Berlin, 1920–23), 204.
82. Ernst H. Kantorowicz, *Laudes regiae: A Study in Liturgical Acclamations and Medieval Ruler Worship* (Berkeley, CA, 1946), 111.

sweet and delicious she could hardly drink it. Asked if any other sister had tasted any of that water, she replied no, because the holy mother Clare immediately threw it away so that there was no more to taste.[83]

And the opposite:

She also said that if Lady Clare saw any of the sisters suffering some temptation or trial, she would call her secretly and console her with tears. Sometimes, she would throw herself at her feet. Asked how she knew these things, she replied that she had seen some of those whom [Clare] had called to be consoled. One of them had told her the lady had thrown herself at her feet. Asked the name of that sister, she replied she was called Sister Illuminata of Pisa, who was dead.[84]

By means of such reversals, Gospel-inspired impulses ultimately create an endless loop; inversion nullifies itself in reversibility. The same circularity, through a permanent reversal of high and low, holds true for the idea of service. In approving Clare's Form of Life two days before her death, on 9 August 1253, Innocent IV (the same pope from the story of the stool) styled himself with the pontifical chancery's usual title: "Innocent, bishop, servant of the servants of God" (*servus servorum Dei*).[85] Alexander IV would do the same in the bull of canonization in 1255, just as so many other popes had done before.[86]

In the Bible, the phrase *servus servorum* appears only once, in the curse that Noah hurls against his grandson Canaan, who had seen him in his nakedness: "Cursed be Canaan! He shall be a servant of servants to his brethren" (Genesis 9:25). In the fourth century, Augustine inverted this curse to call himself "bishop, servant of the servants of Christ."[87] At the turn of the sixth to the seventh century, to counter the proud patriarch of Constantinople's claims to universal (ecumenical) authority with a blast of humility, Pope Gregory the Great carved out the expression "servant of the servants of God."[88] The popes employed the phrase systematically from the ninth century onward, thereby squarely designating papal sovereignty as servitude.

In Clare of Assisi's dossier, male and female servants are everywhere. But of the latter, there are two types. We already know the first. In Clare's Form of Life, we have twice met the "sisters serving [*servientes*] outside the monastery," and

---

83. *Primi documenti*, 175; *CAED*, 180.
84. *Primi documenti*, 171; *CAED*, 178.
85. *Escritos*, 271; *CAED*, 108.
86. *Primi documenti*, 238; *CAED*, 263.
87. Augustine of Hippo, *Epistulae CI–CXXXIX*, ed. K. D. Daur (Turnhout, 2009), epist. 130 (ad Probam novercam Iulianae), 212.
88. Gregory the Great, *Registrum epistularum*, ed. Dag Norberg (Turnhout, 1982).

on two other occasions, more abruptly, "those serving outside the monastery." In the extant Italian version of the canonization process, we have noted three times the simple designation "servants" (*servitiale*), once clarified as "servants of the monastery" and once amplified with the double title "serving sisters" (*sore servitrici*). In Thomas of Celano's Latin legend, they appear only in the chapter on humility, and in particular in the episode concerning foot-washing, where they are three times referred to as *famule*; the recalcitrant sister who launched the kick is called *serviens* or *famula*.

These few occurrences pale in comparison with the avalanche of references to the second type of "servant." These are the women called in Latin *ancille*, *famule*, or *serve*: blunt terms designating both ancient slavery and medieval serfdom. But these women are free, by grace of the phrases which modify their servitude. Yes, they are "servants," but servants "of God," "of the Lord," or "of Christ."

This is the way Francis described them in the embryonic "form of life" that he addressed to them shortly after Clare's conversion ("daughters and servants of the Most High and Sovereign King, the celestial Father"). Cardinal Rainaldo did the same when he approved Clare's Form of Life on 16 September 1252:

> Because you, beloved daughters in Christ, have rejected the splendors and pleasures of the world and, following the footsteps of Christ himself and his most holy Mother, have chosen to live bodily enclosed and to serve the Lord in the highest poverty, so that in freedom of the soul you may be servants of the Lord, we, approving your holy proposal in the Lord, desire with fatherly affection to bestow generous favor upon your wishes and your holy desires.[89]

The difference between "servants of the monastery" and "servants of the Lord" is more than mere nuance. The first designation is social, the second spiritual; the first pertains to the here and now, the second transcends the earthly plane and aspires to the most prestigious models. "Servant of God" (*famulus* or *servus Dei*) or "servant of the Lord" (*famulus* or *servus Domini*): Moses is frequently referred to with these terms, as are sometimes the prophets Joshua and Daniel. The "servant of Christ" (*servus Christi*) is Paul addressing the Romans (1:1) or the Colossians (4:12); the "servant of the Lord" (*ancilla Domini*) is Mary at the moment of the Annunciation (Luke 1:38).

For Alexander IV in the bull of canonization, as for Thomas of Celano in the legend, Clare is the "servant of Christ" (*Christi famula* or *ancilla*) or "servant of God" (*Dei famula*),[90] another way of saying "footprint of the Mother of God," as

---

89. *Escritos*, 272; *CAED*, 108–109.
90. *Primi documenti*, 238–65; *CAED*, 263–71.

the hagiographer calls her in the legend's prologue.[91] She lays claim to this servitude herself, since it represents the highest title precisely because it is the lowest. The same expressions recur in the formula with which she presents herself in her Form of Life, her Testament, and her final blessing to her sisters:

> Clare, unworthy servant of Christ and little plant of the most blessed father Francis.[92]
>
> I, therefore, Clare, servant, although unworthy, of Christ and of the Poor Sisters of the Monastery of San Damiano, the little plant of the holy father.[93]
>
> I, Clare, servant of Christ, little plant of our most blessed father St. Francis, your sister and mother of the other Poor Sisters, although unworthy.[94]

Her horticultural metaphor assures that the link to Francis is not forgotten, even a quarter century after his death. She is a plant, but a "little" plant, as a sign of humility. Since servitude ceased to be degrading as soon as it became service to Christ, and since the title *ancilla Christi* referred to the Savior's mother, it was necessary to add the idea of unworthiness; even this quickly became a mere commonplace. Yet unlike the other sisters, Clare is not content to be the servant of the Lord. Was it not true that he came "not to be served, but to serve" (Matthew 20:28)?

This is the unique status that distinguishes the abbess from her female companions: because she is the superior, she must also be the servant of the community, and not just the "servant of the Lord." In Clare's Form of Life, it is clearly stated that the abbess has authority over all the "subject sisters," who have "renounced their own wills" and are "firmly bound to obey their abbess in all the things they have promised the Lord to observe and which are not against their soul and our profession."[95] Yet by a final reversal, like a counterweight to this obedience and as a kind of institutional version of the washing of feet, the superior is placed below her subordinates:

> Let the abbess be so familiar with them that they can speak and act with her as ladies do with their servant. For this is the way it must be: the abbess should be the servant of all the sisters.[96]

---

91. *Legenda S. Clarae*, 90; CAED, 279.
92. *Fonti legislative*, 22; CAED, 109.
93. Giovanni Boccali, "Testamento e benedizione di S. Chiara. Nuovo codice latino," *Archivum franciscanum historicum* 82 (1989): 287; CAED, 62.
94. Boccali, "Testamento e benedizione di S. Chiara," 293; CAED, 67.
95. *Fonti legislative*, 94; CAED, 122.
96. *Fonti legislative*, 94–96; CAED, 123.

Clare refines this motif of servitude to its highest point in her correspondence with Agnes of Prague. The first letter dates from before Pentecost 1234:

> To the venerable and most holy virgin, Lady Agnes, daughter of the most excellent and illustrious king of Bohemia, Clare, unworthy servant [*famula*] of Jesus Christ and useless servant [*ancilla*] of the enclosed ladies of the monastery of San Damiano, her subject and servant [*subdita et ancilla*] in all things, commends herself totally with special reverence that she may attain the glory of everlasting happiness.[97]

Born in 1205, daughter of King Ottokar I of Bohemia and Queen Constance of Hungary, Agnes remained a virgin, refusing marriage to Emperor Frederick II's son, to Henry III of England, and twice to Frederick II himself. She had other intentions: to entice the Lesser Brothers to settle in Prague, she constructed a church for them and founded a hospital in honor of St. Francis. In this royal woman's presence, Clare could be only a subject and servant, three times over. The second letter was written between 1234 and 1237:

> To the daughter of the King of kings, the servant of the Lord of lords, the most worthy spouse of Jesus Christ, and, therefore the most noble queen, Lady Agnes, Clare, the useless and unworthy servant of the poor ladies, greetings and may you always live in the highest poverty.[98]

By this time, Agnes had taken the decisive step of entering the monastery of St. Francis she had founded, which flanked the hospital in Prague. She had abandoned her earthly royal origins for a celestial union. Henceforth queen by right of her Husband, she can be called his servant, a new and glorious title. The third letter dates from the end of 1237 or the beginning of 1238:

> To the lady she most reveres in Christ and the sister she loves more than all mortals, Agnes, sister in the flesh [*germanae*] of the illustrious king of Bohemia, but now the sister [*sorori*] and spouse of the sovereign King of Heaven, Clare, the most humble and unworthy servant of Christ and servant of the Poor Ladies, [wishes] the joy of redemption in the Author of salvation and every better thing can be desired.[99]

Clare, who had already passed from formal to familiar forms of address in the preceding letter, can now call herself Agnes's sister by virtue of their shared religious choice. If Agnes's biological brother, King Wenceslas, is invoked, she

---

97. *Lettere ad Agnese*, 104; CAED, 43.
98. *Lettere ad Agnese*, 116; CAED, 47.
99. *Lettere ad Agnese*, 126; CAED, 50.

is his sister only in the flesh (*germana*), as opposed to Clare and Christ, her real family, to whom she is the true sister (*soror*).

The fourth letter came just before Clare's death in August 1253:

> To her who is half of her soul and the special shrine of her heart's deepest love, to the illustrious queen and bride of the Lamb, the eternal King, to Lady Agnes, her most dear mother, and her favorite daughter of all, Clare, unworthy servant of Christ and useless servant of his servants in the monastery of San Damiano of Assisi, health and may she sing the new song with the other most holy virgins before the throne of God and the Lamb and follow the Lamb wherever He will go.[100]

The intertwining of spiritual relationships here reaches an rare degree of intricacy: if all these forms of address are added up, Clare is subject, servant, sister, daughter, and mother of Agnes, who is virgin, lady, daughter, and sister of kings of Bohemia, queen herself, as well as servant, daughter, sister, wife (and mother, we learn in the body of the letters) of Christ, of whom Clare is servant and servant of his servants; Clare is also wife of Christ, though she delicately avoids giving herself a title she shares with Agnes.

A complete fusion between the two women? All the familial relationships between Clare and Agnes are reciprocal: they are mother, daughter, and sister to each other. The title of "servant of the Lord" or "of Christ" belongs to both of them, from the moment Agnes leaves her earthly royalty behind. But Clare alone is the servant of Agnes, and it is this inverted privilege that invests her with spiritual authority and real precedence.

Gregory IX also carried on a sustained correspondence with Agnes. On 30 and 31 August 1234, he sent three letters concerning the monastery of St. Francis of Prague, and then three more on 18 May 1235. Between 4 April and 11 May 1238, in the space of a little more than five weeks, he addressed eight letters to Agnes and her sisters, and one more on 18 December of the same year.[101] Such eagerness is puzzling. Was it the result of the Roman See's geopolitical agenda regarding King Wenceslas of Bohemia? Certainly the pope favored anything that countered the power of Emperor Frederick II. But nothing of this political context filters into the content of the letters; the discussion there is confined to the rule followed by the nuns of St. Francis of Prague, dealing with their renunciation of possessions and the mitigation of their fasts. Gregory preached moderation; Agnes wanted austerity and to live without possessions.

---

100. *Lettere ad Agnese*, 138; CAED, 54.
101. BF, 1:134–36, 156–59, 236–44, 258–59.

Still . . . would the pope have shown so much concern for these women who were choosing to wear "the habit of poverty," if they had not been led by the daughter and sister of kings? And how many letters did he address to the truly poor, to those men and women who did not have to debate issues such as liturgical fasts in order to feel real deprivation? The question touches the heart of the Gospel message.

The mentality that emerges from these sources, based on the permanent inversion of words, positions, and gestures, does not obliterate the underlying social reality. In certain ways, it smooths it out. In others, it stirs it up. It always subtly transforms it. The minute episode of Clare of Assisi washing the servant's feet has revealed to us this stirring up, this subtle transformation, this smoothing out. We have closely studied the anecdote in all its implications. It carries deep significance. Now it is time to place it in its wider context.

7. Paradox

Jesus of Nazareth was condemned to death by the prefect of the Roman province of Judea (representing the Emperor Tiberius) and was executed by the Roman punishment of crucifixion. Slowly, with difficulty, Christ triumphed within the very empire that had condemned him. Lactantius as well as Eusebius of Caesarea assure us that the Emperor Constantine personally adopted the religion of Christ in 312. In 313 the Edict of Milan guaranteed "to Christians, as to all, the free ability to follow that religion which each one wishes."[102] In 380, the Emperor Theodosius published the Edict of Thessalonica:

> It is our desire that all the various peoples whom the just measure of our clemency governs should turn to that religion which was delivered to the Romans by the divine Peter, as it has been preserved by faithful tradition, and which is now clearly followed by the Pontiff Damasus and by Peter, Bishop of Alexandria, a man of apostolic holiness; that is, according to the apostolic teaching and the doctrine of the Gospel, we believe in the one deity of the Father, the Son, and the Holy Spirit, in equal majesty, and in a pious Trinity.[103]

Across the entire medieval millennium Christianity was the dominant religion of the West and of the Byzantine East. But the nature of this dominance differed between the two parts of the old Roman world. The logical outcome of the edicts of Milan and Thessalonica in the East was an imperial church serving Byzantine caesaropapism (the fusing of secular government with religious authority). By contrast, in the western half of the empire, the Middle Ages began with the fading away of state power, as the empire disintegrated after 476. The political and ideological system that had gradually come into existence over the fourth century thus found itself deprived of the crucial component for which it had been created, for whose benefit it was meant to function.

Christianity was the dominant religion of the West and of the Byzantine East, but in a manner that was neither exclusive nor unchallenged: the paganism of antiquity did not disappear all at once; Jewish communities expanded in many places; non-Christian cults—Germanic, Scandinavian, Slavic—persisted for a long time in the north and northeast; starting in the seventh century, Islam spread across the entire southern shore of the Mediterranean, in Asia Minor,

---

102. Lactantius, *De mortibus persecutorum*, ed. J. L. Creed (Oxford, 1984) (chap. 48 reports the so-called Edict of Milan); Eusebius of Caesarea, *De vita Constantini*, ed. Bruno Bleckmann (Turnhout, 2007).

103. *Theodosiani libri XVI cum constitutionibus Sirmondianis*, ed. Theodor Mommsen and Paul M. Meyer (Berlin, 1905), 833; Sidney Z. Ehler and John B. Morrall, *Church and State through the Centuries: A Collection of Historic Documents with Commentaries* (New York, 1928), 6–7.

and on the Iberian Peninsula. Moreover, from the middle of the eleventh century on, Christendom was split between Rome and the East, while time and again internal schisms in the West pitted rival popes against each other; doctrinal, moral, pastoral, or cultural disagreements were attacked as heresies; and ancient beliefs persisted. Signs of unbelief sometimes showed themselves too, even at the apex of the ecclesiastical pyramid.

But even without enjoying a religious monopoly, Christianity exercised an indisputable ideological hegemony over the medieval West. As the very words chosen by the guardians of orthodoxy make clear, its rivals—adherents to "superstitions," "heretics," those holding to the "old Covenant," "infidels,"— were integrated into its discourse as proofs of its supremacy. The Christian religion was institutionalized as a church and governed by an established body: the clergy. During the medieval millennium, the church and its clergy were simultaneously the most important landholders, the main possessors of written culture, and (from the clergy's point of view) the essential mediators of the sacred. Medieval Christianity, endowed with a particularly efficient ideological apparatus, thus had all the features of a dominant ideology.

And yet, it faced a serious challenge. The teaching and legitimacy of Christianity rested on a body of texts held to be the expression of divine revelation. In societies where (even allowing for differences of time, place, social status, and gender) those who could read and write were always in the minority, the sacrality of the written word in general and of scripture in particular stood out all the more. The conditions under which writing was produced enhanced its prestige: a Carolingian Bible necessitated the slaughter of hundreds of sheep; it required complicated work to turn hide into parchment; preparation of quires and pages; months or indeed years of copying by hand; a long process of revision; the highly skilled labor of decoration with often costly pigments; and a final expenditure of know-how and precious materials for the binding. The immensity and splendor of the object guaranteed the sacrality of its contents.

But that content was far from uniform. The Christian Bible joined books from the Hebrew Bible, now baptized as the "Old Testament," to the specific contribution of the New Testament. The canon of these books was fixed, for all intents and purposes, by Pope Damasus at a church council held in Rome in 382. For the Old Testament, it included more books than the canon of the Hebrew Bible had done. It left out of the New Testament the apocryphal books, whose memory, however, never completely disappeared. The same Pope Damasus asked Jerome to translate the scriptures from Hebrew and Greek into Latin. In contrast to translating the Hebrew Bible, or later the Qur'an, translating Christian scripture could not be considered sacrilegious for evident reasons stemming from the way it had been received in the Western Empire.

It was a challenge to link together a body of texts formed and translated in this way. The Hebrew Bible could not just be set aside, because Christ had declared:

> Do not think that I am come to destroy the Law, or the prophets. I am not come to destroy, but to fulfill. (Matthew 5:17)

One of the principle tasks of Christian exegesis—to which the Gospel authors themselves had already turned by inserting numerous citations from the Jewish books into their narratives—was to highlight correspondences between the Old and New Testaments, the first prefiguring the second, the Old Testament "type" announcing the New Testament "antitype": "typological" exegesis constantly built these kinds of bridges between the Old and New Covenant.

In the New Testament, the four canonical Gospels shone as the most precious witnesses, because they contained the life, death, and resurrection of Christ, and they preserved his words. Passages from the Gospels (pericopes) were read with particular solemnity at every mass. But the difficulty arose from the diversity of the Gospels. Each book contained episodes with no equivalent in the other three. The recounting of a single episode could diverge notably from one Gospel to another. Three of them—the "synoptic" Gospels—presented strong similarities, while the Gospel of John, distinguished by its attribution to the "disciple whom Jesus loved," showed the highest level of independence.

In seeking to establish dogma based on revelation, the church fathers had confronted these questions from the first centuries of Christianity. Though not imbued with the same sacred aspect as scripture, the works of the Fathers carried great authority. Yet the earliest of the Fathers, and often the most prestigious, had expressed their opinions at a time before orthodoxy had been defined by a series of church councils. Thus they sometimes found themselves in an awkward position after the fact, in relation to the dogma that their debates had helped to forge.

There is "play" in Christian Holy Writ. In Christian scripture, there is play between the canonical body of texts and the apocrypha, between the Old and the New Testaments, between the four Gospels, between the various exegetes, all rendered still less stable by translation from one language to another. Where we expect to find truth and certainties, we instead discover doubt and contradictions. The development of dogma and norms relied on a powerful machinery of textual criticism: in Christian revelation, from the very beginning the relative lay at the heart of the absolute. Peter Lombard compiled many of these divergences in his *Book of Sentences* in the twelfth century. Commentaries on the *Sentences*, obligatory exercises for all scholastic theologians starting in the thirteenth century, added new statements and new problems to the many quandaries they sought to solve.

To avoid too direct a collision between different scriptural passages, one could claim to follow the words of the apostle, "The letter kills, but the spirit gives life" (II Corinthians 3:6) and overcome apparent literal contradictions by seeking a hidden spiritual sense. Based on the four senses of scripture (historical, allegorical, tropological, anagogical), exegesis offered an exceptionally flexible and powerful hermeneutic reading, open to many possible meanings at the same time. But truths open to many meanings are poorly suited to quelling doubt.

At the heart of the debates that sprouted from the soil of revelation, the most vexing questions were considered "mysteries." These were not the secrets of esoteric cults, into which adherents could hope to be initiated and whose very hermeticism guaranteed their validity and established their (only) value. They were rather truths held to be beyond human reason. Yet they were formulated by the human mind, and the church fathers and theologians had never ceased to apply reasoned argument to them: a God who was absolutely one and absolutely triune; a God incarnated, the Son, endowed with a double nature, absolutely God and absolutely man, who every day on the altar took on flesh and blood anew in the mystery of the Eucharist, and who promised salvation through the mystery of the Redemption. The search for the truth led to squaring the circle.

Doubtless, most believers had scant access to the arcane processes by which such meaning was established. But every week they were present for the reading of scripture, particularly Gospel pericopes, from which they gathered up bits and pieces. While the work of exegesis tended toward over-contextualization, the conditions in which simple people listened to Bible readings created a double decontextualization. First, the pericope (the extracted Gospel passage) was the result of a sharp segmentation of the text. Second, for most believers the increasing difficulty of understanding the Latin in which these passages were read limited them to grasping only little bits, like so many bursts imbued with absolute prestige. What did they hear, right from the mouth of Christ? A patchwork of assertions, promises, and precepts, offered in Sunday readings and amplified by preaching, that were capable of shaking the very foundations of worldly order:

> Blessed are you when they shall revile you, and persecute you, and speak all that is evil against you, untruly, for my sake (Matthew 5:11).
> Lay not up to yourselves treasures on earth, where the rust and moth consume and where thieves break through and steal. But lay up to yourselves

treasures in heaven, where neither the rust nor moth consumes and where thieves do not break through nor steal (Matthew 6:19–20).

You cannot serve God and mammon [riches] (Matthew 6:24).

Follow me, and let the dead bury their dead (Matthew 8:22).

For I am not come to call the just, but the sinners (Matthew 9:13).

Do not possess gold, nor silver, nor money in your purses, nor scrip for your journey, nor two coats, nor shoes, nor a staff (Matthew 10:9–10).

Behold I send you as sheep in the midst of wolves (Matthew 10:16).

And you shall be hated by all men for my name's sake, but he that shall persevere to the end, he shall be saved (Matthew 10:22).

Do not think that I came to send peace upon the earth. I came not to send peace, but the sword. For I came to set a man against his father, and the daughter against her mother, and the daughter in law against her mother in law. And a man's enemies shall be they of his own household. He who loves his father or mother more than me, is not worthy of me, and he that loves his son or daughter more than me is not worthy of me. (Matthew 10:34–37)

He that finds his life shall lose it, and he that shall lose his life for me, shall find it (Matthew 10:39).

The Son of man came eating and drinking, and they say: "Behold a man that is a glutton and a wine drinker, a friend of publicans and sinners" (Matthew 11:19).

I praise you, Father, Lord of heaven and earth, because you have hidden these things from the wise and prudent, and have revealed them to the little ones (Matthew 11:25).

Who is my mother, and who are my brothers? (Matthew 12:48).

It is easier for a camel to pass through the eye of a needle, than for a rich man to enter into the kingdom of heaven (Matthew 19:24).

The last shall be first and the first shall be last (Matthew 20:16).

Whosoever will be the greatest among you, let him be your servant, and he that will be first among you, shall be your servant. Even as the Son of man is not come to be served, but to serve, and to give his life for the redemption of many (Matthew 20:26–28).

The publicans and the harlots shall go into the kingdom of God before you (Matthew 21:31).

If any man desires to be first, he shall be the last of all and the servant of all (Mark 9:34).

Beware of the scribes, who love to walk in long robes, and to be saluted in the marketplace, and to sit in the first chairs in the synagogues, and to have the highest places at suppers, who devour the houses of widows

under the pretense of long prayer: these shall receive greater judgment (Mark 12:38–40).
Blessed are the poor, for yours is the kingdom of God (Luke 6:20).
Woe to you that are rich, for you have your consolation (Luke 9:48).
He who is the lesser among you all, he is the greater (Luke 9:48).
Woe to you who are expert in law, because you load men with burdens which they cannot bear, and you yourselves touch not these burdens with even one of your fingers (Luke 11:46).
When you make a feast, call the poor, the maimed, the lame, and the blind; and you shall be blessed, because they have nothing with which to make recompense to you (Luke 14:13).
He who is the greater among you let him become like the youngest, and he that is the leader like he who serves (Luke 22:26).
If the world hates you, know that it has hated me before you (John 15:18).
My kingdom is not of this world (John 18:36).

If, with Hannah Arendt, we accept that an ideology is a system for interpreting the world; that it asserts its power to unlock understanding and explanation of that world, whether visible or invisible, past or future; that it must claim to be incontestable, unfalsifiable, and infallible; that it must be endowed with an internal coherence capable of acknowledging contradiction and integrating it into a demonstration of its own legitimacy; then it is undeniable that medieval Christianity had all the characteristics of an ideology.[104] This is all the more true given that the learned had integrated into their body of knowledge what they had preserved from the science, philosophy, and literature of the Greeks and Romans, whom they held in high esteem and worked to harmonize with Christian doctrine.

If we follow Louis Althusser in thinking that an ideology is characterized by the action of "Ideological State Apparatuses" ("it is ultimately the dominant ideology, precisely in its contradictions, which is realized in the Ideological State Apparatuses"), it is undeniable that medieval Christianity was endowed with a fantastic "Ideological Church Apparatus," in a preeminent, dominating position.[105] This is all the more true since after the deposition of Romulus Augustulus in 476, the successors of St. Peter seized the empty remains of the defunct empire. The Roman Church sometimes took the place of the civil powers, and often competed with them, laying claim to a deeper tradition of longer duration

---

104. Hannah Arendt, *The Origins of Totalitarianism* (New York, 1968), vol. 3, chap. 4, "Ideology and Terror: A Novel Form of Government."

105. Louis Althusser, "Ideology and Ideological State Apparatuses (Notes towards an Investigation)," in *Lenin and Philosophy and Other Essays*, trans. Ben Brewster (New York and London, 1971), 146.

and stronger legitimacy. Following in the footsteps of the emperor, who had now disappeared, the pope claimed the title of *pontifex maximus*, and it would not be until the new *Code of Canon Law* in 1983 that the college of cardinals would abandon the title of "Senate of the Roman Pontiff."

For all these reasons, medieval Christianity was indeed the dominant ideology of the Western Middle Ages. Karl Marx said that "the ideas of the dominant class are the ideas that dominate."[106] Yet in that sense, if we accept that a dominant ideology is not only one that dominates but also one that serves the interests of the dominant class, then describing medieval Christianity as a dominant ideology suddenly seems less satisfying, or at least too simple. Especially since in the West, Christianity was no longer harnessed to the political-ideological system of the empire, the vital force of the Gospel message (to which the church apparatus did not hesitate to turn when countering the claims of state apparatuses) now found itself potentially set free.

For the political and social powers of the Western Middle Ages, Christianity was like a nebulous ideological cloud, which sudden winds might blow in unexpected directions. It had all the characteristics of an ideology through its dominant quality (following Hannah Arendt) and through its apparatus (following Louis Althusser, for whom there was no doubt that the Ideological State Apparatuses picked up where the Ideological Church Apparatus left off), but it had a kind of built-in flaw inherent in its content.

The scriptural patchwork referred to above, when unraveled even a little bit, challenges the two orders that loom over medieval society: the warriors and the priests. It castigates the learned, and, above all, the rich; it mixes virulent condemnation of wealth with repeated glorification of poverty. It exalts the simple over the learned. It sets sinners, publicans, prostitutes, children, the disabled, above the just and the wise. It revels in persecution. It advocates a constant reversal of social and institutional conditions: great and small, first and last, masters and servants.

Certainly the exaltation of humility, poverty, and simplicity could be manipulated to justify domination and exploitation. And it was. Certainly promises about the future inversion of status, of servitude and domination, allowed the least well off to endure crushing economic, social, and cultural oppression while awaiting the Second Coming. Certainly delight in humiliation offered only a bitter reward for people living at the margins. But let's approach the problem from the other direction: If one had to invent an ideology to justify the social order of the Western Middle Ages, is this what one would propose? Would one burden oneself with these goading splinters?

---

106. Karl Marx and Friedrich Engels, "The German Ideology: Part I," in *The Marx-Engels Reader*, 2nd ed., trans. Robert C. Tucker (New York, 1978), 172.

External to Roman culture, founded on an autonomous body of texts generating its own sacrality, the Christian religion was poorly equipped to serve as a dominant ideology in the era following the disintegration of the Western empire. Its very heart, the Gospel message, presented obstacles to anyone seeking to found and maintain a social order upon it. It was indeed churchmen, overwhelmingly, who thought out the medieval social order. But they did this essentially—not exclusively, but systematically—in the service of political power and of the social class to which they belonged.

Nothing would be more simplistic than to turn the Gospel into a revolutionary message. It advocates inversions, but they are not revolutions. Not only does it accept a society dominated by the "first" and the "greatest," but their existence is intrinsic to the relevance of its message. The words of the apostle—"There is neither Jew nor Greek, neither slave nor free, neither male nor female, for you are all one in Christ Jesus" (Galatians 3:28)—offer the utopian horizon of the New Testament, like the classless society for messianic Marxism.

In cyclical fashion, in a surge that was at heart a quest for salvation, men and women, dissatisfied with the world as it was, acting in the name of the Gospel message that claimed to be the foundation of social consensus, would return to its thorniest statements. Through initially halting experiences, from which regular institutions sometimes emerged, they injected a little Gospel leaven into the social lump. They claimed to put the Word into action, "to follow naked the naked Christ." Some were eliminated as heretics, while others were regarded as pastors, as founders, indeed as saints.

In just as cyclical a fashion, a trend would ensue, not of decline, as was long claimed, but of fading away, through social and moral sublimation. The process was simple: the socioeconomic conditions sought in the name of the Gospel's call—poverty, simplicity, lesser-ness (*minoritas*)—would be allegorized as virtues. It was fundamental to this system that humility would no longer be the condition lived by the humble, but rather the virtue of those who applied themselves to the service of the humble, against the social order.

The paradox of medieval Christianity as ideology is that it produced this gap and at the same time allowed it to be reabsorbed into a renewed norm. It maintained a critical relationship with the social system it legitimated. There was neither absolute contradiction nor perfect accord: in the Western Middle Ages, there was "play" between the social order and the dominant ideology. This secret play of doubt, of dissatisfaction, of innovation, created movement. I believe it is not unrelated to the unique position still occupied, for now, by the societies that have emerged from it.

Part Two

Unworthiness in Power

He entered into a certain town and a certain woman named Martha received him into her house. And she had a sister called Mary, who, sitting also at the Lord's feet, heard his teaching. But Martha was busy with much serving. Standing up she said: "Lord, have you no care that my sister has left me alone to serve? Tell her then to help me."

And the Lord, answering, said to her: "Martha, Martha, you are anxious and are troubled about many things; but one thing is necessary. Mary has chosen the best part, which shall not be taken away from her."

—Luke 10:38–42

1. Benedictine Beginnings

The Rule of St. Benedict enjoyed unrivaled prestige in the West throughout the Middle Ages. It was praised by Gregory the Great, and it spread widely in the Carolingian period. Charlemagne's son Louis the Pious, with the help of Benedict of Aniane, insisted that all monasteries in the empire adopt it in 817. From this moment on, every form of regular religious life in the West expressed itself in relation to Benedict's Rule. They either followed it, as at Fleury (Saint-Benoit-sur-Loire), Cluny, and so many other places; or they referred to it while creating something new, as at Cîteaux; or they departed from and claimed to surpass it, even while drawing heavily from it, as with most of the reformed orders in the eleventh and twelfth centuries and right up through the mendicant orders in the thirteenth.

Not having been able to implement her own rule during her lifetime, Clare assumed the direction and government of the sisters of San Damiano as a Benedictine abbess. Cardinal Hugolino's Constitutions, followed by Clare's community in Assisi, were really just specific arrangements to clarify the application of the normative text par excellence that regulated the life of the sisters: the Rule of St. Benedict.

Benedict was born around 490 in Nursia, southeast of Assisi in modern Umbria. He studied at Rome. Dissatisfied, burning with a different ideal, he retired to the harsh solitude of Subiaco, in the hollow of a cave. Tradition has it that some seven centuries later Francis of Assisi stayed there himself. Around 530, Benedict left Subiaco to found the monastery of Monte Cassino, southeast of Rome. It was at this point that he devoted himself to writing a rule for his monks, inspired mainly by the "Rule of the Master," a little-known, anonymous text composed not long before (and I wonder if this "Rule of the Master" was not in fact a first version of the Benedictine Rule; in other words, whether "the Master" was not the young Benedict). Benedict died around 547 or 560.

> The abbot, he who is worthy to be at the head of the monastery, must always remember what his title signifies, and by his acts justify the name of superior.[1]

These are the words that begin chapter 2 of the Benedictine Rule. It is tempting to say simply that these are the words that begin the Rule, since chapter 1 is really a prologue that explains the distinction between four kinds of monks: cenobites, who live in community; anchorites, or hermits, who live solitary lives; sarabaites, rather like religious anarchists without a superior and without a rule;

---

1. *RSB*, 16–17 (chap. 2).

and gyrovagues, dangerous wandering monks. After chapter 1, Benedict focuses his attention and organizational efforts entirely on the first of these categories.

"The abbot, he who is worthy to be at the head of the monastery": the organizational chart starts from the top with the abbot, because, says the Rule, "it is believed that he holds the place of Christ in the monastery."[2]

But right from the opening phrase of the Benedictine Rule's chapter 2, the principle of the precedence of authority is coupled with forceful reminders of the superior's duties, as an antidote to any abuse of power. The phrase "he must" occurs six times and "remember" twice, to say nothing of the veritable avalanche of examples where verbs in the subjunctive mood signal obligation, such as "let him know," which occurs in three places.

These precautions culminate in this passage:

> The abbot must always remember what he is and remember what he is called, and know that more will be expected of a man to whom more has been entrusted.[3]

Not until chapter 64 of the Rule, "On the Election of the Abbot," do we see the inversion of this constitutional vision (if we may apply to monastic norms that vision, so dear to Montesquieu, of the relationship between the legislative and executive powers) and finally learn how the community should choose its superior:

> The man placed in office should be selected either unanimously by the whole community acting in the fear of God, or by a part of the community, even a small part, which possesses sounder judgement.[4]

As far as the choice of the person, only his merit should count, not his rank:

> Goodness of life and wisdom in teaching must be the criteria for the one to be chosen, even if he is the last in community rank.[5]

Or rather, his merit and his knowledge of Revelation should be taken into account:

> He ought, therefore, to be learned in divine law, so that he may know from where to *bring out what is new and what is old* (Matthew 13:52), and be chaste, temperate, and merciful.[6]

---

2. Ibid.
3. Ibid., 20–21.
4. Ibid., 144–45 (chap. 64).
5. Ibid.
6. Ibid., 146–47.

Placing the abbot at the beginning of the Rule makes perfect sense, given the way Benedict composed it. In chapter 1, he had just defined cenobites as the kind of monk "striving under a rule or an abbot."[7] Compared with the three other kinds of monks, who live alone like the anchorites, or in disorder like the sarabaites and the gyrovagues, only the "strong kind, the cenobites," is defined by its organized arrangement.[8] "Under a rule or an abbot": the presence of a superior suffices to define an ordered community. If there is a "below," then there must be an "above." The opposition between high and low is a basic element of all human organization.

Still, the structure of Benedict of Nursia's text, on this particular point, must have seemed odd to one of his most ardent admirers and strongest promoters: Benedict of Aniane. His *Concordance of Rules* brings together other normative sources with the Benedictine Rule, the reference par excellence. In this *Concordance*, the Carolingian reformer thought it necessary to rearrange the elements of Benedict's Rule into an order that seemed more logical to him: he made "On the Election of the Abbot" into chapter 4 and followed it with "What Kind of Man the Abbot Ought to Be" as chapter 5.[9] For the moment, let's just hold on to an idea that must have seemed self-evident, or even like a tautology, in the medieval monastic universe: "The abbot, he who is worthy to be at the head of the monastery." Leadership in the religious community is intimately, intrinsically linked to the dignity of the one who exercises it. Everything flows from there.

> Let the abbot always remember that at the fearful judgment of God he will come under scrutiny on two points: his teaching, and the obedience of his disciples.[10]

Just as the tree will be judged by its fruits, so the superior will be judged by his teaching and by its most evident result, the obedience of his monks. This is the virtue expected of them above all else, as spelled out right from the beginning of chapter 5, "On Obedience," in Benedict's Rule: "The first step of humility is unhesitating obedience." The theological justification follows, balancing the assertion that the abbot is the vicar of Christ in his monastery: "because obedience shown to superiors is given to God."[11]

---

7. Ibid., 14–15 (chap. 1).
8. Ibid., 16–17.
9. Benedict of Aniane, *Concordia regularum*, ed. Pierre Bonnerue (Turnhout, 1999), 51–52, 63–66.
10. *RSB*, 16–17 (chap. 2).
11. Ibid., 38–39 (chap. 7).

Humility, which blends into obedience, is the subject of chapter 7, the longest in the Rule:

> The third degree of humility is that one submits to his superior in all obedience, for the love of God, imitating the Lord, of whom the Apostle says: *He became obedient even to death* (Philippians 2:8). The fourth degree of humility is that in this obedience, when one is presented with difficult, unfavorable orders, or even some injustice, one quietly embraces and endures it without weakening or seeking escape, for scripture says: *Anyone who will have persevered to the end will be saved* (Matthew 10:22). . . . The sixth degree of humility is if a monk is content with the lowest and most menial treatment, and if he regards himself as a poor and worthless workman in whatever task he is given, saying to himself with the Prophet: *I am insignificant and ignorant, no better than a beast before you, yet I am with you always* (Psalms 72:22–23). The seventh step of humility is if one not only admits with his tongue but is also convinced in his heart that he is inferior to all and of less value, humbling himself and saying with the Prophet: *I am truly a worm, not a man, scorned by men and despised by the people* (Psalms 21:7). *I was exalted, then I was humbled and overwhelmed with confusion* (Psalms 87:16). And again, *it is a blessing that you have humbled me so that I can learn your commandments* (Psalms 118:71).[12]

This ladder certainly does not describe a steady progression from one degree to the next. Each of these rungs can and must be climbed simultaneously. Still, a spiritual journey is sketched out, moving from humility to humiliation, from functional obedience to rejoicing in abasement.

This ladder seeks to imitate the one glimpsed in a dream by the patriarch Jacob, on which he beheld "the angels of God ascending and descending" (Genesis 28:12). The abbot himself is also caught up in this continual movement: "Let him also know that he must serve [*prodesse*] rather than prevail over [*praeesse*] others."[13] Benedict borrows this crucial opposition from a sermon by Augustine, employed in turn by Pope Gregory the Great (r. 590–604) in his *Pastoral Care* and by many other monastic thinkers. To be useful, not self-aggrandizing: this is what the Rule of Fructuarius (bishop of Braga, d. ca. 668), which Benedict of Aniane in the *Concordance of Rules* placed side by side with this passage from the Benedictine Rule, expressed in its own way:

---

12. Ibid., 43–45.
13. Ibid., 146–47 (chap. 64).

Let he who is subject to the needy and the poor realize that he is a servant [*ministrum*] rather than a prelate [*praelatum*] by the mercy of Christ.[14]

In fact, it is good for everyone, and thus for all members of the community, to live up to the Gospel verse that opens chapter 7 "On Humility":

> Divine scripture tells us, brothers, that *every one who exalts himself shall be humbled; and he who humbles himself shall be raised up* (Luke 14:11).[15]

"Worthy," "abbot," "obedience," "humility," "humbled," "raised up": These are the key terms of the original magic circle.

In its infinite wisdom the Benedictine Rule (chap. 64) envisions the possibility ("may God forbid!") of an unworthy superior who is elected by the community because he shares its evil ways. In that event, it would fall to the local bishop and the neighboring abbots and Christians to depose him and replace him with "a worthy steward" (*dispensator*).[16]

Here the unworthiness of the superior is specific to the individual; it is an anecdote, an accident to be remedied. But certain monastic communities pushed this paradox to the point of wanting to place at their head, as a matter of principle, members of the community who were a priori unworthy of the charge entrusted to them. Not, certainly, unworthy in terms of personal misconduct. Rather, unworthy because they came from one of the community's internal categories that was considered to be less prestigious than the others. In other words, we are going to collect and consider religious experiences that integrated into their procedures the strict application of the Evangelical inversion by which the last became first.

Doubtless this collection will be somewhat random, more a reflection of personal interest than an exhaustive harvest. The chronological quirks of the thoughts that follow should not be mistaken for a comprehensive survey; they may just as well result from the wandering nature of my engagement. Yet they trace an undeniable path through time, in which texts are in dialogue with other texts over the centuries, and writings and experiences inspire each other in accord with a specific dialectic.

---

14. Benedict of Aniane, *Concordia regularum*, 53.
15. *RSB*, 36–37 (chap. 7).
16. Ibid., 144–45 (chap. 64).

2. Fontevraud

> I ask you, therefore, if it is permitted to me to establish a lay convert as abbess? This way, if there are detractors after the fact, your valid authority will restrain them. I know! The dignity of this order, I know that it calls for a virgin. Furthermore, it is written that whosoever watches over virgins should be a virgin.[17]

In the summer of 1115, Robert of Arbrissel felt his death approaching, and so he gathered his brothers together. According to his second hagiographer, Brother Andrew (the author of the *Supplement to the Story of the Life of Robert*), the founder reminded the brothers of the unusual plan to which they had consented, one that lay at the very heart of the mixed community of women and men installed since 1101 at Fontevraud, not far from the confluence of the Loire and Vienne rivers:

> Therefore consider among yourselves, while I am still alive, whether you wish to persist in your purpose; that is, to obey the commands of Christ's serving women [*ancillarum*] for the salvation of your souls. You know indeed that everything I have built anywhere, with God's help, I have placed under their power and dominance.[18]

The brothers are subject to "Christ's serving women." Robert adds that those who choose not to remain under this subjection have only to change "religion" (in the sense of "form of religious life").

> Having heard his words, nearly all said with one voice, "Far be it from us, dearest father, that we should ever abandon them, since, as you yourself attest, we can in no way do better anywhere else! Far be it from us," they said, "that we should abandon your counsel! On the contrary, we all unanimously and freely promise, before God and his saints, stability and perseverance in the church of Fontevraud."[19]

A few brothers left, but most remained under the power and dominance of the women. Then the old man gathered bishops and abbots from the region. This time, Robert cleverly treated the original inversion inherent in his project as something already settled:

> I sense . . . , brothers, that my end is near, and therefore I have sent for you, so that with your counsel I might be able to provide for the future benefit of our church through the election of an abbess.[20]

---

17. *Deux Vies*, 198–99.
18. Ibid., 192–95.
19. Ibid., 194–95.
20. Ibid., 196–97.

Of course, they all deferred to his decision. He continued:

> You know, my dearest ones, that whatever I have built in this world I did for the sake of our nuns, and that I gave them control over all my resources. And what is more, I submitted myself and my disciples to their service, for the salvation of our souls. So I have decided, with your counsel, to establish an abbess as the head of this community, while I am still alive, lest by some chance—God forbid!—after my death someone might presume to oppose my decision.[21]

It was then that the ailing man raised the question evoked at the beginning of this chapter, the paradox within the paradox: Should the abbess be a lay convert or a virgin? This was a self-conscious transgression, since Robert understood very well that the "dignity of this order," the dignity of this position of leadership, demanded a virgin.

Robert did not come from a Benedictine background. He was the son of the parish priest of Arbrissel, descended from generations of priests. Up until this period, priestly celibacy had been strongly encouraged but not always embraced. Robert himself was a secular (non-monastic) priest of the diocese of Rennes, in Brittany, where he had served as archpriest. He then fled into the solitude of the forest of Craon, in Anjou, to live as a hermit. The first community that he helped to organize, at La Roë, was entirely male. It was initially a community of hermits, but in 1096 it became an abbey of regular canons following the Augustinian Rule.

The same year, he took to the road again to preach to the wider world. A mixed troupe of men and women soon began to follow him. Robert became the target of criticism from the bishop of Angers, Geoffrey of Mayenne, and the bishop of Rennes, Marbode; the latter denounced his mode of dress, his disciples' lack of order, and the way the sexes mixed within the group. In 1101, the master settled his traveling troupe in the little valley of Fontevraud, where the county of Anjou and the diocese of Poitiers met. Fifteen years later, the monastery was flourishing and had expanded into numerous priories (smaller, dependent communities).

Though he was not a Benedictine monk, Robert of Arbrissel knew the Rule of Benedict very well. Fontevraud's cartulary (the compilation of acts and privileges establishing the monastery's rights) proves that at least one copy was definitely kept in the abbey of the Loire valley. According to his second hagiographer, Brother Andrew, Robert referred to this guiding text when he crafted some of the articles of the statutes that he gave to his community:

---

21. Ibid.

This rule concerning clothing was established by him in our religious community, so that in accordance with the authority of St. Benedict, neither the brothers nor our sisters should be faulted for the unaltered color, the coarseness, or the size of their clothing.[22]

In the passage where the founder considers the possibility of placing a female lay convert at the head of the community, the association between "abbess" and "dignity" stems, consciously or not, from chapter 2 of the Benedictine Rule, "what kind of man the abbot ought to be." But times had changed. Robert of Arbrissel was a man of the "Gregorian moment," the decisive move to reform church and society that had been launched by Pope Gregory VII (r. 1073–1085) and pursued by his successors. Thus the founder of Fontevraud introduced a clause entirely foreign to Benedict's thought: the insistence that the superior (here in the feminine) would have to come from one of the abbey's internal categories rather than from another.

Benedictine abbots, as we have already seen, stood out only in terms of their merit and knowledge. This applied equally to their seconds-in-command, the deans. The only way the brothers were ranked was in terms of their order of entry into the community, though the abbot could make prudent modifications to this chronological order in light of individual brothers' merits. The respect due to elders should not stifle the voices of newcomers. Children, novices, the old, the sick: apart from the order of arrival, Benedictine categories were largely biological in nature. The offspring of noble and poor families alike were to be equally welcomed. The community could receive (not without a certain hesitation) priests from outside the monastery; the abbot could also encourage one or another of the brothers to enter the priesthood or the diaconate. But in either case the most important thing was that priestly status not become an excuse for pride, just as artisans should not put on airs due to their skills. Entry to the monastery, at least according to the Rule, wiped out all other distinctions. There is a real transparency to the ideal Benedictine vocation.

The reforming Gregorian movement was the papacy's battle to rid itself of the German emperors' oversight and of the influence of princes, to free bishops from the power of counts, and to liberate parish priests and monks from the grip of secular lords. It proclaimed, loud and clear, the "liberty of the church." It fought simony (influence peddling in exchange for ecclesiastical office) and Nicolaism (priestly marriage). The latter, of course, had produced Robert of Arbrissel.

---

22. Ibid., 208–9.

Moreover, the Gregorian reform included the desire to enmesh the entire social body in ecclesiastical netting, as seen in the fight against marriage between even distant relatives and the affirmation of marriage as a sacrament, monogamous and indissoluble. Lacking physical weapons, the reforming clergy moved the fight to the level of morality and developed a keen sense of individual guilt, opening up paths to repentance and conversion. Robert, a preacher's son converted to reform, was the living symbol of this renewal.

The Gregorian reform can be reduced to two elements, without really knowing which one was cause and which effect. On one hand was the struggle between evangelical and worldly values. On the other was the fight between two apparatuses competing for power ("the two lights," "the two swords")—that is, the apparatus of the church and the apparatus of the re-emergent states, building on the foundation of the feudal system. The first undertaking, concerning moral questions, implied a notable growth of the pastoral function in order to bring the behavior of Christians into line with the ever more stringent code set out by the church. The second undertaking, ideological and political, culminated in the "Investiture Controversy": Who had the right to invest bishops with their office, the prince or the pope?

The reforming papacy from this point on was profoundly centralizing. Reform was also a way of quietly reducing the autonomy of local churches, of drawing them closer to their mother, the holy Roman Church, which identified itself, and itself alone, as the universal church. Some reforming popes, first and foremost Gregory VII himself, dreamed of a centralized theocracy, with the pope, the true successor to the emperor, directing Christendom in God's name from the Roman See. At the turn of the eleventh and twelfth centuries, faced with resistance from powerful laymen, the popes grew more conciliatory. A division took shape between what pertained to spiritual power and what remained in the hands of temporal power.

Eventually, the Gregorian impulse introduced a de facto distinction between the sacred and the profane, though this distinction did not abolish all traces of the original link, since, as Giorgio Agamben aptly puts it, "secularization acts within the conceptual system of modernity as a signature, which refers it back to theology."[23]

The Gregorian reform marks one of the decisive turns not only in the history of the Middle Ages, but in the entire history of the West. It is the emblematic epiphenomenon, the epiphany, of the ideological paradox of Christian

---

23. Giorgio Agamben, *The Signature of All Things: On Method*, trans. Luca d'Isanto with Kevin Attell (New York, 2009), 77.

society that we are trying to grasp here—that is, the exacerbated tension between the dominant religion and the social order it is supposed to protect as an ideology.

In its desire to take in hand all of Christian society and while proclaiming its eminently universal mission, the church sought to address each of its constituent categories: it divided the social body in order to better rule each part. Within this larger movement, the monastic vocation offers the best example. In theory, the Benedictine Rule launched an appeal to all of Christendom. The Gregorian reformers shattered this universal call by multiplying divisions along the lines of social, moral, or canonical statuses. The thinkers and actors of the reforms expressed totality through a profusion of internal categories, creating or reinforcing complementary binary distinctions intended to articulate unity through multiplicity. The reforming spirit, at least in its initial phase, functioned in such a binary mode.

Traces of this spirit are apparent at Fontevraud, perhaps more than elsewhere:

> "There are also my priests and my clerics, there are also the holy virgins, widows and chaste women, persevering night and day in praises of God; there are my beloved sick men and women."[24]

These are the categories that, according to the *Supplement to the Story of the Life of Robert*, the founder could congratulate himself on having assembled at Fontevraud, including male and female lepers welcomed to the priory of Saint-Lazare. And he organized them in this manner, according to the *Story of Master Robert* written by his first hagiographer, Baudri, the archbishop of Dol and former abbot of Bourgueil:

> Nevertheless Robert separated the women from the men, and sentenced to the cloister, so to speak, the women, who were consigned to prayer; the men he delivered up to labor. He did so not without discernment, it seemed, for he committed the gentler and weaker sex to psalm-singing and contemplation, and the stronger sex to the duties of the active life. Laypeople and clerics went about together, except that the clergy sang psalms and celebrated the mass, while the lay folk voluntarily submitted to labor.[25]

The fundamental division was into four: clerics and laymen on the male side, virgins and chaste women on the female. The latter, those who had known

---

24. *Deux Vies*, 252–53.
25. Ibid., 162–63.

male company but now found themselves freed by widowhood or by mutual consent and who had converted to religious life, made up the category of lay converts at Fontevraud. The term "convert" here has its older meaning: one who has known the world and converted from it, with no implications for her social background. Thus it was to one of these women that Robert intended to entrust the office of abbess.

He explained himself to the assembly of prelates gathered in the summer of 1115:

> "But how will any cloister virgin, who knows nothing except how to chant psalms, be able to manage our external affairs suitably? How can she effectively treat earthly matters, she who has always been accustomed to spiritual labor? How, I say, will she who knows nothing but the joys of contemplation shoulder the burden of the active life? By what logic will a tongue accustomed from childhood to speaking with the Lord in prayer, to singing, or to reading, respond concerning external affairs? . . . Therefore, I do not want to entrust this office to any cloistral virgin lest I appear (let it never be so!) to destroy what I built, for indeed I could be blamed if I knowingly gave the charge of what I built with God's aid to one who does now know how to manage. . . . Let Mary attend ceaselessly to celestial concerns, but let us choose Martha, who knows how to minister wisely to external affairs."[26]

The oldest statutes for Fontevraud, which I have recently brought to light,[27] allow us to expose the archeological layers underlying this decision, known through the hagiographic account. An original article (which must have been drawn up by Robert between 1106 and 1112), predating the rewriting of the statutes necessitated by the designation of the abbess in 1115, indicates in effect that "one of the two cloistral prioresses should be a *conversa*."[28] Two prioresses had therefore been appointed at the founder's side; one was required to be a convert, the other not.

Again, it is necessary to turn to the hagiographic texts and the cartulary. The first of these prioresses had been Hersende, widow of the lord of Montsoreau. She represented, at the center of the religious community, the small group of original lay donors, masters of neighboring castles who guaranteed

---

26. Ibid., 198–99.
27. Jacques Dalarun, "Les plus anciens statuts de Fontevraud," in *Robert d'Arbrissel et la vie religieuse dans l'Ouest de la France. Actes du colloque de Fontevraud, 13–16 décembre 2001*, ed. Jacques Dalarun (Turnhout, 2004), 139–72; revised in Jacques Dalarun, *Modèle monastique: Un laboratoire de la modernité* (Paris, 2019), 87–127.
28. *Deux Vies*, 390–91.

Fontevraud's protection. She was then joined by Petronilla, herself the widow or separated wife of the lord of Chemillé. Thus at the outset the two prioresses had belonged to the same social class and to the same category of converts, which necessitated the requirement expressed by the statutes (assuming that they were then written in this form).

After Hersende's death, Petronilla was joined by Angarde, whose status (convert or virgin) is not made clear. Between 1101, the date of Fontevraud's foundation, and 1109/1113, the period during which Hersende died, a generation of *nutritae*, girls raised in the cloister from childhood, had reached an age when they would be able to take affairs in hand. The article in the statutes seems to be formulated in such a way as to fight against the temptation to name both of the prioresses from among the virgins. Logically, one would expect that Angarde would have been a virgin, balancing out Petronilla, the convert. In this case, Robert's dilemma in the summer of 1115 would become clear: Which of my two assistants should I choose as my successor?

The *Supplement to the Story of the Life of Robert* indicates that Robert paused before naming Petronilla of Chemillé. The statutes preserve a more solemn trace of her election and fix the limits of her power:

> Petronilla, chosen by Master Robert and made abbess by the common will and pious request of both the nuns and the religious brothers, shall have and hold full power to rule the church of Fontevraud and all places belonging to this same church. They should obey her and revere her as their spiritual mother, and all business of the church, spiritual and secular, is to remain under her management or that of anyone to whom she shall delegate responsibilities and as she will establish.[29]

Following her election, and completing the statutes, Petronilla very diplomatically granted to the other prioress, the one over whom she had been chosen, the title of "grand prioress" and made her a kind of deputy:

> This same abbess, looking to the future, decreed the following: the grand prioress is to be received everywhere, both in the church of Fontevraud and in all houses belonging to that church, and they are to obey her, and she is to have power second to the abbess in transacting the affairs of the church.[30]

---

29. Ibid., 396–97.
30. Ibid.

The grand prioress was indeed the abbess's substitute in transacting business, as well as her place-holder in the event of her death. But she was not her designated successor:

> And when the abbess dies, the grand prioress should keep the dignity of her position and have full power of ruling the church until another abbess takes the succession from among the *conversae*, as our master Robert established.[31]

Because if the grand prioress came from the other category of nuns, the virgins, then she could not fit the founder's insistence that the abbess be chosen from among the converts.

The prescription to choose the abbess from among the converts lasted only until the death of Petronilla of Chemillé in 1149. The transition passed smoothly with the election of her successor, Mathilda of Anjou. Daughter of Count Fulk V of Anjou, Mathilda was the widow of William Ætheling, King Henry I of England's heir apparent who died in the wreck of the White Ship in 1120. But she was also a virgin, since the marriage had never been consummated. All the subsequent abbesses were selected from among the virgins. As for the mix of men and women in the community and the submission of the men to the women, these elements lasted right up to the dissolution of the congregation during the French Revolution.

We know Robert of Arbrissel's most important acts, and they fascinate us. His motivations, however, largely escape our grasp. In trying to explain the most striking of his choices, the submission of the men to the women, all sorts of hypotheses have been proposed: a revolutionary desire to promote women or a respect for social hierarchy (since most of the nuns were indeed from a higher social position than the brothers), the influence of "courtly love" (service to a lady out of love for the Lord) or a model of evangelical reversal (according to which the last should be first and the first should be last)? Concerning the three decisive choices that marked the founding of Fontevraud—mixing the sexes, giving women the dominant position, and choosing the abbess from among the converts—here is what the early sources have to tell us.

Mixing the sexes? *The Story of Master Robert* says simply: "It was fitting that the women should stay with the men."

Submission of the men to the women? The brothers' statutes describe it this way:

---

31. Ibid.

II. UNWORTHINESS IN POWER

Master Robert gave these precepts for living rightly and obeying the Lord and the blessed Mary and serving the nuns of Fontevraud to the priests, clerics, and laymen who had received the habit of holy life through his teaching and promised of their own free will and out of pure love that they would serve the nuns under the bonds of obedience unto death and, with the reverence of due submission, to perform this submission not only at Fontevraud but in all the houses belonging to it.[32]

To serve the nuns "under the bonds of obedience unto death" is an echo of the Benedictine Rule, itself based on a verse of the Epistle to the Philippians 2:8: "He humbled himself, becoming obedient unto death." Below the abbess, the women are collectively superior to the men. The *Supplement to the Story of the Life of Robert* hammers home the founder's instructions to his brothers at the end of his life:

"You know the precepts I have given you: *do them and you will be saved* (Ecclesiasticus 3:2). You also know that I have commanded you to obey the female servants of Jesus Christ throughout your entire lives, for the salvation of your souls, and to serve them out of love for their bridegroom Jesus, and you will be rewarded for it in the blessed realm of Paradise."[33]

Finally, on the last point, the choice of a convert as abbess, the *Supplement to the Story of the Life of Robert* and the statutes offer somewhat different reasons. According to the hagiographer, a practical argument prevailed in Robert's decision: a virgin raised in the cloister would know nothing about how to manage the abbey's possessions. The passage concludes with an evangelical justification that turns scripture on its head, but in accord with the valorization of the active life characteristic of the Gregorian period: let us leave Mary to sigh after the heavens; Martha, unworthy though she might be, will know how to administer temporal affairs.

The statutes go farther. Petronilla is more than just an administrator. She has "full power" over Fontevraud and its priories, and the cartulary provides abundant testimony to the historical reality of this omnipotence. She is venerated as "spiritual mother" of both the brothers and the sisters, and she holds authority over spiritual as well as temporal affairs. Martha governs Mary's part as well as her own. At Fontevraud, the world is decidedly turned upside down.

---

32. Ibid., 398–99.
33. Ibid., 278.

3. The Paraclete

Fontevraud's inverting project, its project of inversion, received a commentary in the least-read letter of the most celebrated letter collection of the Middle Ages: letter 8 of the *Correspondence* between Peter Abelard and Heloise. Or at least this is the hypothesis that I think I can propose.

Born at Le Pallet, near Nantes in Brittany, Peter Abelard was supposed to become a knight, like his father. Instead, he threw himself into a life of study with a warrior's ardor. His masters were Roscelin of Compiègne, William of Champeaux, and Anselm of Laon, whom he never ceased to contradict. He founded his own school in Paris, on Mount Sainte-Geneviève, where he taught philosophy with great success. In 1117–1118, he seduced Heloise, the niece of his landlord, the canon Fulbert. A son, Astralabe, was born from this relationship. The lovers married in secret, and Heloise retired to the monastery of Argenteuil, where she had passed her childhood. Fulbert took his revenge by ordering family retainers to seize and castrate Peter Abelard. Peter then became a monk at the Benedictine abbey of Saint-Denis, just north of Paris. There he devoted himself to theology, opposing Bernard of Clairvaux and William of Saint-Thierry. In 1122 he founded the hermitage of the Paraclete, in Champagne; then from 1125 to 1133 he served as abbot of Saint-Gildas de Rhuys, in Brittany. During this time he gave the Paraclete to Heloise and her nuns, who had been driven out of Argenteuil. It was also during this time that he exchanged numerous letters with his wife.

The *Correspondence* as a collection was doubtless organized after the fact, perhaps lightly revised in form and certainly pared down from the mass of missives Peter Abelard and Heloise had exchanged. But it rests on a real exchange of letters between the two spouses at the beginning of the 1130s: scholarship can have no further doubt on this point. After having subjected the oldest surviving example of the *Correspondence* (manuscript 802 of the municipal library of Troyes) to a minute examination, with the help of Patricia Stirnemann and other colleagues, I have suggested that the collection could have been edited in 1237, as a fresh copy of the original dossier preserved until then at the Paraclete.[34] This edition would have been produced at the request of the contemporary abbess of the Paraclete, Ermengarde, in the milieu of the cathedral chapter of Notre-Dame, under the authority of the bishop of Paris, the prestigious theologian William of Auvergne.

Peter Abelard's long letter recounting his misfortunes to an anonymous friend, known as the *Story of My Calamities*, is traditionally considered letter 1

---

34. Jacques Dalarun, "Nouveaux aperçus sur Abélard, Héloïse, et le Paraclet," *Francia. Forschungen zur westeuropäischen Geschichte* 32 (2005): 19–66; revised in Dalarun, *Modèle monastique*, 129–56.

of the *Correspondence*. It contains the core of what we know about Peter's life. In letter 2, Heloise, who by chance (she says) has just become aware of the first letter, complains of having been neglected. She is still in love and asks her husband to help her and her sisters to come closer to God. In letter 3, Peter apologizes, but in a distant tone. He presents himself as condemned to a looming death and asks that the nuns of the Paraclete pray for him! Letter 4 is traditionally considered the most beautiful of the exchange. Heloise laments having brought about her lover's ruin and regrets the marriage that ended in such a fashion, but cannot free herself from the memory of past pleasures. In letter 5, Peter repents of having been a bad husband, lustful and violent. He assures Heloise that she has made the right choice by becoming the Lord's bride.

In letter 6, Heloise deplores, with some exaggeration, the fact that none of the church fathers ever sought to establish a rule of life specifically for women. After painting a grand historical panorama of female religious life in letter 7, Peter Abelard accepts the challenge in letter 8, in which he conceives the project of a rule for a mixed community of men and women, united by a common ideal. But nothing is ever created out of thin air. In this case, Peter (as the *institutor*, the one who conceives of the institution) could lean on the Benedictine Rule. He also says that he was inspired by "the best customs of monasteries," including what had been instituted "for nuns." Is it not highly probable that Peter Abelard had in mind the case of Fontevraud—the double monastery that was receiving so much attention in the kingdom of France in these first decades of the twelfth century?

> Finally, why do they [my detractors] refrain from accusing the holy Fathers themselves, when we have often read or seen how they founded monasteries for women too and ministered to them there, following the example of the seven deacons, who were appointed to wait at table and look after the women? The weaker sex needs the help of the stronger, so much so that the Apostle lays down that the man must always be over the woman, as her head. As a sign of this, he orders her always to have her head covered. And so I am much surprised that these customs should have been recently established in convents, that is, of putting abbesses in charge of women just as abbots are set over men, of binding women by profession according to the same rule, for there is much in the rule which cannot be carried out by women, whether in authority or subordinate. In several places too, the natural order is overthrown to the extent that we see abbesses and nuns ruling the clergy, who have authority over the people. And we see that they have opportunities of leading them on to evil desires

insofar as they prevail over [*praeesse*] them more closely and cause a heavy yoke to weigh upon them.³⁵

The last part of this passage from the *Story of My Calamities* has been interpreted as an allusion to Fontevraud, and rightly so. This is how Robert of Arbrissel's foundation was perceived by a contemporary. The first thing that astonished Peter was that abbesses governed their sisters with the prerogatives of an abbot. The second aberration was that the two sexes submitted to the same rule. The third and greatest scandal (which surely points to Robert of Arbrissel's foundation) was that abbesses and their nuns—exactly as in the statutes of Fontevraud—gave orders not just to men but to clerics and exercised absolute power over them. "Full power," one is tempted to translate the Latin, echoing Master Robert's statutes. This was unquestionably a reversal of the natural order of things for Peter Abelard.

Peter Abelard was certainly familiar with the case of Robert of Arbrissel. In a letter to Gilbert, bishop of Paris, written in the first months of 1120, he expressed indignation at attacks launched by Roscelin of Compiègne, his former master at Tours and Loches:

> This man [Roscelin] had the audacity to fashion an arrogant letter against that outstanding herald of Christ, Robert of Arbrissel.³⁶

Several months before, Roscelin had indeed addressed a letter of rare violence to his former student. He primarily attacked Peter Abelard, but also dealt Robert of Arbrissel a back-handed blow:

> Indeed, I saw that Lord Robert had welcomed women fleeing from their husbands, even as the latter sought to reclaim them. Refusing to obey the bishop of Angers, who ordered him to return them, he obstinately kept them to the end of their lives. Consider how unreasonable this is! Because if a woman denies what she owes to her husband and for that reason he is driven to commit adultery, the fault is greater for the one who drives him to do so than for the one who commits the act. It is the woman then who is guilty of adultery in leaving her husband, who then sins out of necessity.³⁷

---

35. J. T. Muckle, ed., "Abelard's Letter of Consolation to a Friend (*Historia Calamitatum*)," *Mediaeval Studies* 12 (1950): 208–9; *Letters of A and H*, 39.
36. Peter Abelard, *Letters IX-XIV. An Edition with an Introduction*, ed. E. R. Smits (Groningen, 1983), 280 (letter 14); *Letters of Peter Abelard: Beyond the Personal*, trans. Jan M. Ziolkowski (Washington, D.C., 2008), 195.
37. Roscelin de Compiège, "Epistola XIV," *PL*, vol. 178, cols. 361–62.

Roscelin concludes: "Therefore, either the two must separate, or they must remain united." But if Peter Abelard criticized Robert of Arbrissel in his *Story of My Calamities*, why had he rushed to his defense a decade earlier? The answer is that the *institutor* of the Paraclete did not condemn the founder of Fontevraud altogether. Both men had set out on the difficult path of offering an institutional and practical framework for women, allowing them to live out their religious conversion. Peter Abelard admired and respected Robert of Arbrissel, but this did not stop Peter from debating with him, inch by inch, point by point, article by article, just as he was accustomed to construct his thought, always in contradiction, often carried away by the force of polemic.

Letter 8 of the *Correspondence* is, to my mind, a veiled *disputatio* with the founder of Fontevraud. Peter Abelard would have known (this is still my supposition) the original statutes of the abbey of the Loire valley (and this would be an additional indication that the epistolary exchange dates to the 1130s). Our polemicist accepts some elements and rejects others. He applies to female religious life the method of his famous work of dialectic, *Sic et Non (Yes and No)*. Robert's normative text is the springboard for Peter's thought, its foundation and its foil. We will concern ourselves here only with what relates directly to our subject: the manner in which the idealized Paraclete was to be governed.

To do this, it is necessary to disentangle the combination of statuses, functions, and powers, first among the women and then between the two sexes, as they are found in letter 8. The ideal female community is formed of "cloistral nuns" and "converts," but in the "new" sense of convert (religious women of a lesser social and legal status), not in the sense of the converts of Fontevraud:

> All the other nuns, whom we call the cloistral sisters, perform their service for God diligently, like knights. As for the converts, who, renouncing the world, dedicate themselves to serving the nuns, in a kind of religious (though not a monastic) habit, they hold a lower rank, like foot soldiers.[38]

On this point, the weight of social origins bears down with all its force. Knights versus rank and file soldiers: Peter could hardly have put this more clearly, being himself the son of a knight. But the same distinction, so dear to Robert of Arbrissel, appears among the "cloistral nuns"—virgins and matrons. In his preceding letters, Peter Abelard had offered a conventional, not very convincing praise of virginity, which really only revealed his preference for women who had known "real life," like the Ethiopian woman in the Song of Songs or the Magdalene. How can we not see here a plea in favor of the path chosen by members of his own family? Peter's mother, Lucy, had entered a monastery late

---

38. Ep. 8, 252; *Letters of A and H*, 145.

in life, after having separated from her husband, Beranger, when he himself entered religion. Peter's wife, Heloise, had likewise reentered Argenteuil after spending the intervening years of her youth in the heart of Paris. The main argument in favor of experienced women was their age, in the same way that Christ himself had preferred Peter to John. This issue then led to the question of government.

The military metaphor continues:

> As in the armed camps of the world, so in the camp of the Lord, that is, in monastic communities, people must be appointed to hold authority over the rest. In any army there is one commander over all, at whose bidding everything is carried out.[39]

Contrary to what the attack against abbesses in the *Story of My Calamities* might lead one to think, the same principle applied to female communities:

> Similarly in convents it is also necessary for one matron to preside over all; the others must do everything in accordance with her decision and judgment, and no one must presume to oppose her in anything or even to grumble at any of her instructions.[40]

Pointing to a citation from St. Jerome's letter to Rusticus,[41] widely known within monastic culture, Peter Abelard's justification falls under the heading of natural law; after all, do not wild animals, bees, and cranes, have leaders too?

Then the philosopher again grows indignant:

> And so we are greatly surprised that the pernicious practice has arisen in the church of appointing virgins to this office rather than women who have known men, and often putting younger over older women.[42]

The words and tone are similar to those used to attack Fontevraud implicitly in the *Story of My Calamities*. But the target has changed, because now Peter Abelard is in perfect accord with Robert of Arbrissel's speech from the summer of 1115, when he had asked whether it was permitted to him to appoint a convert as abbess. Nevertheless, the justification is different. While the founder of Fontevraud recognized his own transgression (virgins would be more worthy of this office, but still . . .) and put forth an argument based on technical competence, the founder of the Paraclete retreats to reasons of authority and propriety: the young should not take precedence over their elders.

---

39. Ep. 8, 250; *Letters of A and H*, 142–43.
40. Ep. 8, 251; *Letters of A and H*, 143.
41. Jerome, *Lettres*, ed. Jérôme Labourt (Paris, 1949–1963), 1: 126.
42. Ep. 8, 252; *Letters of A and H*, 145–46.

Just as with the relationship between the sexes, Peter Abelard does not want to disturb the order that he sees as natural.

The superior of his ideal female community should be called deaconess rather than abbess for the same Gospel-inspired reason that led Robert to refuse the title of abbot:

> But do not wish to be called Rabbi. For one is your master; and you are all brothers. And do not want to call anyone father upon earth; for one is your father, who is in heaven. Neither be called masters; for one is your master, Christ. He that is the greatest among you shall be your servant. And whosoever shall exalt himself shall be humbled: and he that shall humble himself shall be exalted. (Matthew 23:8–12)

Thus, like the abbess at Fontevraud, the deaconess of the Paraclete should be a mature woman, converted from the world. She should govern surrounded by her six female officers, taking counsel from all or some of the sisters, but making decisions on her own. She should be distinguished by her life, her teaching, and her age (the argument about worthiness, so dear to Benedict, is evident here). It is better to avoid looking for a deaconess among noble and powerful women, who would tend to be proud of their lineage and to cultivate their family's interests more than the monastery's (this is still a Benedictine argument). Nevertheless, she is to be chosen from among the "cloistral nuns," not from the obscure mass of "converts."

We have already seen Peter Abelard scandalized by monasteries where women commanded men. In letter 4, Heloise had concurred, calling on him to guide his spiritual daughters and refusing the precedence that he had seemed to grant her through his use of the intricate art of epistolary convention:

> I am surprised, my only one, that contrary to custom in letter-writing and, indeed, to the natural order of things, you have thought fit to put my name before yours in the greeting which heads your letter, so that we have the woman before the man, wife before husband, servant before lord, nun before monk, deaconess before priest, and abbess before abbot.[43]

The two lovers might seem completely conformist, were their repeated appeals to "natural order" not linked to their desire to root their thoughts in reason. What made their love celebrated across the ages was precisely the way they so desperately needed to reason through it. Their love of debate made their lovemaking famous.

---

43. J. T Muckle, "The Personal Letters between Abelard and Heloise," *Medieval Studies* 15 (1953), 77; *Letters of A and H*, 63.

In letter 8, Peter Abelard addressed the subject of the best architecture for female monasteries. The deaconess and the nuns should be freed from all practical tasks for which they were unsuited. The presence of two categories of men was thus essential: "The monks are necessary especially to celebrate mass, the lay monks for heavy work."[44] Note that, in Peter Abelard's mind, it is self-evident that the (choir) monks are priests, because they are intended to celebrate mass. A sole pastor will direct the men and the women of the mixed community, a pastor who must obviously be a man, since as the Apostle Paul put it:

> Let the man be the head of the woman, as Christ is the head of the man and God is the head of Christ (cf. I Corinthians 11:3).

Could anything be more diametrically opposed to Robert of Arbrissel's initial choice, that of the submission of the men to the women?

There is, though, a reversal in Peter Abelard's letter, prepared in advance by invoking St. Jerome's words to Eustochium, a consecrated virgin (whose name is known to us only in this Latin neuter form): "Surely I must address as 'lady' the bride of my Lord."[45] A single flock and a single shepherd, but with this distinction:

> We want the provost of the monks, whom they call the abbot, to prevail over [*praeesse*] the nuns in such a way that those who are the brides of the Lord, whose servant he is, he recognizes as his ladies, and so is glad not to prevail over [*praeesse*] but to serve [*prodesse*] them.[46]

The slide from "prevail over" (*praeesse*) to "serve" (*prodesse*), from "be eminent" to "be useful," from "be before" to "be for": this, we recall, is the properly understood role of the abbot according to Benedict, in turn drawing inspiration from Augustine: "Let him also know that he should serve rather than prevail over." Is the origin of this reversal drawn from the Gospels? Is it Augustinian, Jeromian, Benedictine, or courtly? In any case, here the provost has become the servant of his ladies.

Food, clothing, money: just as at Fontevraud, everything will be placed in the hands of the serving women of Christ. "And what is surplus to the sisters' requirements can be made over to the brothers."[47] This echoes the statutes of the brothers of Fontevraud:

---

44. Ep. 8, 258; *Letters of A and H*, 155.
45. Muckle, "The Personal Letters," 83; *Letters of A and H*, 73; Jerome, *Lettres*, ed. Labourt, 1:112.
46. Ep. 8, 259; *Letters of A and H*, 157.
47. Ep. 8, 259; *Letters of A and H*, 157.

II. UNWORTHINESS IN POWER

Let them lead a cloistered and communal life, without personal possessions, contenting themselves with what the nuns will give them.[48]

The men of the Paraclete will guarantee the protection of the sisters, particularly their chastity:

All the brothers, in making their profession, shall bind themselves by oath to the sisters, promising not to consent to their oppression in any form and to guarantee their bodily purity, as far as they can.[49]

All of this leads Peter Abelard to arrive at a new judgment, which, in the desire to protect the weak from the strong, ends with the complete inversion of the initial formulation:

But so that the men, being stronger than the women, shall not try to oppress them in any way, we make it a rule that they shall impose nothing against the will of the deaconess, but do everything at her bidding, and all alike, men and women, shall make profession to her and promise obedience. For peace will be more soundly based and harmony better preserved if less is allowed to the stronger, while the strong will be less likely to refuse to obey the weak if they fear their violence less.[50]

Because, concludes Peter Abelard in an echo of Matthew 23:12, in a move perhaps again borrowed from Benedict of Nursia (and which seems, in the end, to clarify Robert of Arbrissel's decision): "Certainly the more a man has humbled himself before God, the higher he will be exalted."[51] In the end, the idealized Paraclete, like Fontevraud, becomes a world turned upside down.

In Peter Abelard, the philosopher, the theologian, the polemicist, and the star-crossed lover tend to obscure the man of the Gospel. He is all of the former, but the latter as well. Like Robert of Arbrissel, he tried to build, as he says in letter 5, "a religious community of the Poor of Christ."[52] In letter 7, he makes Christ the founder "of the order of nuns."[53] In letter 8, he refers to the "discipline of the Lord, that of the evangelical rule," and he adopts as his own Jerome's adage, "forsaking everything we follow naked the naked Christ."[54]

---

48. *Deux Vies*, 398–99.
49. Ep. 8, 260; *Letters of A and H*, 158.
50. Ep. 8, 260; *Letters of A and H*, 158.
51. Ep. 8, 260; *Letters of A and H*, 158.
52. Muckle, "The Personal Letters," 85; *Letters of A and H*, 76.
53. J. T. Muckle, "The Letter of Heloise on Religious Life and Abelard's First Reply," *Mediaeval Studies* 17 (1955): 253; *Letters of A and H*, 112.
54. Ep. 8, 243; *Letters of A and H*, 131–32.

In contrast to Fontevraud, the idealized Paraclete imagined by Peter Abelard never existed except as an epistolary fiction. The historical Paraclete, that of "the most wise Heloise," the one governed by the *Institutions*, was a female monastery, and then soon a congregation with its dependent priories and its indispensable brothers, priests, and converts. It was never truly a double monastery in the way that Fontevraud was, nor in the way that Peter Abelard had wished.

The thoughts of the two men clarify each other. Robert of Arbrissel did not hesitate to raise the question of the superior's worthiness. Peter Abelard wanted to subordinate everything to the principle of propriety. Yet this evident divergence arrives at the same configuration: abasement in obedience, exaltation in abasement.

4. Grandmont I: Facts

> At all costs, we forbid that women should be received into this religious community.[55]

Unlike at Fontevraud or the Paraclete, at Grandmont the status of women was never an issue. It must be said that—according to the rule of this Limousin community, written shortly before 1156 under the guidance of the fourth prior, Stephen of Liciac, and based on earlier instructions given by the founder, Stephen of Muret—the hermits of Grandmont did not burden themselves with much.

They were to have no lands beyond a small hermit's enclosure, no churches, no animals; they were to form no confraternities with other religious communities, to obtain no charters, to engage in no legal cases; they were to avoid begging and all conflict with the "ordinary" (the bishop upon whom a community depended) or with other monastic houses; they were not to leave their hermitages (the "cells") to visit the sick or to tend to the needs of the poor; nor were they to accept religious coming from other congregations, or men of less than twenty years of age, or the sick, or lepers; they were not to go out to preach or to hear preaching, nor to confess outside the hermitage . . .

Even in its earliest version, written while Stephen of Liciac was prior (1139–1163), the *Life of the Venerable Man Stephen of Muret* presents too many chronological problems to be followed with any confidence.[56] At most, we can accept that the founder was from an elite background, son of the viscount of Thiers in the Auvergne; that in his youth he made a pilgrimage to the south of Italy, where he met Calabrian hermits who had a profound influence on him; that he was taken under the protection of the reforming archbishop Milo of Benevento in 1074–1075; that he stayed for a time at the papal court during the reign of Gregory VII (1073–1085); and that he probably became a deacon but refused the priesthood out of humility.

The foundation of the hermitage of Muret, an archipelago of cells in the wooded solitude northeast of Limoges, goes back to around 1078. After the founder's death, in 1124, the brothers moved a short distance to Grandmont, to avoid any quarrels with the Benedictine monks of the nearby monastery of Ambazac.

Unlike Robert of Arbrissel or Peter Abelard, Stephen of Muret left no writings. His teachings, collected within the circle around his close disciple Hugh Lacerta (d. 1157), a former knight turned lay brother, were given the title *Book on*

---

55. *RS*, 86.
56. *Vita venerabilis viri Stephani Muretensis*, ed. Jean Bequet, in *Scriptores ordinis Grandimontensis* (Turnhout, 1968), 101–37.

Doctrine or Book of Sentences—"Book on Doctrine," that is, on the teachings of the master; "Book of Sentences," that is, gathering the words of wisdom that he had offered. If all religious institutions assume the appearance of a social utopia, Stephen's foundation seems to belong to a kind of utopian socialism, evidently inspired by the Acts of the Apostles: "Any good is better if it is in common than if it is not."[57]

Stephen of Muret's culture was only superficially Benedictine, and more than one aspect of his religious experience flew in the face of monastic practices of his day. His meeting with the Calabrian hermits, themselves in touch with Greek tradition, must have made him receptive to Eastern monasticism. His sources among the church fathers should be sought in the writings of Augustine, and especially in those of Gregory the Great, the only author to have had a perceptible influence on his formation. Beyond that, it was the Gospel and nothing but the Gospel. His creed is summed up in the famous formulation that opens the *Book on Doctrine*: "There is no other rule but the Gospel of Christ."[58] And further:

> Everything is taken from the common rule, that is, the Gospel, and no man will be saved, except one, that is, Jesus Christ with his members.[59]

Like the men and women who followed Robert of Arbrissel or Peter Abelard, the Limousin hermits claimed no title other than "Poor of Christ."[60] Stephen of Muret's thought, as it has come down to us, seems abrupt and marked by strong contrasts, but it does not lack finesse or discernment. Alongside these traits is a powerful penchant for paradox:

> It is closer to perfection to accuse oneself of doing good, than of evil.[61]
> For a just man, it is closer to perfection to receive alms so he might live, than to give them.[62]
> No pilgrim is more fully on the right path than the one who is heading to his own church.[63]
> It is a greater sin to kill one's enemy than one's friend.[64]
> In many ways, the good man and the bad are alike.[65]

---

57. LD, 52.
58. Ibid., 5.
59. Ibid., 5–6.
60. Ibid., 24.
61. Ibid., 22.
62. Ibid., 23.
63. Ibid., 29.
64. Ibid., 36.
65. Ibid., 37.

II. UNWORTHINESS IN POWER

God will be honored in the reprobate in the same way as in the elect.[66]

Let's come to the Rule of Grandmont. Its prologue ends like this:

> Let all goods thus be in common for you, let there be mutual charity and reciprocal affection among you. And let none of you think that anything belongs to you, but rather love one another, obey one another.[67]

The body of the Rule then begins with three chapters dedicated entirely to obedience. Right from the first chapter, the submission owed to the other brothers is added to that owed to God and to the superior (the "pastor"):

> Each time the faithful disciple willingly carries out the commandment of the pastor or of the brothers, God forgives him his sins.[68]

The Benedictine Rule does contain this prescription:

> Not only should everyone display the good of obedience to the abbot, but let the brothers also obey one another, knowing that by the path of this obedience they will reach God.[69]

But the Rule of Grandmont gives the idea of reciprocal obedience greater importance by placing it at the very beginning of the text. Chapter 2 plays with a paradox, in which one can probably see the founder's thought at work, but which does not stray from the demands of traditional monastic asceticism:

> Moreover, the disciple should take care never to love that which his pastor orders for him.[70]

At the other end of the text, chapter 59 goes beyond the principles of hierarchical obedience, in a passage that harkens back to the prologue:

> Thus to observe fraternity in the religious community, it is fitting that one should prevail over the other in honor, and vice versa, and that *he that is the greater among you, let him become as the younger; and he that is the leader, as he that serves* (Luke 22:26); let each one, out of goodness, willingly serve all the others.[71]

---

66. Ibid., 42.
67. *RS*, 67–68 (cf. Acts of the Apostles 2:44, 4:32).
68. Ibid., 70.
69. *RSB*, 158–59 (chap. 71).
70. *RS*, 70–71.
71. Ibid., 95–96.

We have to wait until the last quarter of the Rule, in chapter 54, "On the Treatment of Clerics and Converts," to see the community's internal categories outlined. Free from all practical tasks, the clerics have chosen the "better part," in imitation of Mary, the sister of Martha and Lazarus (referring to Luke 10:42). Consequently, says the Rule, "let them administer the spiritual domain," and let nothing distract them from the divine office.

> That is why we naturally entrust the temporal care of the cell to the converts alone; and since they [the converts caring for the cell], in their work and in doing other tasks, prevail over the other brothers—that is, the clerics and the [other] converts—not by domination, but by charity, let humility, the guardian of all the virtues, be preserved intact.[72]

The scriptural argument follows:

> Because the Creator of all things was himself obedient to his creatures, that is, to Mary and Joseph, as the Gospel says: *and he was subject to them* (Luke 2:51).[73]

Of course, it would be better if no one had to deal with secular affairs; but since it is necessary, let the converts deal with the outside world.

As in the Benedictine Rule, the designation of the superior comes at the end of the Rule of Grandmont. But the desire to distance the Rule from monastic tradition is apparent here. This desire echoes the preoccupations of Robert of Arbrissel or of Gilbert of Sempringham (1085–1189), who wanted no other title than that of "master," or of Peter Abelard, who preferred "provost" to "abbot," and "deaconess" to "abbess":

> We prescribe to you thus, again, that your pastor should never be called abbot, but only prior.[74]

This prior is not to be chosen from outside the community; nor is his election to be subject to any external influence. Once elected, he is to do everything possible to avoid leaving the enclosure of Grandmont. Finally we come to the procedure for his selection, in chapter 60, "On the Election of the Prior":

> When it is necessary to elect the prior, let two brothers come to Grandmont from each cell, as they are accustomed to come two by two to the assembly [*ad conventum*]. Let those who stay behind in each place promise to those who go that they will abide by the decision made by the whole

---

72. Ibid., 92.
73. Ibid.
74. Ibid., 97.

assembly. Once the assembly is gathered, after the invocation of the Lord's name, let twelve faithful and careful brothers of the religious community, that is, six clerics and six converts, be designated to elect the prior. After they have heard from the mouths of all that no one will contradict their decision, they shall retire to discuss the question among themselves. Let a pastor be elected who has previously been a faithful disciple of this religious community, such that, considering the others in his own estimation, according to what is necessary, he will provide to each what is useful. If, among these twelve, certain of them are in disagreement with the election, they must give way to the greater part, understood as the more faithful and the more sound, considering nothing but the common utility, while those who are in disagreement are to be removed from the council [*a consilio*] and even from the assembly, so that everything may proceed without them. From the assembly, however, let there be added to the council a number equal to those who have been removed, of both clerics and converts, so that the election still takes place with twelve electors.[75]

This is the system, in its broad outlines. Let's submit it to an examination that tries to peel back its layers, that reveals its internal contradictions, and that above all assesses its originality and its coherence.

---

75. Ibid., 96–97.

5. Grandmont II: Conjectures

The term "convert," as we have seen, referred to two successive realities in the medieval monastic context. The older usage referred to adults who had once lived in the world. They were converted from the world, as opposed to those who had lived in the cloister from a young age, "oblates" who had been offered to monasteries by their families. As late arrivals, these "old-style" converts did not become clerics, but their social status was not necessarily lower than that of their brothers, the clerical monks.

The emergence of "new-style" converts is characteristic of the monastic reforms of the eleventh and twelfth centuries. They are recorded, as we have said, at Vallombrosa, Camaldoli, Hirsau, the Grande Chartreuse, Cîteaux, Prémontré, and Sempringham. Intimately linked to the wider Gregorian reform, which developed a sharp sense of individual responsibility, these monastic reforms generally rejected the offering of young children to monasteries. The category of oblates faded away.

And so among adult recruits the distinction took hold between those who were literate in Latin—having received instruction, for example, with a clerical tutor or at a cathedral school—and those who were not. This division between the literate and the illiterate, the learned and the simple, inevitably reflected social reality. It also implied a distribution of tasks at the heart of the community.

The new converts formed a category of second-class religious, dedicated to manual labor, while the choir monks devoted themselves to study and the divine office. Peter Abelard unapologetically justified the double presence of "monks" and "converts" at his idealized Paraclete in this way. At Fontevraud, if the female converts were still "old style"—women who had known the world before their conversion—the male converts were indeed "new style," in opposition to the clerics.

This was certainly a class divide, yet this new status of converts did offer a recognized framework for a religious life to men who, without it, would have been relegated to the fate of rural laborers working the lands of monastic lordships. This is how the monastic reforms were intimately linked to the Gregorian reform. It was no longer just that the church would march toward its triumph as one undifferentiated entity, but that each and every one of its members, converted and repentant sinners, could find a place in the economy of salvation. To go from "all together" to "each and every one": this could have been the slogan of the reform movement.

This kind of convert, however, confused canonical order by introducing an interloping subcategory, neither fish nor fowl, between the two main "kinds of Christians." Gratian's *Decretum*, compiled in the 1140s from patristic writings, papal decrees, conciliar canons, and episcopal or synodal statutes, reflects this confusion:

> There are two kinds of Christians. There is one kind which, given over to the divine office and dedicated to contemplation and prayer, should be kept free of all the tumult of temporal affairs; these are clerics and people vowed to God, that is, converts. Indeed, *kléros*, in Greek and Latin, is the drawing of lots. For this reason men of this kind are called clerics, that is, those elected by lot. For God elects them as his own. They are kings, because they rule themselves and others in terms of virtues; and thus the kingdom of God is theirs. And this is shown by a crown [the tonsure] on their heads. They receive this crown through the institution of the Roman Church, as a sign of the kingdom which they await in Christ. The shaving of the head is the putting aside of all temporal goods. For food and clothing, they content themselves with possessing no personal property; they must have all in common.
>
> There is another kind of Christian; these are the laypeople. *Laós*, indeed, means the people. To them it is permitted to possess temporal goods, but only to make use of them; there is nothing more miserable than to neglect God for money. To them it is allowed to take a wife, to cultivate the land, to judge between one man and another, to engage in legal processes, to make offerings at the altars, to pay tithes; and thus they can be saved, provided that they avoid vice and do good.[76]

The converts are here classed with the clerics, but without being totally integrated into them, since converts are added to the category of clerics without being merged with it: "clerics and people vowed to God, that is, converts." In many congregations, the latter were also called "lay brothers," which only reinforced the ambiguity.

Let's return to Grandmont. Grandmont, or should we say Muret? This unique community requires us to adopt a somewhat unorthodox methodology. The difficulty stems from the fact that we have no direct sources to inform us of its history before Stephen de Liciac's term as prior in the middle of the twelfth century. For the period from the hermits' installation at Muret at the end of the 1070s up to the death of Stephen of Muret in 1124 and the move to Grandmont, there is a complete documentary blank.

---

76. *Corpus iuris canonici*, ed. Emil Friedberg, (Leipzig, 1879), vol. 1, col. 678 (part 2, cause 12, question 1, chap. 7).

The founder's spirituality rejected written texts on principle: no archives concerning land or legal cases survive before the beginning of the thirteenth century; no documents offer a solid basis for a sociology of recruitment; even the form of life remained uncodified, since it was limited to precepts from the Gospels. In fact, the example and oral admonitions of the founder—in the Eastern tradition of aphorisms—took the place of a rule. Cells were certainly dispersed, but only across a limited area, and so there was no need to create a normative rule or a liturgical *ordo* for far-flung daughter houses. Hence the documentary silence, so frustrating for the historian.

Let's start from the following premise. The *Book on Doctrine* is also called the *Book of Sentences* because it was said to preserve the teachings of the late founder. We will therefore assume that it preserves the memory of Grandmont before Grandmont, of the period when the hermits' community was still established at Muret. At the same time, we will also assume that the Rule of Grandmont, written down nearly eighty years after the establishment at Muret, testifies, at least in its normative measures, to the institutionalization of the community after the death of Stephen and the move to Grandmont. The danger is that this distinction might really reflect only the difference between the two genres of texts: a spiritual source with the *Book on Doctrine*, a normative source with the Rule.

Let's nevertheless risk this conjecture, in order to make the silence speak. The result is the emergence of two layers in this imagined archeology, which we will call "Muret" and "Grandmont," the layer of origins and the layer of institutionalization, respectively. What follows is only an attempt to sketch their contours.

What was the reality regarding clerics and converts at Muret and then at Grandmont?

The *Book on Doctrine*, which we are assuming reflects the primitive phase, reveals no trace of such a division. That there were men from both of these categories among the hermits of Muret, however, is shown by the case of Stephen himself, presented in his *Life* as a deacon, and by that of his companion Hugh Lacerta, referred to as a convert. Hugh had been a knight. The fifth prior of Grandmont, Peter-Bernard of Boschiac, had likewise been a knight and even married before entering Grandmont. The converts of Muret were thus not necessarily from the humblest social backgrounds. It was possible for them to have led another existence in the world and only later convert to religious life. In sum, they were old-style converts, like the original female converts at Fontevraud. But they enjoyed an internal mobility in terms of canonical status: after his entry to Grandmont, Peter-Bernard of Boschiac became a priest and so ceased de facto to be a convert.

If the *Book on Doctrine* does not attest to a distinction of status between clerics and converts, neither does it present the evangelical figures of Martha and Mary in functional opposition. Thus we can assume that at Muret the existence of clerics and converts corresponded to personal status, but that this distinction was not necessarily static and did not divide the community into two blocks with different functions. The time of origins may have been one of relative fluidity, when the principle of reciprocal obedience was not yet expressed through abrupt reversals of rigid categories.

The original project rested on a fundamental principle that precluded the adoption of such roles: the community was a single whole, the body of Christ. It prevailed over individuals but did not obliterate them, because it was important that each person within the group should find the function best suited to his talents. The *Book on Doctrine* puts it this way:

> [God] grants one virtue to one person, and another to another; in the end the whole of a religious community forms Jesus Christ.[77]

Therefore, obedience was not owed to one category more than to another, nor even to the pastor alone. It was constantly reciprocal, since it was "mutual charity," as the spiritual echo preserved in the Rule's prologue puts it.[78] The ideal community was founded on a multidirectional exchange of obedience, ensuring that there was neither dominator nor dominated—or rather that there was no dominator but only dominated, with each person eternally fulfilling the virtue of humility toward all, a humility that was also a "sentiment of reciprocal affection"[79] of each toward the others. This anthropology, which can rightly be regarded as that of the founder, was in harmony with an eschatology from which it certainly emerged:

> It will be wonderful, with other good things, in heavenly joy! All the elect will be equal there; no one will take precedence over another, even if he has been born and died first. It will not seem to anyone that they arrived there late. Because everyone will see all at once how, by divine providence, they will have been present in the heavenly kingdom before the beginning of the world.[80]

At Grandmont, by contrast, the dichotomy between clerics and converts took shape and hardened: the Rule clearly indicates the presence of the two categories. Both groups entered the community as adults, since it was prohib-

---

77. *LD*, 14.
78. *RS*, 68.
79. Ibid.
80. *LD*, 42.

ited to accept anyone under the age of twenty. Insofar as "old-style" converts tended to disappear (not entirely, it is true) from religious congregations over the course of the twelfth century and give way to "new-style" converts, we can suppose by analogy that the same phenomenon eventually occurred at Grandmont, too. The division between the canonical statuses gradually began to reflect social reality.

Such an evolution in recruitment might explain the hardening of the divide between clerics and converts. As long as the social background of the converts was not uniformly more modest than that of the clerics, the distinction of personal status did not imply a separation into two discrete blocks; other kinds of solidarities held sway, carried over from the secular world. But as soon as canonical status became more firmly based on social condition, the two blocks took shape and solidified.

The Rule of Grandmont decreed that the clerics were charged with carrying out the divine office and that no practical cares should distract them from it. The connotations of the two kinds of task, practical and spiritual, are consistent throughout the Rule: Mary's part is better; Martha is less fortunate. What is more, the clerics of Grandmont are compared to Christ in person, but only to be assigned Christ's status in relation to his parents: "submissive," "subject."

The exchange of reciprocal obedience between individuals is henceforth expressed by the codified relationship of the two canonical categories, but with their respective worth reversed. Real power is given to the converts, while insisting that their share is in fact the worse; the Rule places the clerics in a position of undeniable subordination, while trying to persuade them that this is cause for rejoicing.

There still remains the question of the prior. Since it seems that Stephen guided Muret from beginning to end, the question applies only to Grandmont.

The only condition for eligibility was that the prior had to belong to the community. The Rule of Grandmont does not state whether the person chosen must come from one category rather than the other. The very fact that the prior had to supervise the other brothers and "provide for each one's necessities" connected him to the role of the converts.[81] But by virtue of his permanent location at the heart of Grandmont's enclosure, he was more closely linked to the lot of the clerics, who left external contacts to the converts. In fact, the priors of Grandmont were chosen from among the clerics, and even more specifically from among the more limited number of priests. This is further evidence for the radical change from Muret to Grandmont, since the founder himself had not been a priest.

---

81. RS, 97.

The Rule does not mention the length of the prior's mandate. It does not seem, however, that he held this function for life, since the phrase "as long as he will be bound by the chain of Christ" is applied to the prior, in passing.[82] He could in fact be condemned and removed from office: if he took it into his head to stray from the straight path, "without doubt, he will be anathema, as will be anyone who agrees with him."[83] And further:

> If your pastor tries to turn you from this path of truth toward another direction, and leaving aside these institutions he will not in any way listen to your counsels, then by the authority of God we order you resolutely to expel him totally from your company as an apostate, rather than, by his fault, stray from this path.[84]

In the Benedictine Rule, this kind of power to deal with a wayward superior was granted only to prelates and Christians *outside* the monastery. At Grandmont, the flock could set itself up as judge of its shepherd, a notable dent in the principle of hierarchical obedience. Before John XXII imposed the title of abbot there in 1317, eleven out of twenty-two priors of Grandmont left office during their lifetimes, nine resigning and two being deposed, as a result of the internal turbulence that beset the congregation.

The prior's election was to be left up to the brothers, without any outside pressure. The electoral procedure was decidedly unusual. There could be no question of gathering the opinion of "the entire unanimous community" in the spirit of the Benedictine Rule, because Grandmont's community of hermits was dispersed in its cells. Nor could it be a matter of calling together the superiors of these micro-establishments (like the abbots in the Cistercian customs), since the scattered brothers had no superior except for the prior of Grandmont.

So two brothers came from each cell to participate in the assembly (*conventus*), which played a role roughly comparable to the Cistercian general chapter. The two envoys were those who "are accustomed to come two by two to the assembly"[85]—that is, already accustomed to come there for other purposes besides the election of the prior.

Were these two from the start designated by the other inhabitants of the cell? Were they merely charged with conveying the will of the group, or once designated, did they have freedom to maneuver and exercise their own judgment? The latter hypothesis—which implies an embryonic delegation of power and hence a principle of representation—seems more plausible, because the

---

82. Ibid.
83. Ibid.
84. Ibid., 98.
85. Ibid., 96.

brothers who remained behind had to promise to accept the result of the election, even, by implication, if it should turn out to go against their wishes. This precaution was certainly intended to avoid the secession of a cell that refused to recognize the choice of "the whole assembly."[86] But it also shielded the delegates from the reproaches of the brothers from their own cell.

Even if this type of numerical calculation was not common at the time, it was important that the cells should remain close to a common model and that each one should contain roughly the same number of individuals, so that the electoral procedure remained fair. Once the assembly had gathered, it was necessary that twelve electors "be designated" (*designentur*); the passive voice suggests that the assembly chose them. Thus it turned over its elective power to a small chosen group at its heart, whose members could be called "grand electors."

But let's be clear: in the Middle Ages, the idea of an "election" was not necessarily the same as our modern experience of casting ballots. Debate, strenuous disagreement, dispute, arguments from authority, arguments from inspiration (a phrase such as "after the invocation of the name of God,"[87] or, in Benedict's Rule, "inspired by the fear of God," was never just an empty formula), and recourse to all manner of signs could sway the decision.

At this point in the procedure we can see the practice of delegation and the idea of representation showing through again, because all the members of the assembly (*conventus*) had to promise not to oppose the decision of the smaller council (*concilium*); they agreed in advance to accept the decision of those they had empowered. But this cascade of promises (the brothers to their delegates, the delegates to the grand electors) proves the extent to which these pioneering steps were not self-evident, since it was necessary to shield them from challenges even before any such problems arose.

The most striking element of this system is the parity between the six clerics and the six converts at the heart of the smaller council. This equality of representation did not reflect the numerical relationship between the two categories, since we know that the clerics were in a clear minority in Grandmont's early days. If their number grew across the twelfth century, it never equaled that of the converts. So representation was equal in terms of statuses, not of individuals.

In fact, this parity of statuses, maintained at the heart of the council, already existed in the wider assembly. Each cell necessarily included brothers from both statuses. And of the two brothers who represented a cell at the assembly, custom

---

86. Ibid.
87. Ibid.

dictated that there should be one cleric and one convert; this automatically created a perfect equilibrium, in terms of the two statuses, within the assembly.

Let's return to the electoral procedure. The twelve "great electors" of the council retired to confer. If they agreed, the affair was settled, and the prior was elected. But the Rule provided for cases of disagreement. Indeed, such disagreement could hardly help but arise, due (among other factors) to the battles for influence between the two categories present in the council. To make things even more challenging, the council consisted of an even number of great electors. Among other crises, the converts' sudden deposition of the prior William of Treignac required the intervention of Pope Urban III in two letters dated 14 and 15 July 1186.[88]

According to the Rule of Grandmont, if unanimity could not be reached, then the "greater part" should hold sway in electing the prior. But the "greater part" did not simply mean the numerical majority as we would understand it. The Rule specifies that the greater part is "understood as the more faithful and the more sound," evidently echoing the Benedictine notion of the "small part, which possesses sounder judgment." The "greater part" was thus the more distinguished, the more prestigious part, which counted for more in the moral sense, qualitatively rather than quantitatively.

In a measure unique to Grandmont, dissidents (who could, after all, make up the majority in the modern sense) were expelled from the council and even from the assembly. Thus the urgency of deciding what constituted the "greater part" is apparent. How much weight should be given to the priests and clerics? What attributes conferred the exercise of day-to-day management and through it, inevitably, of power? In any case, it was not a good thing to be designated as the "lesser part" at Grandmont. The council was then restored to its full number, presumably through a new recourse to the assembly's preference. But did the assembly really have any choice but to reinforce the "greater part," which had already won the day within the group of great electors and to transform a moral into a numerical majority? Any other choice risked provoking a hopeless crisis. Note that even when making this substitution, the principle of parity between clerics and converts was scrupulously respected.

Compared with Stephen of Muret's foundation, Robert of Arbrissel's seems almost simple; at least at Fontevraud the superiority of the women was unabashedly stated and the system, whatever one thought about it, held firm. At Grandmont, by contrast, conflicts were so incessant that the community was suppressed in 1772. This strange institution is remembered mainly for the parity granted to its converts, or indeed for the practical superiority given to

---

88. *PL*, vol. 202, cols. 1415–18.

them. It is true that this principle gave the congregation of hermits a checkered history; this was noted by contemporaries, for instance in the 1217 revolt of the converts, which Pope Honorius III suppressed with his letter of 1 March 1219.[89] Due in large part to the parity of statuses that held sway, the system at Grandmont was such that only outside intervention could resolve the internal conflicts and impasses that resulted.

If the converts of Grandmont were mainly rustics in their social origins, if their status stemmed from their humble background, then there is a notable whiff of class warfare here, the driving force and the expression of which were rooted in the Gospel. Despite a determined desire to turn its back on the Benedictine tradition (though doubtless it was more a question of that tradition as it was understood at Cluny), Grandmont revived an original monasticism—that of Benedict among others—that did not equate monastic status with the priesthood or with being a cleric. Grandmont was indeed an expression of the Gregorian reform as a return to evangelical origins and affirmation, but also in that it resisted the groundswell that, since at least the Carolingian period, had glorified clerical status and even more so the priesthood.

But the real originality of Stephen of Muret's project lies at a deeper level, in the repeated affirmation of the community's true sense—a community without high or low, where the risk of negating the individual is avoided by considering each person's attributes, thereby allowing the body as a whole to find a more just use for each of its members, as explained in chapter 10 of the *Book on Doctrine*: "On the Knowledge Necessary to Serve God in a Reasoned Manner."[90]

In Robert of Arbrissel's journey (because it is better illuminated by the sources, but also because, unlike Stephen of Muret, he did not refuse to take charge of both sexes), we can see that the reproachful letters of Geoffrey of Mayenne, Marbode of Rennes, and Geoffrey of Vendôme forced the founder himself to oversee the transition from intuition to institution.[91]

How did the evolution between what we have called, for the sake of convenience, Muret and Grandmont play out? With no sources to enlighten us, we simply do not know. As its principles took shape around the middle of the twelfth century, Grandmont appears as a step forward in the history of the founder's original project. Fluidity gave way to categorization, which necessitated the pioneering invention of experimental forms of representation for these categories. In this evolutionary hypothesis, the unusual place granted to the converts would be only the most palpable expression, in the categorical language typical of the

---

89. *Bullarium, diplomatum et privilegiorum sanctorum Romanorum pontificum,* ed. Luigi Tomassetti, 3rd ed. (Turin, 1858), 350–55.
90. LD, 14–15.
91. *Deux Vies,* 503–77.

time, of a more general, more profound principle of greater importance, which we believe to be fundamental to the Gregorian reform: each and every person is called to salvation.

In the complicated storyline, heavy with consequences for the history of the congregation, by which administrative functions with lesser moral worth were assigned to the converts while clerics charged with exalted spiritual functions were effectively subordinated, we seem to read the remnants of an impulse to celebrate the equal dignity of all God's creatures; of a Creator who, according to the psalmist, cited in chapter 59 of the Rule of Grandmont, pushes his kindness to the point of making his creatures into gods:

> *I have said: You are gods and all of you the sons of the most High* (Psalms 81:6). We do not say this to you out of pride, but so that brother should serve and obey his brother, out of humility and affection.[92]

---

92. *RS*, 96.

6. Preachers

In August 1233, in Bologna, Brother John of Spain testified in the canonization process for Dominic, the Castilian canon, committed combatant against the so-called Albigensian heresy, and founder of the Order of Preaching Brothers (better known as the Dominicans) who had died in 1221. John of Spain presented himself as an early companion and close associate of the man he called "the planter and first master of this Order."[93] Not only was he an eyewitness to the facts he reported, but he even claimed to have conferred with Dominic about them.

John stressed the future saint's diligence in prayer, his austerity, the ascetic bent that drove him to discipline himself with an iron chain (one of the rare facts that John related without having seen it with his own eyes), and his concern for the salvation of others. He reported that, against the advice of the count of Montfort, the archbishop of Narbonne, and the bishop of Toulouse, Dominic had sent him—John of Spain, himself—to Paris with five other clerics and a convert, so that they could study, preach, and found a convent there. This was indeed done at the convent of Saint-Jacques (named after the old chapel given to the preachers in Paris). He specified, however, that Dominic taught them to disdain "everything temporal" and to love poverty and that he encouraged them to dispose of any possessions given to them anywhere.[94] John adds:

> And so that the brothers might devote themselves more intensely to study and preaching, the said Brother Dominic wanted the illiterate converts of his order to prevail over [*preessent*] the literate brothers for the administration and representation of temporal affairs. But the clerical brothers did not want the converts to prevail over them, lest the same thing happen to them that had happened to the brothers of the Order of Grandmont with their converts.[95]

John of Spain was careful to be precise, especially about chronology. Testifying about the moment when he had taken the habit, he declared that he had entered the order "in that year when the Order of Preaching Brothers was confirmed at the council of the Lord Pope Innocent III," adding "as he firmly believed, concerning the time."[96] This specific reference indicates the year 1215, when Dominic tried to gain approval for his project, in the autumn, just before the opening of the Fourth Lateran Council. John adds that he received the habit

---
93. *ACSD*, 142.
94. Ibid., 144.
95. Ibid., 144–45.
96. Ibid., 142.

from the hands of Dominic in person and made his profession to him in the church of Saint-Romain of Toulouse—"It will have been eighteen years ago at the next feast of St. Augustine."[97]

If one wanted to be a little hard on our witness and highlight the flaws in his testimony, one could argue that in 1215 John did not enter the "Order of Preaching Brothers" properly speaking, because this designation did not appear until a letter of Honorius III dated 11 February 1218. One could moreover object that in 1215, far from confirming the "Order of Preaching Brothers," Innocent III showed a prudent reserve concerning Dominic's project. And since John testified on 10 August 1233 and the feast of St. Augustine is on 28 August, his profession at Saint-Romain eighteen years earlier would have taken place on 28 August 1215. But if he entered religious life in 1215, it is more logical to think that his actual vows would have been pronounced the next year, following a year as a novice—all the more so since, according to the Master General Jordan of Saxony in his precious *Booklet on the Beginnings of the Order of Preachers*, the church of Saint-Romain in Toulouse was not given to the brothers (sixteen of them at the time, specifies Jordan) until the summer of 1216.[98] The donation was indeed made in July 1216 and confirmed by Pope Honorius III on 22 December, though perhaps the friars could have been using it a year earlier.

These are minor faults, attributable to the inevitable embellishments of memory. They take nothing away from the value of John of Spain's testimony. He does not give a date for the sending of the brothers from Toulouse to Paris, but we know that this crucial event happened on 15 August 1217 and that the donation of Saint-Jacques occurred in 1218. Let's note in passing the clear mention in John's deposition of the opposition shown by Count Simon of Montfort and Bishop Fulk of Toulouse to Dominic's project—understandable, given that the little local battalion was about to escape their control and take on a universal vocation. The hagiographic works relating Dominic's life are much more circumspect on this point.

In his *Booklet on the Beginnings of the Order of Preachers*, Jordan of Saxony confirms John's testimony that seven brothers were sent to Paris. He even gives their names. First were "the abbot" Matthew, Bertrand, John of Navarre (our John of Spain), and Lawrence the Englishman. Then, in a second expedition, came Dominic's own brother Mannes, Michael of Spain, and a Norman convert named Odier. Concerning the election of the canon Matthew at the head

---

97. Ibid., 142–43.
98. *LP*, 46–47; Jordan of Saxony, *On the Beginnings of the Order of Preachers*, ed. and trans. Simon Tugwell (Chicago, 1982), 11.

of the community, Jordan of Saxony comments on the title that was applied to him:

> He was the first and last in this order to be called "abbot"; because afterward, to instill humility, the brothers preferred that the one who prevailed [*preesset*] over them be called not "abbot" but rather "master" of the order.[99]

John of Spain did not give a date for the attempt to confer the administration of the order on the converts. It probably took shape in Dominic's mind between 1216, when the Customs were being drawn up, and May 1220, when the first core of the Constitutions was established during the first general chapter in Bologna. Since John of Spain was not present at Bologna in 1220, perhaps the conflict took place at the local chapter meeting in Paris in 1219. The revolt of Grandmont's converts—as we have seen—was at its height between 1217 and 1219, which tallies perfectly with John's testimony. For the brothers gathered in general chapter at Bologna in 1220, this conflict was still the front-page news of the day.

And so we come to the heart of the affair. It is obviously presented to us in a partial and indeed partisan manner. John identifies himself as a "priest of the Order of Preachers." Only the voice of the clerics comes through here—or, more precisely, the voice of the canons, since Dominic had not instituted a new rule, properly speaking, but rather had slipped his brothers into the mold offered by the life of regular canons, governed by the venerable Augustinian Rule. It was they, the canons, who refused to accept the supremacy of the converts ("the clerical brothers did not want the converts to prevail over them"), not being willing—they argued—to suffer at the hands of their converts what the clerics of Grandmont had just endured at the hands of theirs.

What were Dominic's intentions? His idea was not just a passing thought, whim, or dream. "The said Brother Dominic wanted": this was a firm desire, opposed by an equally resolute will: "but the clerical brothers did not want." This was a conceptual conflict, a conflict of interests, between the founder and a group of brothers, the dominant group in terms of numbers and prestige, who did not intend to see that dominance called into question.

The clerical preachers were well aware of the tribulations roiling Stephen of Muret's foundation, and they explicitly referred to them as a deplorable example to be avoided. Dominic certainly knew the Rule of Grandmont. Was it under its influence that he conceived the idea of entrusting the order's administration to the converts? John of Spain does not say so. But we should note how closely the

---

99. *LP*, 48; Jordan of Saxony, *On the Beginnings of the Order of Preachers*, 13.

formulation of Dominic's desire (though filtered through John's oral deposition and without there being an exact textual parallel) echoes the Rule of Grandmont's chapter 54, "On the Treatment of Clerics and Converts." In both cases, preference is given to the converts for the administration and representation of temporal affairs, and this step is understood as relieving the clerics of a burden.

Why did Dominic seek such an arrangement, before being forced to give up the idea? On this point we can follow John of Spain's testimony without hesitation. The converts were "illiterate," the clerics "literate." The clerics should thus dedicate themselves even more, "more intensely," to study. In the founder's mind, study was intrinsically linked to preaching, an activity so fundamental that it gave the order its name. Starting with a letter from Pope Honorius III dated 21 January 1217, the term "preachers" was used to refer to the brothers of Saint-Romain of Toulouse. This preaching was the main weapon in the campaign of re-conquest against heresy.

Like many other witnesses, John of Spain went on to say that Dominic urged the brothers to study "the New and the Old Testament."[100] He reported that the master always carried with him the Gospel of Matthew and the letters of Paul. He adds: "He studied them a great deal, so that he knew them practically by heart."[101] This meant that Dominic could compete with the practices of Albigensian or Waldensian preachers, attested by many sources. It was essential not to allow the Albigensians and Waldensians to be the only ones to announce the Gospel, the Good News, but rather to fight them on their own turf. To do this, it was necessary to know the texts as well as they did, better if possible, and thus to devote oneself to study. Yet this study had to come without coveting the ownership of books, which one should be ready to sell in an instant, as Dominic did, to feed the poor.[102] One had to sacrifice everything for study and for preaching, because these were the keys to the salvation of others—sacrifice everything, that is, except the poor.

Dominic in fact felt trapped between two imperatives, both of which lay at the heart of his community's mission: on the one hand, carrying out a campaign of evangelical re-conquest through the spoken word, which required intellectual performance; on the other, remaining faithful to the less educated brothers who had come to him, but who were less suited for preaching. His solution to the dilemma was crystal clear: let the converts relieve the educated brothers of all other preoccupations. The two statuses within the order could thus contribute jointly, in complementary fashion, to the great common goal:

---

100. *ACSD*, 147.
101. Ibid.
102. Ibid.

"so that the brothers might devote themselves more intensely to study and preaching." This was an entirely functional reasoning, producing a satisfying division of tasks, in just the same way that the choice of a convert as abbess had been justified at Fontevraud. Dominic's motivation does not seem to have been to invert the two statuses, to humble the first and to exalt the last.

Yet this is exactly how the clerics of the order interpreted his proposal. A telltale word jumps out twice from John of Spain's testimony, first to describe the master's intention and then his sons' refusal: *preessent*. The Latin verb *praeesse* means not only "to prevail over," but "to be ahead of," "to be in charge of," "to take the lead over." In Dominic's mind, the converts' supremacy would certainly have been limited to the administration of temporal affairs, yet he still expressed the relationship in hierarchical terms. He could have adopted Benedictine vocabulary and wished that the converts "be useful" (*prodessent*) to the literate brothers, without them "taking the lead over" them; that they should serve rather than prevail over them. Compare Dominic's formulation to the one employed in the *Life* of Abbot William of Hirsau (d. 1091) to describe the same type of relation:

> The kind father, burning with zeal for the care of souls, was the first to bring it about that the monks should make use of [*uterentur*] the faithful ministry of the lay converts in the administration of exterior affairs, and that, reciprocally, these same lay converts should receive from the monks what related to the care of souls.[103]

There were multiple possibilities for expressing this same exchange of services. "The converts prevail over"; "the monks make use of." The limit of what was acceptable lies somewhere between these two subjects governing these two verbs.

If the acts of Dominic's canonization process had not been preserved, if John of Spain had hesitated to compromise the harmony that necessarily envelops the memory of the servant of God in a canonization (with the untimely reference to a remembrance that he cannot have been the only one to have recalled, but that he was in fact the only one to report), we would never have known about this thwarted constitutional desire expressed by the founder of the Order of Preachers. Nothing related to this passage in John of Spain's deposition appears in Dominic's legends, and the order's legislation gives no hint of power ever having been conveyed to the converts.

Another witness in the canonization process, however, deserves our attention. This is Brother Rudolph of Faenza, rector and chaplain of San Nicolò of Bologna, who testified right after John of Spain, still in August 1233. He too

---

103. *PL*, vol. 150, col. 914.

stressed how important it was to Dominic that the preachers should suffer the least possible distraction from their main mission:

> He also says that [Dominic] did not want the brothers to concern themselves with temporal affairs . . . except those who had been made responsible for the care of the house. But he wanted the others always to apply themselves to reading, prayer, or preaching. And if he knew that a brother was suitable for preaching, he did not want anyone to impose any other duty on him.[104]
>
> He also says that [Dominic] was very fervent, devoted, and diligent in his sermons and confessions. Often he would weep during his sermons, and move to tears those who were listening. He says also that at the time when the first chapter of the Preaching Brothers was celebrated in the city of Bologna, the said Brother Dominic said before the brothers: "I deserve to be deposed, because I am useless and lax." And he humbled himself deeply in all things. Since the brothers did not want to depose him, it pleased Brother Dominic that diffinitors [elected delegates] should be instituted, who had power, as much over him as the others and over the whole chapter, to make rulings, to define, and to order as long as the chapter lasted.[105]

Rudolph starts with the subject of preaching, but then jumps suddenly to the chapter of 1220. What particularly caught this witness's attention was Dominic's call for his own removal from office, and then the humiliation he imposed upon himself. The traditional interpretation has been to see here a ritual proclamation of unworthiness by a worn out but universally accepted founder. But, reading between the lines, might it not be that Dominic offered his resignation, that the clerics did not accept it, and that they instead placed him under the strict control of the "diffinitors"? Like it or not, he was forced to accept this control: "It pleased Brother Dominic." We might go so far as to suppose, given the chain of themes and events in Rudolph of Faenza's testimony, that the question of the converts (which, thanks to John of Spain, we know was intimately linked to the subject of preaching) was at the heart of the conflict.

The Institutions issued by the chapter held at Bologna, the first general chapter ever held by the Order of Preachers, have not come down to us intact. The only surviving witness is the version in the early Dominican Constitutions, preserved in a manuscript from the convent of Rodez, which essentially combines the Customs of 1216, the Institutions of 1220, and many additions of subse-

---

104. *ACSD*, 150–51.
105. *ACSD*, 151.

quent chapters. The paramount importance of preaching is underlined in the prologue to the Constitutions:

> In the convent the superior is to have the power to dispense the brothers when it will seem useful to him, especially in things which seem likely to obstruct study or preaching or the profit of souls. Because it is known that our order was founded in the beginning for preaching and the salvation of souls. And our studies ought to tend principally and ardently and in the highest degree to these ends, so that we might be useful to the souls of our neighbors.[106]

The text of the Constitutions ends with a *Rule of Our Convert Brothers*. Inspired by Premonstratensian legislation, chapter 37 of the second part of this collection deals mainly with the specific prayers that the converts should recite during the office or at meals, as well as with their dress, which differed slightly from that of the canons. It also stipulates:

> As to converts who currently have psalters, let them be permitted to keep them only for two years, starting now; and to the other converts, we forbid psalters. . . . Furthermore, no lay brother shall become a cleric or dare to occupy his time in reading books for the purpose of study.[107]

Outside of chapter 37, the distinction between the various categories of brothers comes up three times elsewhere in the text.

> Let the prior of the convent not receive anyone as a convert and no one as a canon, without having first asked for and received the agreement of the entire chapter or its greater part.[108]
>
> The novices, both clerics and lay brothers, for a year shall not be sent to far-off places, except in cases of necessity, nor shall they take on any office.[109]
>
> From the feast of St. Denis [9 October] to Advent, for the anniversary of the [deceased] brothers, let each cleric say a psalter, each priest celebrate three masses, and the lay brothers say fifty Our Fathers.[110]

But chapter 31 of the second part, which deals with "Preachers" and does not say a word about converts, includes a passage that reveals the outcome of our story:

---

106. *CP*, 5.
107. Ibid., 23–24.
108. Ibid., 9.
109. Ibid., 10.
110. Ibid., 20.

Those who are assigned to the office of preaching or to study shall be free from the responsibility or assumption of administrative duties in temporal affairs, so that they may more effectively and better accomplish the ministry of spiritual affairs assigned to them; except in the case where there is no one else to take care of these matters, for one must sometimes occupy oneself with the necessities of the day.[111]

The exact parallels with John of Spain's testimony speak volumes. "Preaching," "study," "administration," "temporal affairs": the two sources deal with the same question. Chapter 31 of the Constitutions was compiled in 1220, reflecting the lost text of the Institutions of that year (which do not survive). So it was indeed at the assembly of Bologna, in 1220, that Dominic's desire was definitively rejected. In both the text of the Constitutions and the testimony of John of Spain, the assumption is the same: the brothers charged with preaching, and to that end applying themselves to study, must be free from all temporal administration in order to better devote themselves to their spiritual ministry.

Beyond this common assumption, however, the perspectives part ways. The debate must have been particularly heated at the Bologna chapter. Dominic offered his resignation. A crisis was barely averted. Instead of adopting the solution desired by the founder—that the converts take on the care of practical tasks—the Constitutions drawn up at Bologna opened up the opposite possibility—namely, that if there were no other options at hand, the preachers could carry out both temporal and spiritual functions, under the theory that it was good to deal occasionally with everyday realities. From the point of view of the canons, they risked taking on a heavy burden. But so what? In their eyes, the worst had been avoided. Those who want to hold onto power at any cost must be willing to pay the price. The converts became in all respects second-class brothers, and subsequent general chapters even tried to limit their recruitment.

In other respects, the legislation of the preachers rises as a splendid institutional edifice, the most impressive of any such legislation left to us by the Middle Ages in terms of democracy and representation. But it was built to the disadvantage of the simple and in direct opposition to what could have been the cutting edge of Dominic's project: a government based on service, rooted in a complementarity of vocations.

---

111. Ibid., 22.

7. Lesser Brothers I: Writings by and about Francis

In the final dossier we will consider, the Franciscan dossier, no single source directly addresses the question of inverted obedience, the subject whose thread we are following. We will have to read between the lines and make the silences speak in constructing a hypothesis.

Francis was born in the city of Assisi around 1181. Son of a cloth merchant, he entered the family business while dreaming of becoming a knight. Around 1206, he converted to the call of the Gospel, and two years later companions began to join him. In 1209, the little group received Innocent III's oral approval for its embryonic form of life. The brotherhood grew; the brothers took the name of "Minors" ("Lesser" Brothers). Francis left for Egypt and the Holy Land in 1219–1220. When he returned, he found the community changed and resigned his office as minister general in discontent. A rule was drafted in 1221, but did not receive pontifical approval. For this reason it is referred to as the *Regula non bullata*, that is, the rule not officially confirmed by a "bull," the official seal of the papacy. A revised version was finally confirmed in 1223 by a bull of Pope Honorius III, which is why it is known as the *Regula bullata*, the "confirmed" or "sealed" rule. Francis, who at the end of his life suffered from fleshy protrusions on his hands and feet and a wound in his right side, passed away during the night between 3 and 4 October 1226.

At the beginning of his religious conversion, around 1206, he briefly took on a sort of hermit's dress, and in certain ways his early brotherhood resembled a group of hermits. Indeed, the simplest, clearest form of government Francis ever imagined is found in his Rule for Hermitages:

> Those who wish to stay in deserted places, in a religious way, let them be three brothers or at most four; let two of them be the mothers and have two sons, or at least one. Let the two who are mothers lead the life of Martha, and the two sons lead the life of Mary; and let them have an enclosure in which each one may have his cell in which he may pray and sleep, . . . Let the sons from time to time assume the role of the mothers in their turn, for a period of time as they will decide best.[112]

Prayer is the unique goal. Obedience is due only to the minister (a superior who contents himself with the title of "servant"), which guarantees the attachment of this basic unit of collective life to the larger community of brothers:

---

112. *Scripta*, 344; *FAED*, 1:61–62.

II. UNWORTHINESS IN POWER

> And let the sons not speak with anyone except with their mothers and the minister and the custos, when it will please them to visit with the Lord's blessing.[113]

There is neither high nor low here. There are no hierarchical bonds. The two roles—mother and son—are held by each brother in turn. It is a dream, an ideal blueprint; an absolute brotherhood defined by a relative motherhood. The spirit is that of Robert of Arbrissel's troupe before its installation at Fontevraud, or of Muret before Grandmont. The brothers are distinguished from each other only by the roles they temporarily take on, not by permanent individual statuses.

When he left the world of the hermitages and had to confront questions that affected larger numbers of brothers, as in the *Regula non bullata* (the Rule completed in 1221), Francis was inspired by the same spirit:

> Likewise, let all the brothers have no power or control in this instance, especially among themselves.[114]
>
> Let each one cherish and care for his brother as a mother cherishes and cares for her son, in those matters in which God will give them grace.[115]

But in carrying out the work of legislation, the Poverello (as Francis came to be known) also returned, inevitably, to the model of monastic community life, with touches resembling the Benedictine tradition. So in his *Admonitions*:

> He leaves all that he possesses and loses his soul and body, he who offers himself totally to obedience in the hands of his prelate. And whatever he does and says which he knows is not contrary to the will of this prelate is true obedience, provided what he does is good. And should he see that some things might be better and more useful for his soul than what a prelate commands, let him willingly offer his wishes to God as a sacrifice; and, instead, let him earnestly strive to fulfill in acts the prelate's wishes. For this is loving obedience, because it pleases God and neighbor.[116]

Yet giving oneself over to obedience is matched by a crucial caveat, not found in the Benedictine Rule:

> But if the prelate commands something contrary to his soul, even though he may not obey him, let him not, however, abandon him.[117]

---

113. *Scripta*, 344; *FAED*, 1:62.
114. *Scripta*, 250 (chap. 5); *FAED*, 1: 67.
115. *Scripta*, 258 (chap. 9); *FAED*, 1: 71.
116. *Scripta*, 356 (chap. 3); *FAED*, 1:130.
117. *Scripta*, 356 (chap. 3); *FAED*, 1:130.

The "subject" here preserves his freedom of judgment and his right to use it. The individual thus benefits from a sort of conscience clause, whose halting emergence we have already seen at Grandmont.

As for the superior, even more than in the earlier monastic tradition, probably more than ever before, he must remember that his office is a service—a service signified by Christ's gesture toward his disciples on the evening of the Last Supper—as repeated in a passage from the *Admonitions* that we have already discussed:

> *I have not come to be served but to serve* (Matthew 20:28), says the Lord. Those who have been placed over others, let them glory in that position as much as if they had been assigned the duty of washing their brothers' feet.[118]

In a deeply evangelical choice, the term "minister" is used in Francis's legislation, often in the pairing "minister and servant," to designate the one whom we can hardly dare call the superior. Francis had learned well the Benedictine lesson on the degrees of humility—and he certainly also knew Bernard of Clairvaux's commentary in the *Treatise on the Degrees of Humility*. But he supercharged these teachings, pushing the principle to its limits.

Subordination applies to each brother, who is required to submit not only to every human creature but even to wild animals, according to the call to "Holy Obedience" in the *Salutation of the Virtues*:

> Holy Obedience confounds every corporal and carnal wish, binds its mortified body to obedience of the Spirit and obedience to one's brother, and he [the subject] is submissive to everyone in the world, not only to people but to every beast and wild animal as well, so that they may do whatever they want with it insofar as it *has been given* to them *from above* by the Lord (John 19:11).[119]

As if to forestall any hint of revolt in the "absolute subject" (who is all the more firmly subjected by this), submission applies even more to the superior, who must live out his office in humility and reach the height of humiliation, as Francis prescribed in the *Letter to a Minister*:

> About the state of your soul, I say to you as best I can, that all that impedes you from loving the Lord God, and whoever has become an impediment to you, whether brothers or others, even if they cover you with blows, you should consider as a grace. And may you want it to be this way and not

---

118. *Scripta*, 358 (chap. 4); *FAED*, 1:130.
119. *Scripta*, 48–50; *FAED*, 1:165.

otherwise. And do this from true obedience to the Lord God and to me, for I know with certitude that this is true obedience. And love those who do those things to you and do not wish anything different from them apart from what the Lord God shall have given you. And love them in this and do not wish that they be better Christians.[120]

The concluding clause of this passage is so startling that since the Middle Ages copyists have suppressed the "not," so that it would read "wish that they be better Christians." But this was not the Poverello's teaching: the minister should want no reward except humiliation.

This crushing subjection applies above all to Francis himself, as shown by the edifying anecdote he imagined while defining *The True Joy*, a bitter jubilation that the founder had to experience when rebuffed like the lowest of lepers:

> I return from Perugia and arrive here in the dead of night. It's winter time, muddy, and so cold that icicles have formed on the edges of my habit and keep striking my legs, and blood flows from these wounds. Freezing, covered with mud and ice, I come to the gate and, after I've knocked and called for a long time, a brother comes and asks: "Who is it?" "Brother Francis," I answer. "Go away!" he says. "This isn't a decent hour to be wandering about! You can't come in!" When I insist, he replies: "Go away! You are simple and illiterate! Don't come back to us again! We are such that we don't need you!" I stand again at the door and say: "For the love of God, take me in tonight!" And he replies: "I will not! Go to the Crosiers' place [a religious hospital for lepers close to Assisi] and ask there!" I tell you that if I am patient and do not become upset, in this lies true joy, and true virtue, and the salvation of my soul.[121]

Like the congregation of Grandmont and the Order of Preachers, the community of Lesser Brothers did not burden itself with the question of women. The two extant rules insist on scrupulous avoidance of contacts with the other sex and of the "care of nuns." Yet Dominic and Francis themselves welcomed women: Dominic in the female monastery of Prouille, which was in fact the first establishment he founded of any kind; and Francis at San Damiano, where (as we have seen) he installed Clare and her sisters. But as soon as their orders came into existence, the monastic logic of wariness toward the opposite sex took hold. Neither the Lesser Brothers nor the Preachers became a double order. In both cases, the female "branch," called the "Second Order," was a separate institution, even if it preserved privileged ties with the male order.

---

120. *Scripta*, 164; FAED, 1:97.
121. *Scripta*, 417–18; FAED, 1:166–67.

Even if there was no mixing of the sexes, at the heart of the Lesser Brothers there was a diversity of canonical statuses, just as with the Preachers. Some were clerics, others lay brothers. All were to apply themselves to the Divine Office, but each category according to its own abilities, as the *Regula non bullata* prescribed:

> Let all the brothers, clerical or lay, recite the Divine Office, lauds and prayers, as they are required to do.[122]

This distinction was never challenged. With the same rigor as the early Constitutions of the Preachers, the *Regula bullata* (the Rule confirmed in 1223), prescribes that if a brother is illiterate, he should remain that way.[123]

Francis knew perfectly well the seven orders of the clerical hierarchy: priest, deacon, subdeacon, acolyte, exorcist, reader, porter. Over and over again he insisted on the respect due to priests, to their sacred hands that touched the body and blood of Christ. The Eucharist and confession gave them their prestigious position, and no one should presume to judge them. Not only was the Eucharist at the center of Francis's devotion, but it lay at the heart of his theological and ecclesiological thought. He rebuilt the church from that sacrament, which is also a mystery, the endless repetition of the astonishing abasement of the Son in his Incarnation. The Eucharist required consecration, which implied the priesthood. The moral worth of an individual priest was beside the point; what counted was that their order had been instituted and guaranteed by the holy Roman Church.

Francis often folded priests into the larger category of clerics, who should also be honored. As a deacon, he himself belonged to this larger category, which he insisted must, more than others, venerate the body and name of the Lord. Rarely, very rarely, the founder adopted a warning tone with priests or clerics, reminding them of the higher obligations to which their status called them.

Were the community's two categories assigned specific functions beyond the Divine Office? We find no explicit mention of this. The *Regula non bullata* does, however, offer the following formulation: "all my brothers: preachers, prayers, workers, clerics as much as lay brothers."[124] The first three terms ("preachers, prayers, workers") designate functions; the last two ("clerics as well as lay brothers"), statuses. If Francis had the slightest conception of the three orders into which feudal society was divided ("those who pray, those who fight, those who work"), it is interesting to note that, in their projection at the

---

122. *Scripta*, 246 (chap. 3); FAED, 1:65.
123. *Scripta*, 334 (chap. 10); FAED, 1:105.
124. *Scripta*, 268 (chap. 17); FAED, 1:75.

II. UNWORTHINESS IN POWER

heart of the religious community, the preachers fill the warriors' place; this is not without a certain connection to Dominic's conception of preaching as battle. Should we try to find a correlation between function and status? If so, then preaching and prayer would pertain to the clerics, and work to the lay brothers. The context, however, does not justify such an extrapolation.

In the *Regula bullata*—the Rule that finally received official papal approval—the minister general is not required to have any particular status. Concerning the ministers (meaning the ministers of the provinces of the order, the "provincials"), it is mentioned in passing that they can be priests or not.[125] From this point of view, too, Francis in the end comes back to the spirit of the Benedictine Rule, in which priesthood is a personal status that is not taken into consideration when structuring the community.

In their early days, the companions of Francis of Assisi formed a local group of lay penitents, with no distinction of status. The oldest legends make this clear.

In the *Life of the Blessed Francis*, composed by Thomas of Celano in 1228–1229, and in *The Beginning of the Order*, composed by Brother John around 1240–1241, when the recruitment of the first companions around 1208–1209 is related, not a single one of them is referred to as a priest or cleric. This is in contrast to the priest Sylvester, who joined them soon after but who at first played a far from positive role: out of greed he tried to swindle Francis on the price of the stones purchased to restore San Damiano.

In *The Beginning of the Order* (also known as *The Anonymous of Perugia*), when asked "to what order do you belong?" these odd vagabonds answer: "We are penitents, and we were born in the city of Assisi."[126] In 1209, during the meeting between Innocent III and the little battalion of penitents from Assisi, brought to the pope by Cardinal Giovanni of San Paolo, the brothers were given permission to preach anywhere. Brother John adds:

> And as for Cardinal Giovanni of San Paolo, because of the devotion that he had for the Brother [Francis], he caused the whole group of twelve brothers to be tonsured.[127]

This detail is of great canonical importance, because the "first tonsure," as long as it is "given according to the form of the church," confers de facto clerical status: a letter of Innocent III to the archbishop of Rouen, dated 1 September 1210 and made available in the *Decretales* of Gregory IX, attests to this fact.[128] The episode of Francis and his companions receiving the tonsure at

---

125. *Scripta*, 330 (chap. 7); *FAED*, 1:103–4.
126. *FF*, 1326 (chap. 5); *FAED*, 2:43.
127. *FF*, 1339 (chap. 7); *FAED*, 2:51.
128. *Corpus iuris canonici*, ed. Friedberg, vol. 2, col. 129 (book 1, title 14, chapter 11).

Rome is taken up again by the *Legend of the Three Companions*, compiled between 1244 and 1246:

> The blessed Francis and the eleven other brothers received the tonsure that the cardinal had obtained for them, because he wanted all twelve to be clerics.[129]

Evoked in a rather enigmatic manner in the *Memorial* written by Thomas of Celano in 1246–1247 ("Francis began, with the authority now granted him, to preach passionately and to scatter the seeds of virtue, visiting towns and villages"[130]), the episode of the tonsure was elaborated in the *Legenda maior*, finished in or just after 1262 by the minister general Bonaventure, which attributes the impetus to Innocent III:

> He approved the Rule, gave a mandate to preach penance, and caused small tonsures to be given to all the lay brothers who had accompanied the servant of God, so that they could freely preach *the word of God* (Luke 11:28).[131]

Bonaventure was not only an eminent theologian at the University of Paris, but also the order's minister general. He was thus both overseer and servant of the whole Order of Lesser Brothers. He is often called the "second founder" of the order on account of his legislative work. It was important for him that this consecration should have been bestowed directly by the pope upon all the brothers, who in reality were all laymen at that point. We can see in this passage the desire for normalization that Bonaventure often showed both as a theologian and as minister general. But it was also important to him that the tonsure should have been "small," so that these illiterate men would not be completely confused with real clerics.

If we have to follow one of these accounts, it should be *The Beginning of the Order*. It is more plausible that Cardinal Giovanni of San Paolo, who had taken the risk of facilitating the meeting between Francis and Innocent III, would have been the one who tried to normalize the canonical position of the penitents of Assisi.

Even after Francis's group had returned from Rome and installed itself at Rivo Torto (near Assisi) in 1209–1210, the *Life of the Blessed Francis* shows that there was still no priest among the companions:

---

129. *FF*, 1424 (chap. 12); *FAED*, 2:98.
130. *FF*, 460 (chap. 11); *FAED*, 2:256.
131. *FF*, 802–3 (chap. 3); *FAED*, 2:548–49.

They would often confess their sins to a certain secular priest, whose deeds had earned him a very bad reputation and who was despised by everyone else because of the enormity of his misdeeds.[132]

The *Life of the Blessed Francis* reveals that the brotherhood continued to recruit from among both clerics and laymen, which fits with the fact that this distinction appears in both extant Rules, in Francis's *Testament*, and in his *Letter to the Entire Order*.

In the *Assisi Compilation*, which mostly reflects memories gathered by Brother Leo between 1244 and 1246, John the Simple's conversation with Francis provides a nice portrait of one of these illiterate brothers, in a mirror effect between the Poverello and the real poor that Giacomo Todeschini has illuminated:[133]

> One day, the blessed Francis went to a church in a village near the city of Assisi and began to sweep it. Immediately the rumor spread through the village, especially because those people enjoyed seeing and hearing him. A man named John heard it, a man of amazing simplicity, who was plowing his field near the church, and he immediately went to [Francis]. Finding him sweeping the church, he said to him, "Brother, give me the broom because I want to help you." Taking the broom from him, he swept the rest. When they both sat down, he said to the blessed Francis: "Brother, for a long time now I've wanted to serve God, especially after I heard talk about you and your brothers, but I didn't know how to come to you. Now that it has pleased God for me to see you, I want to do whatever pleases you." Considering his fervor, the blessed Francis rejoiced in the Lord, especially because he then had few brothers, and because it seemed to him that, on account of his pure simplicity, he would make a good religious.[134]

Finally, the *Life of the Blessed Francis* confirms that the Poverello was a cleric, and more specifically a deacon, in 1223, although we have no evidence at all to establish the circumstances under which he received this major order, just below that of the priesthood.

In sum, the legends shed little light on our question, which we might formulate like this: In an order where clerics, some of them priests, rubbed shoulders with lay brothers, did these canonical statuses ever coincide with the

---

132. *FF*, 320 (chap. 17); *FAED*, 1:223.
133. Giacomo Todeschini, *Visibilmente crudeli. Malviventi, persone sospette e gente qualunque dal Medioevo all'età moderna* (Bologna, 2007).
134. *FF*, 1553 (chap. 61); *FAED*, 2:163.

functions exercised by the brothers, especially with their governmental functions? The oldest Franciscan chronicles, less restrained than the hagiographic texts we have just studied, open up essential aspects of life in the provinces, of life in the order, of the daily life of the brothers. It is to them that we now must turn.

8. Lesser Brothers II: Chronicles

In the *Chronicle* he dictated to Brother Baldwin of Brandenburg in 1262, Jordan of Giano recounted the arrival of the Lesser Brothers in Germany. Brother Jordan, originally from Umbria, was already a cleric when he set off—reluctantly—for this distant land in 1221. In 1223, he was promoted to the priesthood. He was generally careful to note the status of the brothers mentioned in his *Chronicle*. Let's follow it, in order to try to clarify three main points: the composition of the teams of brothers working in Germany; the possibilities for internal mobility from one status to another; and the promotion to positions of responsibility in the order as a function of personal status.

The little squad that headed to Germany in 1221, led by Caesarius of Speyer, was composed of twelve clerics, three of whom were priests, and five lay brothers. The same year, at Würzburg, Caesarius of Speyer recruited a cleric who soon became a priest, as well as two lay brothers. In 1222, at the provincial chapter of Worms, clerics and lay brothers were already both present in large numbers, but the brothers of Worms and Speyer included so few priests that only one novice was available to celebrate mass and hear confessions. In 1223, the team that left for the new custody of Saxony included eleven brothers. We know the specific status for nine: four clerics, two of whom were priests, and five lay brothers, one being a tailor. They were joined by new recruits at Hildesheim, among whom were a canon, a school master, and a knight.

In 1224, we find other references to "mixed" teams, such as the one Jordan of Giano led himself, which was composed of five clerics, two of whom were priests, and three lay brothers. In 1225, an exploratory mission to Thuringia was entrusted to lay brothers, followed by a priest empowered as a preacher. The same year, the group sent to Nordhausen was made up entirely of lay brothers, so that Jordan ran himself ragged hearing all of their confessions. Four more lay brothers founded the first house of brothers at Mülhausen.

It would be pointless to propose a statistical analysis of such limited numbers. Yet for the teams that have just been mentioned and whose make-up can be detailed, the clerics, about a third of them priests, slightly outnumber the lay brothers: in total there are twenty-two clerics, seven of whom are priests, compared with seventeen lay brothers. But this percentage of laymen is surely too low. For one thing, Jordan of Giano tends to pass them over in anonymity. For another, he refers repeatedly to problems posed by having a large number of lay brothers and too few priest brothers. Hence the need for internal promotion, such as the young cleric who quickly became a priest and preacher, and the four other clerics whom Caesarius of Speyer decided to raise to the priesthood.

Concerning positions of responsibility at the heart of the German province, these were held by brothers of all statuses, but in notably unequal proportions. One of the provincial ministers was at least a subdeacon (Caesarius of Speyer), and the other a priest (Albert of Pisa). Two provincial vicars were clerics, one of whom was a priest. All five custodes (brothers responsible for the custodies, intermediate jurisdictions between the provinces and the individual convents) for whom the status is given were clerics, including three priests. We have to descend to the level of the guardians (brothers in charge of individual houses) to find one lay brother along with three clerics, two of whom were priests. Moreover, once the priest Albert of Pisa was promoted to the rank of provincial minister in 1223, these provincial responsibilities became the exclusive preserve of the priests.

This same Albert of Pisa had to speak sharply to the priest Nicholas of the Rhine—whose boundless humility caused our chronicler Jordan of Giano to regard him as both highly admirable and impossibly exasperating—in order to get him to accept the charge of custos:

> So, you don't want to be a "lord"! Are we "lords," we who hold offices in the order? Admit your fault immediately, brother, because you have considered the order's offices as lordships and prelacies, when in fact we can say that they are burdens and servitudes.[135]

The *Treatise on the Arrival of the Lesser Brothers in England*, written by Thomas of Eccleston over a period of years from 1231 to 1258, forms the English counterpart to Jordan of Giano's German *Chronicle*. Here it was also a "mixed" team of four clerics, including two priests (one of whom, we learn, was castrated), and five laymen, who landed at Dover in 1224. In this first group, one of the priests and one of the lay brothers were still novices. Rapid recruitment in England changed this picture. Twelve clerics were welcomed into the order, one being an abbot and seven university masters, compared with four laymen, one referred to as "a playful layman" and the three others as "knights." In contrast to Jordan of Giano, Thomas of Eccleston offers a true case of mobility (in addition to the promotion, doubtless from within the group of clerics, of a novice who received the status of acolyte and then priest):

> There was also a very delicate boy who was received as a lay brother. The glorious Virgin then appeared to him and put her finger to his mouth as a sign of preaching and teaching; he was accepted not only as a preacher and an eminent lector, but also as an important figure in the government of the order.[136]

---

135. *CFJ*, 44 (chap. 49); *XIIIth Cent. Chronicles*, 56.
136. *AA*, 109–110 (chap. 15); *XIIIth Cent. Chronicles*, 175.

Oddly, the beneficiary of these developments (whose story is unique in the two chronicles) is not named, and it took an appearance of the Virgin Mary to justify such an unprecedented promotion.

Concerning the exercise of responsibilities, let's take several cases mentioned in the course of Thomas's narrative. The first provincial minister of England, Agnellus of Pisa, was a former custos of Paris and a deacon who only reluctantly accepted the priesthood:

> Brother Agnellus, when he had for a long time been minister of England and in the order of deacons, did not want to be promoted to the priesthood, until the general chapter, by the intermediary of the provincial chapter, made sure to command him [to do so].[137]

Thomas cites three other provincial ministers: Albert of Pisa (again) and Haymo of Faversham for England, Richard of Ingworth for Ireland. They were all priests. For Albert of Pisa, this was his seventh post as a provincial minister. In 1230, Agnellus of Pisa appointed a priest and a lay brother as his co-vicars; just before his death, he named a priest as vicar "insofar as he had the power to do so."[138] At lower levels, we find the cases of a lay custos and two other lay brothers promoted as guardians, compared with one cleric referred to as holding the same office. Doubtless these instances reflect the heroic beginnings of the order in England. One of these lay brothers who became a guardian was the Lombard Henry of Treviso. He had learned to read at night in the church of St. Peter in Cornhill (London), later became provincial vicar, but eventually came to a bad end:

> At last, however, not being able to stand such good fortune but rather demoralized and becoming a stranger to himself by these honors, he miserably apostatized from the order.[139]

Thomas of Eccleston testifies to the appearance of two functions that Jordan of Giano mentions only indirectly: preachers and lectors (the latter were educated brothers assigned as teachers at each Franciscan community). If Thomas gives scant information about the status of the brothers appointed to these offices, this is because it was self-evident that they were recruited only from among the clerics. This was especially true for the lectors of the prestigious *studia* of Oxford and Cambridge, where the brothers were educated at the heart of the universities. Next came the confessors:

---

137. *AA*, 97 (chap. 14); *XIIIth Cent. Chronicles*, 165.
138. *AA*, 95 (chap. 14); *XIIIth Cent. Chronicles*, 165.
139. *AA*, 14 (chap. 2); *XIIIth Cent. Chronicles*, 102.

There were also many brothers who, though they did not hold the office of preaching or teaching, did hear the confessions of both religious and secular people, in various places, thanks to the gracious favor of the prelates, obeying an order of the provincial minister.[140]

This remark suggests that the role of confessor was a consolation prize for those who had not achieved the other two offices, those of preacher and lector, which shows how the latter two offices were prized. This in turn proves that the offices of preacher and lector—more prestigious than the position of confessor, which was necessarily filled by a priest (at least to grant absolution)—were sought after by the priest brothers. The office of lector was itself an asset when it came to moving up to positions of higher responsibility in the Order of Lesser Brothers.

Beyond the lively pictures they paint for (respectively) Germany and England, Jordan of Giano and Thomas of Eccleston also relay information about the wider order. Jordan, for instance, gives an indication that Francis was indeed a deacon, and as early as 1221, by relating that Francis read the Gospel during the chapter meeting of that year. Jordan further tells us about the intellectual formation of Francis's first vicar, Peter Cattani, appointed in 1220, who was "expert in law and master of laws,"[141] and of the minister general elected in 1227, John Parenti, "citizen of Rome and master of laws."[142] Jordan also narrates the deposition of John Parenti in 1232 and his replacement by Elias.

The latter figure particularly held Jordan's attention. In 1221, at the death of Peter Cattani (the first vicar whom Francis had named after his own resignation as minister general), the founder had chosen Elias to succeed Peter as vicar. In 1227, a year after Francis's death, Elias convened a general chapter in which he hoped to be confirmed as minister general, but the chapter instead chose John Parenti. In 1230, at a new general chapter, Elias tried in vain to return to power. He finally succeeded at the next chapter, in 1232, from which point he led the order until 1239.

Jordan of Giano's *Chronicle* refers repeatedly to aspects of Elias's bad government: soliciting financial contributions to build the basilica of San Francesco in Assisi, neglecting to convoke general chapters, abruptly transferring stubborn brothers, allowing visitators to abuse their powers in the provinces, making arbitrary nominations to different levels of responsibility in the order, causing provinces to proliferate pointlessly. Growing discontent among some of the brothers led to an appeal to the pope and ultimately to Elias's abrupt deposition in 1239 and his replacement with Albert of Pisa.

---

140. *AA*, 75 (chap. 12); *XIIIth Cent. Chronicles*, 148.
141. *CFJ*, 9 (chap. 11); *XIIIth Cent. Chronicles*, 26.
142. *CFJ*, 46 (chap. 51); *XIIIth Cent. Chronicles*, 58.

Thomas of Eccleston, specifying that Elias had been a "scribe at Bologna,"[143] also recounts his attempted coup during the general chapter of 1230, when the common mass of brothers supported him against the provincial ministers and particularly the university masters. Thomas credits the deposition of this unworthy minister general in 1239 to Haymo of Faversham and repeats the accusations already made against Elias by Jordan of Giano: scandals, tyranny, abuses by the visitators, multiplication of provinces. To these he adds Elias's harshness, love of comfort, accumulation of wealth, and use of a palfrey or charger. Under the close supervision of Pope Gregory IX, Albert of Pisa was elected in 1239 to replace the ousted minister:

> So the minister general celebrated mass, and said to the brothers who were not part of the chapter: "You have just heard the first mass ever celebrated in the order by a minister general. Go now to your places, with the blessing of Jesus Christ!"[144]

One cannot help but catch a whiff of revenge here. If Albert of Pisa could pride himself on being the first priest at the head of the order, it was because he followed four superiors—Francis, Peter Cattani, Elias, and John Parenti—who had never risen to the priesthood.

These two chroniclers, Jordan and Thomas, give many indications of a latent internal conflict between priests and laymen in the Order of Lesser Brothers. But their tone is one of regret, always hiding the implications of a rift they found troubling, probably because they knew it to be contrary to the original spirit of the brotherhood.

As early as 1220, Jordan of Giano indicates that it was a lay brother who made the voyage east to alert Francis to the statutory reforms undertaken by the vicars he had left behind in Italy:

> Concerning these Constitutions, a lay brother was outraged by the fact that these vicars presumed to add something to the Rule of the holy father. He took these Constitutions with him and crossed the sea, without authorization from the vicars.[145]

Describing the English provinces, Thomas of Eccleston reveals in passing:

> At the time of Brother John, Brother Elias ordered that the brothers should wash their undergarments themselves; the brothers of the administration of England therefore washed theirs, as had been ordered;

---

143. *AA*, 79 (chap. 13); *XIIIth Cent. Chronicles*, 152.
144. *AA*, 82–84 (chap. 13); *XIIIth Cent. Chronicles*, 156.
145. *CFJ*, 11 (chap. 12); *XIIIth Cent. Chronicles*, 27.

but the brothers of the administration of Scotland held out until they received a written reminder from him.[146]

Listing the lectors of Oxford, Thomas arrives at Richard of Cornwall, whose career the chronicler links to that of Elias, and about whom he relates this story:

> When this Richard came to England, he told in the chapter at Oxford how, when a brother at Paris was caught up in ecstasy, it seemed to him that Brother Giles [of Assisi], a lay brother but a contemplative, had sat at the lectern, teaching about the seven authentic petitions of the Lord's prayer, all his hearers being brothers who were lectors in the order. When St. Francis entered, he first stood silent, then exclaimed in these words: "O how shameful it is for you that such a lay brother should exceed your merits in heaven above! And because," he went on, "knowledge puffs up, but charity edifies, many clerical brothers are venerated down here but are counted as nothing in the eternal kingdom of God."[147]

Around 1240, when the provinces were asked to indicate passages in the Rule that required clarification, Francis again intervened in a dream:

> That very night St. Francis appeared to Brother John of Bannister and showed him a deep well: Brother John said to him, "Father, behold, the fathers want to explain the Rule; it would be much better for you to explain it to us." The saint replied, "My son, go to the lay brothers and they will explain the Rule to you."[148]

We have to turn to a third chronicler, Salimbene of Adam, to see this crisis burst out into the open. Under the title *The Book on the Prelate*, this priest brother dedicated a section of his richly detailed *Chronicle*, written between 1283 and 1285 and continued as far as 1288, to an indictment of Elias. He claimed that the latter had been called Bonusbaro in the world and had made mattresses and taught children to read the psalter in the city of Assisi. Here is a collection of Salimbene's most illuminating passages concerning our subject:

> The second fault of Brother Elias was that he accepted many useless men into the order. I lived in the convent of Siena for two years, and I saw twenty-five lay brothers there. Then I lived in Pisa for four years, and I saw thirty lay brothers living there.[149]

---

146. *AA*, 52 (chap. 9); *XIIIth Cent. Chronicles*, 136.
147. *AA*, 65 (chap. 11); *XIIIth Cent. Chronicles*, 145.
148. *AA*, 88 (chap. 13); *XIIIth Cent. Chronicles*, 158.
149. Salimbene, *Chronica*, 145–46; *Chronicle of Salimbene*, 79.

II. UNWORTHINESS IN POWER

In like manner, if it is indeed true that Brother Elias admitted large numbers of lay brothers so that he could better hold power over such men or so that brothers received by him would fill his hands with wealth, then we may say with justification that he was rightly deposed from his ministry.[150]

The third fault of Brother Elias was that he promoted unworthy men to offices in the order. For he placed lay brothers in the positions of guardians, custodes, and ministers, which was absurd, since there was an abundance of good clerics available in the order. I myself was under the authority of a lay custos and more than one lay guardian. I was never governed by a lay minister, but I have seen many of them in other provinces.[151]

Indeed, under Elias's governance there were many tonsured lay brothers, as I saw with my own eyes when I was living in Tuscany, and yet they were totally illiterate.[152]

In that time indeed lay brothers were honored more highly than priests. And in a hermitage where, save for the teacher and the priest, all were lay brothers, they wanted the priest to take his turn in the kitchen.[153]

For they were always conspiring against us. I remember that once at the convent of Pisa, they wanted to put on the chapter's agenda a motion whereby for every cleric admitted to the order, a lay brother would have to be admitted too. But they were not listened to nor satisfied, because it was so foolish.[154]

The ninth fault of Brother Elias was that he sent commands throughout the whole of Italy to all the sturdy lay brothers whom he considered supporters, instructing them to be sure to attend the general chapter [of 1239], because he knew that the ministers were gathering together against him. Indeed, he hoped that the lay brothers would defend him with blows from their staffs. Having learned of this however, Brother Arnulf brought it about, with Pope Gregory's consent, that only those brothers that the Rule specified should attend the general chapter, with suitable and proper companions. He also had all the orders sent to the lay brothers by Elias annulled.[155]

---

150. Salimbene, *Chronica*, 148; *Chronicle of Salimbene*, 81.
151. Salimbene, *Chronica*, 148, *Chronicle of Salimbene*, 81.
152. Salimbene, *Chronica*, 149; *Chronicle of Salimbene*, 82.
153. Salimbene, *Chronica*, 150; *Chronicle of Salimbene*, 83.
154. Salimbene, *Chronica*, 150; *Chronicle of Salimbene*, 83.
155. Salimbene, *Chronica*, 245; *Chronicle of Salimbene*, 150.

9. Lesser Brothers III: About Face

That is the gist of what the sources have to say. How should we interpret the conflict that Jordan of Giano and Thomas of Eccleston allow to simmer just beneath the surface of their texts and that Salimbene of Adam then angrily exposes? Let's try to arrive at an answer by posing two questions: What exactly was Elias's attitude during his generalship? And what were the positions of the three categories present in the order: priests, clerics who were not priests, and lay brothers?

If we take at face value Salimbene of Adam's most explicit accusations—"he promoted unworthy men to offices in the Order," "lay brothers were honored more highly than priests"—we might wonder whether Elias gave in to a temptation similar to the one Dominic flirted with for the Order of Preachers: entrusting the administration of the Order of Lesser Brothers to the lay brothers, on the model of Grandmont, which was well known to them at the time. But this hypothesis will not hold up. For one thing, we know for certain that Elias as minister general named clerical or priest brothers to important offices, including Albert of Pisa (his own eventual successor) as provincial minister of England. For another, Salimbene's bad faith is obvious when he reproaches Elias for encouraging what was really just a strict application of the Rule for Hermitages: the priest who was to do the cooking in the hermitage only ever had to play the role of Martha "in his turn."

But it is true that Elias had to face an unprecedented challenge. Everything stemmed from the choice to embrace preaching. And this choice, which brought the vocation of the Lesser Brothers closer to that of the Preachers, was indisputably made by Francis himself. If the brothers were going to carry the Gospel out into the world, then they would have to study scripture; hence the rise of the clerics, the creation of places of study (the *studia*), and the leading role lectors came to play in the training of the brothers and, more generally, in the life of the order.

Priests were already necessary within the community to administer the Eucharist and absolve sins; when priests were lacking, the brothers' sacramental life suffered severely. If the brothers also wanted to hear the confessions of lay people—the logical outcome of their sermons urging repentance and evangelical conversion—a growing number of them were going to have to enter the priesthood; hence the growth in the number of priest brothers, usually through the promotion of clerics recruited as such from the time of their novitiate. The recruitment of men who had already been ordained as priests, mentioned in the early years, must have become more rare. These evolutions were already apparent in Francis's day. Doubtless he eyed them with distrust, but all in all he accepted them.

Moreover, the order was not evolving in a vacuum. The 1220s and 1230s were the decades when university life in the West made its most impressive leap forward. The number of clerics in medieval society increased. At the beginning of the 1210s, the original group of penitents forming around Francis in Assisi probably would have had difficulty recruiting a large number of clerics in that modest Umbrian town. In the following decades, at Paris, Bologna, Oxford, or Cambridge, clerics naturally flocked to the *studia* (the order's centers for advanced study), which offered a thrilling renewal of theological studies and of intellectual methods. The convent of Pisa's proposal, denounced by Salimbene of Adam, had been intended to ensure parity in recruitment between laymen and clerics. But by the 1230s such parity had become a pipe dream.

In this new context, the political intentions of the minister general were surely not to harden the regulations, to bring about a kind of statutory stiffening similar to what may have happened during (what we have called) the passage from Muret to Grandmont, or to institute a categorical reversal by giving the lay brothers supremacy over the clerical brothers, in order to preserve at any cost the original spirit of fluid permeability (even if it meant losing that fluidity itself). We should rather assume that Elias sought to maintain the status quo just as it had been established in Francis's day, but that this was enough to cause discontent, indeed scandal, because the world had changed around the order, and the order, inevitably, had changed with it. The status quo was that priests were not to claim that their priesthood exempted them from domestic chores, dishwashing and cooking, within the community; that brothers of any status could be promoted to any kind of office; that all were allowed to participate in general chapters.

Does this mean that there were no grounds for the accusations against Elias? One does not have to be the hero of a Dostoyevsky novel in order for a single act to result from two impulses, one praiseworthy and the other less so. Part of the minister general's attitude was certainly calculating: the lay brothers with their stout staffs could make strong allies against the elite class of university men that was assuming an ever more powerful place in the order. Elias's autocratic tendencies are undeniable. But Francis's hand-picked successor also displayed a desperate, anachronistic defense of the founder's original message. This defense can also explain, in part, Elias's autocratic rigidity.

What was the attitude of the priests? It would hardly be fair to attribute to all of them the insufferable arrogance of Salimbene of Adam as he looked back from old age on the memories of his youth. They cannot all have regarded their lay brothers as useless mouths to feed. But they could all feel, like Jordan of Giano, the burden that fell on them when the percentage of priests was too low. The priests must inevitably have applied a new kind of logic, that of efficiency, to the internal life of the brothers' community as well as to pastoral services they provided to the faithful. And thus it was also out of efficiency, as much as out of general arrogance, that they sought to avoid anything that took them away from their sacramental or pastoral tasks. Hence the brothers of the province of Scotland—it must have been the clerics in general and the priests in particular—preferred to wait for a new round of orders rather than to lose precious time in washing their own undergarments.

Nothing proves that all the priests in the order opposed Elias's views. And yet, the university-educated clerics, who were usually priests, were certainly decisive in strengthening the faction opposed to the minister general. Their impact can be seen as early as 1230, at the time of Elias's attempted coup. It is apparent the same year in the make-up of the delegation that obtained Gregory IX's letter *Quo elongati*; educated priests, including Haymo of Faversham and Anthony of Padua, went to the pope to ask to be freed from some of Francis's prescriptions. It can be perceived in the revolt that took shape around 1237, in which Haymo of Faversham played a crucial role. It is evident in the *Commentary on the Rule* offered by four university masters in 1241–1242. Reacting against Elias's generalship, this *Commentary* argued that the general chapter should tightly control the minister general. It sought to place the order under the leadership of the provincial ministers, men from a university background who had by this time begun to constitute the effective machinery of provincial government.

The university-educated clerics were well aware of the Preachers' model and felt a certain desire to emulate it. Since the two orders sought the same ends, they tended to evolve in the same ways in terms of recruitment and mode of government. And certain lay brothers' wandering vagrancy, their rough dress, their incomplete separation from secular society, indeed their simplicity, all these things must have seemed at least embarrassing, if not scandalous, to the educated elite of the order. Some of these elites, however, could still recognize the simplicity of Francis in the lay brothers. The priest Nicholas of the Rhine's exasperating humility may have been merely a part of his personality, a personal virtue pushed to extremes. But it may also be an indication that some priests did not think that priestly status systematically entitled them to monopolize the order's offices. In that case, Albert of Pisa's sharp rebuke of Nicholas of the Rhine would take on a whole different aspect.

All of this having been said, if the original ideal envisioned any brother being able to exercise any office regardless of his status, there was still one responsibility that up until 1239 had not been evenly shared among the order's several categories: that of minister general. Francis, Peter Cattani, Elias, John Parenti: vicar or minister, whatever title they went by, none of them had been a priest. Was this pure chance? This series rather suggests that the model of a non-priestly founder led to the selection of his successors from the same category. The remark attributed to Albert of Pisa following his election ("You have just heard the first mass ever celebrated in the order by a minister general") may strike us as haughty, but it might also have expressed the sense that equity had finally been achieved.

At the other end of things, what did the lay brothers think? Owing to the very nature of their status, we have no direct written account from these men who were prohibited from writing. The career path of Henry of Treviso, the self-taught lay brother, guardian, then provincial vicar, is exceptional. Its outcome speaks volumes: flush with an honor that far exceeded his personal status, unable to cope with the promotion his energy had earned him, he lost his head and left the order. So we have to read the sources with close attention. The lay brother who took the trouble to cross the sea in 1220 and warn Francis of the order's drift was surely thinking that these changes, which would bring the brotherhood closer to the Cistercian model, were out of step with the project he had signed up for. So he put all his hopes in Francis.

It is striking to see that in the two episodes recounted by Thomas of Eccleston that seem to echo lay voices—Brother Giles of Assisi holding forth from his lectern and Brother John of Bannister dreaming of Francis's comment on the Rule—it is the founder in person who appears to defend the simple. It is tempting to add to this same category a brief story recorded by Thomas of Celano in the *Memorial*. This story is as much the expression of fears felt in the 1240s as it is a real memory of Francis's life. Nevertheless it again places the humblest brothers under Francis's patronage:

> When St. Francis was being shaved, he would often say to the one who shaved him: "Be careful: don't give me a big crown! Because I want my simple brothers to have a share in my head." Really he wanted the order to be held in common by the poor and illiterate and not just by the rich and learned. *"With God,"* he would say, *"there is no respecting of persons* (Romans 2:11); the minister general of the religion, the Holy Spirit, rests equally upon the poor and the simple." He wanted to put these words in the Rule, but the fact that it was already sealed by papal bull prevented it.[156]

The audacious lay brothers described by Salimbene could also claim to follow the founder's informal dress and speech, or more directly the example of Brother Giles of Assisi, who retired to hermitages after Francis's death, probably in order not to be compromised by the order's evolutions of which he disapproved.

---

156. *FF*, 612; *FAED*, 2:371.

In the story that Richard of Cornwall told to the chapter meeting at Oxford (a stronghold of the educated brothers) and that he presented as a message coming from a brother of Paris (another eminent place of study), Giles of Assisi benefited from a remarkable inversion of roles. He "sat at the lectern," thus occupying the position characteristic of a master facing his disciples, who were however "lectors in the Order." "A lay brother but a contemplative," Giles taught them by commenting on the seven petitions in the *Our Father*, just as Francis himself had proposed in the *Exposition on the Our Father* for the lay brothers' meditation. The episode is surely a moral reminder of an original simplicity, countering the growth of studies and ranks; a lesson, in all senses of the word, given by the simple to the learned.

As for the other anecdote related by Thomas of Eccleston, in which Francis advises John of Bannister to ask the lay brothers to comment on the Rule, surely we must read this as more than just an edifying tale. It emerged at exactly the moment when the lay brothers were being permanently marginalized within the order. Consequently it is reasonable to suppose that Francis's message, given to John of Bannister in his sleep, bore more explicitly institutional implications: go ask the lay brothers what they think of being cast aside!

For in the end the image of the late founder had less force than the actions of the living, and the opinion of the uneducated was doomed to rejection when faced with the words of the learned. The measures imposed following the deposition of Elias in 1239 are striking: forbidding the recruitment of anyone lacking a high level of education or not likely to increase the order's renown; forbidding the appointment of lay brothers to offices in the order. In a letter of 21 August 1252, when he wanted to indicate the brothers now relegated to the smallest share, the term "converts" flowed from Pope Innocent IV's pen,[157] presumably by accident and due to an assumed similarity with monastic orders such as the Cistercians or with the "converts" of the Preachers. The slip is nonetheless telling.

But in an earlier letter, dated 1 December 1248, the same Innocent IV protected from any excommunication or interdict affecting places where Lesser Brothers lived "those who, in [their] houses, serve [*servientes*] in useful functions," "the servants [*pueri*] assigned to [their] service."[158] These were probably the lay servants for whom no religious status offered protection from the thunderbolts of the church. It is as though, two decades after his death, Francis's spirit had well and truly passed out of the world for a second time.

Truth be told, it is not certain that the few anecdotes that support the lay brothers' cause really come from them, or directly from them. There is in fact

---

157. *BF*, 1:622 (no. 424).
158. Ibid., 1:523 (no. 290).

a third category of brothers that we tend to forget and who were doubtless also marginalized after 1239: the clerics who were not priests. More than either the priests or the lay brothers, this group could claim to follow the model of a founder who had been a deacon. Caught between the other two canonical categories, they were also best placed to try to defend the idea of a balance between statuses at the heart of the Order of Lesser Brothers. Probably many of them hoped to be promoted to the priesthood, as the logical outcome of the progression of clerical orders and as the best way to serve the ideal for which they had joined the order. This must have been particularly true for young men recruited from the universities; from the moment of their novitiate, they were already potential priests.

But others, especially among the older brothers, probably saw their status as an end in itself and, following Stephen of Muret's lead, did not seek the priesthood. Agnellus of Pisa is the most obvious example. It is striking that the provincial and general chapters would have thought it necessary to promote him from deacon to priest despite his hesitation—and this was before Elias returned to power in 1232—as an essential upgrade of his personal canonical status appropriate to the role he occupied at the head of the English province.

What about at the highest level, that of the vicar general or minister general? Here the gaps in the evidence are the largest, making it impossible to offer a group portrait of the order's leaders. As surprising as it may seem, we do not know the exact canonical status of Albert of Pisa's predecessors. Peter Cattani, Elias, John Parenti (to whom Peregrine of Bologna, with no proof whatsoever, attributes a son, doubtless as a pure extrapolation from the name "Parenti") were all educated men. They were learned in law, presumably civil law. Was the battle between non-priests and priests also a conflict between legal scholars and theologians? If they were not priests, were not Peter, Elias, and John probably clerics, like their common predecessor Francis? It is tempting to think so, but we cannot be certain, and these areas of obscurity limit our understanding of the competition between categories within the Order of Lesser Brothers.

It is beyond doubt, however, that these categories lie at the root of many divisions within the order. They cannot explain them all, because interpretations of the Lesser Brothers' vocation also varied according to generation, nation, and place. In the end, as a certain number of anecdotes in the chronicles prove, a brother could choose not to identify with the interests of his own category, and many other factors could complicate the tensions between these tendencies. For instance, although neither one was a priest, John Parenti and Elias were bitter rivals. We will never know all the twists and turns of that story. But we do know its outcome: "the abundance of good clerics" no longer had to endure the domination of "unworthy men."

Shortly after 1244, the priest Brother Leo, Francis's close companion in the last years of his life, compiled his memories, which were later edited into the *Assisi Compilation*. Describing the ideal mode of life in the convent of the Portiuncula, he put words in Francis's mouth that can hardly have been his and that appear to mock the principle of alternating service advocated in the Rule for Hermitages:

> Let the clerics be chosen from among the holiest and most upright brothers, and those who know how to say the office best in the whole order, so that not only other people, but also the brothers will gladly listen to them with great devotion. And let some holy lay brothers, discerning and upright men, also be chosen, who may serve them. I also wish that none of the brothers or any other person enter that place except the minister general and the brothers who serve him. And let them not speak to anyone except the brothers who serve them and to the minister when he visits them. I likewise want the lay brothers who serve them to be bound not to pass on to them any word of news of the world they have heard, which is not useful to the soul.[159]

These "holy lay brothers" were remnants of the order's earlier history. From 1239 on, according to the new Constitutions, no one could be received into the order if he was not a master of arts, medicine, or law; if he did not have a degree in theology; if he was not a well-known preacher or a famous lawyer; or if, whether cleric or layman, his entrance would not particularly edify the people and the clergy. Brother John the Simple would certainly have been excluded by such criteria. Would Francis himself have been accepted? Or, thirteen years after his death, would the founder of the Order of Lesser Brothers have been denied entry? In that case, he would have had the consolation of his own ready-made words:

> "Go away! You are simple and illiterate! Don't come back to us again! We are such that we don't need you!" . . . I tell you that if I am patient and do not become upset, in this lies true joy, and true virtue, and the salvation of my soul.[160]

---

159. *FF*, 1538–39 (chap. 56); *FAED*, 2:156.
160. *Scripta*, 417; *FAED*, 1:166–67.

10. Experiments

Religious institutions are remarkable laboratories for the formalization of social and political life, like micro-societies in test tubes. Comparing the dossiers of these diverse communal experiences—Fontevraud, the Paraclete, Grandmont, the Preachers, and the Lesser Brothers—helps us understand each one of them better. At the same time, such a comparison can shed light on processes of much wider importance, following the approach developed by Gert Melville and the "Dresden school" of monastic history (in turn loosely inspired by the sociologist Max Weber).

On the subject of obedience, the Benedictine Rule had established the essential points. A community must be governed. Yet the obedience owed to the superior is more than just an inevitable result of natural law. Exalted as a manifestation of humility, this obedience has spiritual value because it represents the submission of creatures to the Creator, of Christians to Christ. But, marked out by his personal dignity as vicar of the Son, the superior is more servant than sovereign, a steward of the only King. He must live out his office as service, in turn modeling himself on the figure of Christ-as-servant. The five subsequent religious experiences on which we have focused did not challenge these premises. On the contrary, they were characterized by a search for ways to push them to their limits.

They all had at least one thing in common (even if they had no exclusive claim on this point): they rejected the term "abbot" to refer to the superior. For if these institutions never challenged the Benedictine spirit, they certainly sought to distance themselves from Benedictine practices of their own time. The Carthusians (directed by a prior), the Gilbertines of Sempringham (directed by a master), and the Trinitarians (the first to have adopted the title of minister), would offer further examples of the same principle.

The puzzle pieced together by the series of communities studied here lets us understand the working out of a project and the stages of an experimental process. Each dossier opens up some aspect of this process, but almost always in a fragmentary fashion, rarely putting the project's overall coherence on view. In the spirit of evangelical renewal that was characteristic of the Gregorian moment, but that also irreversibly infused the following centuries, these communal religious experiences passed through a pre-institutional phase, characterized by complete openness to all social statuses. The animating spirit was that of the Acts of the Apostles. Nothing was to be owned individually. There was to be no correlation between social origins, level of education, canonical status (or, indeed, whether one was a man or a woman), on one hand, and the distribution of offices or the exercise of responsibilities within the group, on the other.

Utopia gave way to institutionalization. In each of these communities, in a more or less clear-cut manner, at least two categories emerged: men and women at Fontevraud and the Paraclete, clerics and lay brothers with the Grandmontines, Preachers, and Lesser Brothers. In dividing by sex as well as status, Fontevraud and the idealized Paraclete went so far as to trace out a world in four dimensions. In this sense, these institutions took part in the same movement as the overwhelming majority of reformed congregations born in the eleventh century onward. They shared this character as double or even quadruple communities: Vallombrosians, Camaldolese, Carthusians, Premonstratensians, Cistercians, the monks and nuns of Aubazine, Gilbertines . . .

But the five dossiers chosen for study here are unique in the way these communities apportioned the responsibilities of government. To fight against the combined effects of growing numbers and passing time, the project that emerged in practically all of these institutions was to entrust—or to want to entrust—governance to the category that seemed, adopting Benedictine vocabulary, the less worthy of the two to exercise it. This meant female converts (double unworthiness!) at Fontevraud, and in a more roundabout way at the idealized Paraclete. It meant convert brothers at Grandmont and with the Preachers. Since they could not maintain their original fluidity in the face of success and the passage of time, these communities tried to preserve the spirit of complete openness and mutual humility by inverting a hierarchy that was assumed to be natural. With the Lesser Brothers, neither Francis nor Elias resorted to this extreme measure. Instead, it was precisely the original moment that they tried for thirty years to preserve, against the turning tide and the headwinds of time.

With the exception of the Dominican sources, too thin in reporting what was after all only an abandoned project, these dossiers systematically use the two evangelical sisters of Lazarus—Martha and Mary, representing the two aspects of the apostolic life, action and contemplation—to distinguish responsibility for temporal affairs from spiritual matters. The part given to Martha is not exactly the same from one dossier to another: temporal administration at Grandmont and in Dominic's project; full power, both temporal and spiritual, at Fontevraud. This evangelical allegory had to be deployed with delicacy. Those who lost control or power had to be persuaded that they had received the better part and that it would have been bad form for them to complain; those to whom governance was entrusted had to be convinced that it would be a mistake to boast about it.

Moreover, a range of arguments was used across these diverse institutions—at least according to the surviving sources. Robert of Arbrissel, the Rule of Grandmont, and Dominic all stressed the functional value of such a division, though Robert did slip in the idea of the converts' unworthiness, while Peter Abelard was the only one to stress the idea of the humiliation of the men. On the other hand, it is certain that across the long lives of these religious institutions all the "Mary's" (virgins of Fontevraud, clerics of Grandmont, clerics of the Preachers and Lesser Brothers, even if the latter were the least threatened) certainly felt the sting of humiliation.

Consequently, these audacious experiments have another point in common: they all ended in more or less marked failure. Peter Abelard's vision of the Paraclete never saw the light of day; Dominic's wishes were rejected (harshly, as we have argued) in 1220; Grandmont suffered from continual conflicts; if Robert's wishes were respected concerning the choice of an abbess, her status as a convert did not last beyond Petronilla of Chemillé.

Furthermore, the balanced bipolarity of the communities wore down over time. The lay brothers saw not only their positions but their numbers diminish within the Preachers and Lesser Brothers, only a handful of men lived at the real Paraclete, and the brothers of Fontevraud never attained numbers comparable to those of their nuns. From this point of view, the converts of Grandmont showed themselves the most tenacious, but their history was a long and irreversible process of being brought to heel.

In fact, only Robert of Arbrissel's project succeeded across the centuries (except for the abbess having the status of a convert). At least three reasons for this success are apparent. First, Robert was careful, while still alive, to create written statutes for his institutions, a rather rare step for a monastic founder to take at the beginning of the twelfth century. Second, ahead of his time, he entrusted the abbess who succeeded him with full power over a rigorously centralized congregation. Third and finally, since the reversal of gendered categories actually reinforced the reality of social class, the transgression seemed less serious to the ecclesiastical authorities and the lay powers.

A century later, on the other hand, it is striking to see that Dominic and Francis, two founders whom the historiography sometimes likes to lump together and sometimes to split apart, had to confront in the same year—1220—the same question concerning the increasingly priestly make up of their orders. They tried to offer the same resistance by the same means—the threat of resignation—but neither achieved any more success than the other. With the Preachers, realism quickly won out, and Dominic gave in. With the Lesser Brothers, the resistance of Francis and Elias only delayed by two decades the same outcome.

Utopias, hopeless battles—were all of these daring innovations in vain? No. They serve as invitations to a reflection on power and obedience. That the social body in its entirety, and each social group specifically, must be founded on the principle of authority—doubtless this is one of the most widely shared ideas across societies. For St. Jerome, the assertion was obvious, because natural law—from the lore of bestiaries to the lessons of Roman history—had proved its necessity. So there must be a governor, the governed, and a tie of obedience between them. Peter Abelard expressed this idea clearly with his military metaphor.

If constituent bodies seek a governor as the foundation and ultimate symbol of their constitutions, subjects nevertheless show contradictory reactions to being governed. On the one hand, a substitute father or mother is reassuring. On the other, the one who dares to raise his head above the others, even for a moment, has to pay the price, real or symbolic, of this transgression. Athenian magistrates did not always meet happy ends; tyrants lived in fear of the plot that would bring them down; kings usually escaped the scaffold, yet had to submit to their own constraints, particularly in order to guarantee legitimate descendants or in the name of protocol; beneath the level of serious political debate, the leaders of our present democracies see their faults caricatured, while their private lives spill out into the public arena, sometimes at their own initiative. Those who govern are the first to be alienated by the system.

Christianity offered the medieval world a remarkable way out of this eternal dilemma. Renouncing sovereignty, the Son of God had become human, drained the cup to the dregs, and died on the cross. Marcel Gauchet—who has described Jesus as "a messiah turned upside down"—focuses on this reversal:

> Christ, or the figure of an apparent defeat . . . which is in reality a victory. For the pagans of antiquity, the fact that Christ had gone unrecognized, had been treated as a criminal, and had been crucified, showed his insignificance and the absurdity of his followers' faith. In fact, the opposite could be proven true! From the religion of the weak and of slaves came a civilization of unmatched power, of which the consistent genius was to stand the appearances of power on their head.[161]

Christ existed in embryonic form in all medieval pastors; we might think, on the political level, of the superabundant authority that captivity (likened to martyrdom) granted St. Louis, as William Chester Jordan and Jacques Le Goff have shown.[162]

The superiors of religious communities, first and foremost, thus had at their disposal a model that was exceptional, in the end even incongruous. Certainly their authority had to be justified by their merit and knowledge. But the reward

---

161. Marcel Gauchet, *La Condition historique. Entretiens avec François Azouvi et Sylvain Piron* (Paris, 2003), 102–3.

162. William Chester Jordan, *Louis IX and the Challenge of the Crusade. A Study in Rulership* (Princeton, NJ, 1979); Jacques Le Goff, *Saint Louis*, trans. Gareth Evan Gollrad (Notre Dame, IN, 2009).

for their preeminence, paid for in advance, was the humility from which they could never escape in the exercise of government.

Humility, of which Christ was the shining example, thus carried two charges. For subjects, it merged with obedience. For superiors, it was the antidote to the pride that could have taken hold of them, a sort of preemptive, voluntary, sacrificial rite. At its height, all members of the community, governors and governed, could live out their various positions under the sign of the same virtue, which guaranteed their communion. For the subject confronted with an over-mighty authority, for the superior crushed by the weight of a responsibility that was quite literally a burden, reassuring humility might indeed shade into bitter humiliation; the reward would only be greater in heaven.

The Gregorian moment sought to restore the evangelical message to the contemporary world and the high monastic tradition, using the common denominator of the apostolic life. It sought to make sure that everyone, regardless of his or her condition, sex, or status, could find a place within the economy of salvation. The promise that the last would be first was no longer understood only in a moral sense. It took on social meaning. The twelfth and thirteenth centuries in their totality—church and kingdoms, convents and cities—displayed extraordinary institutional inventiveness, and the religious communities we have studied certainly had no monopoly on this quality; we might think of the chapter meetings of the Cistercians or the Premonstratensians, of the growing complexity of papal and royal administrations, or of the political life of the Italian communes.

But because they shared the fact of having chosen, or of having tried to choose, the great challenge of categorical reversal, the religious foundations of our sample functioned as laboratories of institutional experimentation. They were not satisfied to promise that some day the last would be first. In designating their superiors, they declared, or sought to declare, that the last *were* first, right here and right now.

At Grandmont, we have witnessed an original reflection at work, concerning the distinctive potential of each person within the group. This vision avoided the pitfalls of implementing a destructive leveling, on one hand, or of reinforcing dominant social prejudices, on the other. Dominic and Francis in turn fought to defend this idea of complementary abilities. At Grandmont, again, we have glimpsed how, through trial and error, a delegation was appointed to designate the superior, establishing the representative nature of the delegates. The Preachers and Lesser Brothers developed this principle further. These three male institutions introduced the possibility that the superior's mandate might not necessarily be for life. In the ties between governors and governed, we have seen the right to remove one's superior appear at Grandmont, then be justified by the conscience clause of the Lesser Brothers.

All of the institutions we have considered declared a preference for government as service. Such a declaration could certainly be found in older rules, but this idea reached its most perfect expression with Francis. Robert of Arbrissel, for his part, deserves special mention for having confronted—and resolved on the local level—the question of women's religious life in general and of the "care of nuns" in particular, a challenging issue that the other foundations preferred to see addressed outside their strict enclosures.

Were these complete failures? To reach that judgment would be to forget that, in the diverse institutions we have considered, memories of their origins remained vivid and capable of inspiring returns to the strict observance of founding ideals. It is undeniable that institutional development—a fragile balance between volatile impulses, practices, rites, codes, tensions, constraints, and pressures—involves a continual return to the beginning. This is perhaps even more true for religious communities than it is elsewhere.

Because they invented new modes of collective life, these medieval experiments, when considered together (and even including their missteps), offer a series of lessons to anyone willing to listen. Their history teaches, as a cautionary tale, that a corollary to the democratic functioning of a collectivity is often an elitist closing off of its recruitment. It is so much easier to get along with people of the "right" standing and the same education. There is a tension between the strength of the democratic processes operating at the heart of a system and the democratic openness of that very system. The true democratic challenge is not to achieve just one or the other of these two senses of democracy (procedural strength versus popular openness), but to hold tight to both ends of that chain.

By refusing to equate the length of a mandate with the lifespan of an individual, by allowing the governed to contest the decisions of their governors, the institutions studied here undermined the idea that some people are destined to dominate and others to submit. Above all they dared to try to promote unworthiness to power. For this promotion of unworthiness carried within itself the beginnings of the idea of promotion based on competence. Know-how was called to take the place of the ambiguous notion of worthiness, which could so easily reflect only one's standing in the world.

These medieval communal experiences teach us that individuals should never be conflated with their status, nor confused with the offices they hold; that distinction should be based only on usefulness to the community; that one does not possess an office, but rather holds it for a certain time; that government is neither power nor prominence, but should be only service. In this sense, these experiments of the past can still have a promising future.

Part Three

Maternal Government

And he spoke to them this parable, saying, "What man of you, if he has a hundred sheep, and if he shall lose one of them, would not leave the ninety-nine in the desert, and go after the one that was lost, until he finds it? And when he has found it, lay it upon his shoulders, rejoicing? And coming home, call together his friends and neighbors, saying to them, "Rejoice with me, because I have found my sheep that was lost?" I say to you, that even so there shall be joy in heaven upon one sinner who does penance, more than upon ninety-nine just who do not need to repent.

—Luke 15:3–7

1. Treasure Trove[1]

The last several decades have witnessed a vast project to publish the courses Michel Foucault gave at the Collège de France between January 1971 and June 1984.

His 1977–1978 course was published in 2004,[2] then translated into English in 2007 as *Security, Territory, Population*.[3] The publication was described as "the most literal transcription possible" of "the words spoken publicly by Michel Foucault."[4] The project evidently ran up against a clause in the author's will: "No posthumous publications." In their foreword, without explicitly acknowledging that difficulty, the series editors addressed it implicitly by indicating that "strictly speaking it is not a question of unpublished work, since this edition reproduces words spoken publicly by Foucault," and they stated that they had the permission of the author's heirs.[5]

Without entering into the underlying debate, I will claim the right of treasure trove in order to extract a small sample from the exhumed thought of Michel Foucault—an "exaction," to borrow a medieval term that originally had no moral connotations.

The 1977–1978 course begins on 11 January 1978. Michel Foucault announces that it will be devoted to the study of an idea he has already sketched out (in his 1975–1976 course, and in *The Will to Knowledge*, already published in 1976 and first translated into English in 1978[6]): "bio-power,"

> namely, the whole set of mechanisms through which the basic biological features of the human species will be able to enter a political realm, of a political strategy, of a general strategy of power; in other words, how,

---

1. The chapter title in French, "Aubaine," means "windfall" with the broader sense of "unexpected gift." The third paragraph, however, makes a metaphorical reference to the *droit d'aubaine*, the right of the local lord or the king, in pre-Revolutionary France, to appropriate the property of a foreigner who died within his territory. The English legal concept of "treasure trove," according to which lost treasure could be claimed by the finder but hidden treasure belonged to the crown, thus seems a usable parallel.
2. Michel Foucault, *Sécurité, territoire, population. Cours au Collège de France, 1977–1978*, ed. Michel Senellart, general eds. François Ewald and Alessandro Fontana (Paris, 2004).
3. Michel Foucault, *Security, Territory, Population: Lectures at the Collège de France, 1977–1978*, ed. Michel Senellart, general eds. François Ewald and Alessandro Fontana, trans. Graham Burchell, English series ed. Arnold I. Davidson (New York, 2007). Although translations in the present volume are greatly indebted to Burchell's (and footnotes direct the reader to his published version), they are often somewhat more literally faithful to the French, especially where it has been necessary to highlight terms and phrases central to Jacques Dalarun's analysis.
4. François Ewald and Alessandro Fontana, "Forward," in Foucault, *Security, Territory, Population*, xv.
5. Ibid., xvi.
6. The study, first published in English as *The Will to Knowledge*, forms part of Foucault's three-volume *History of Sexuality* and is now most readily available as *The History of Sexuality, Vol. 1: An Introduction*, trans. Robert Hurley (New York, 1990).

starting from the eighteenth century, society, modern Western societies, took on board the fundamental biological fact that human beings are a species.[7]

Foucault indicates that he does not intend to propose "a general theory of what power is," but to devote himself to an analysis of "a whole set of mechanisms and procedures that have the role or function and theme, even when they are unsuccessful, of securing power."[8] To define what "security" might mean, he identifies three elements in the reaction to violating a prohibition: "the legal or juridical mechanism," "the disciplinary mechanism," and "the apparatus of security."[9] These elements are better regarded as "forms": "It is not a question of the legal age, the disciplinary age, and then the age of security,"[10] insofar as traces of the most recent mechanisms can already be found in the earliest period; these forms only cause the dominant one to emerge within a system at a given moment.

At the end of the lecture on 11 January and in the next two lectures on 18 and 25 January 1978, Michel Foucault turns to general aspects of the apparatus of security, beginning with questions of space:

> To summarize, let's say then that whereas sovereignty capitalizes a territory, raising the major problem of the seat of government, whereas discipline structures a space and addresses the essential problem of a hierarchical and functional distribution of elements, security will try to plan a milieu in terms of events or series of events or possible elements, of series that it will be necessary to regulate within a multivalent and transformable framework.[11]

Foucault then examines the relationship to events. Using the example of food scarcity, he shows the difference between the mercantilists' disciplinary mechanism and the physiocrats' apparatus of security. He distinguishes between the older notion of "the people" and the emergence of "the population" as a political subject, between centripetal discipline and centrifugal security, between regulation and laissez-faire; and he demonstrates the essential link between the apparatus of security and freedom of movement.

---

7. Foucault, *Security, Territory, Population*, 1.
8. Ibid., 1–2.
9. Ibid., 5–6.
10. Ibid., 8.
11. Ibid., 20.

Finally, Michel Foucault envisions the normalization inherent in mechanisms of security, from which emerges a new political technology, government, which is applied to the population:

> Population is not, then, a collection of juridical subjects in an individual or collective relationship with a sovereign will. It is a whole set of elements within which we can note constants and regularities, even in accidents, within which we can identify the universal of desire regularly producing the benefit of all, and with regard to which we can identify a number of variables on which it depends and which may modify it.[12]

Across these first three lectures, Foucault traces out a distinction between the series discipline-people-sovereignty and the series security-population-government. This leads him to devote his fourth lecture, on 1 February 1978, to the problem of government. He notes that the question of government (of self, of souls, and of behaviors, of children, of states) emerges in the sixteenth century. This period—from the sixteenth right up to the end of the eighteenth century, with the dissolution of feudal structures and the emergence of the major modern states—saw the flourishing of an abundant literature on the subject, expressed as revulsion with Machiavelli's *The Prince*, because, notes Foucault, "to be skillful at keeping one's principality, is not at all to possess the art of governing."[13]

The idea of government takes on multiple aspects: government of the self, which relates to morals; government of the family, which relates to economy; government of the state, which relates to politics. At heart, governing a state is a matter of applying the family father's economy on a larger scale. In contrast to sovereignty, the objective of government is not to impose law on human beings, but to arrange things. Although it began to be expressed in the sixteenth century, this art of governing was not really applied before the end of the eighteenth, for various historical reasons. Its development was linked to demographic expansion and thus "to the emergence of the problem of population."[14] The family at that point ceased to be a model for government and became instead an element of the population to be governed.

In short, the transition from an art of government to a political science, the transition from a regime dominated by structures of sovereignty to a regime dominated by techniques of government, happens in the

---

12. Ibid., 74.
13. Ibid., 92.
14. Ibid., 104.

eighteenth century around population, and consequently, around political economy.[15]

Again, Michel Foucault warns against the error of thinking that sovereignty, discipline, and governmental development followed one after the other. Decrying the "overvaluation of the problem of the State,"[16] he returns to the title given to this year's course, *Security, Territory, Population*, and says that he would have preferred the idea of a history of "governmentality," in which he sees "the lines of force, that for a long time, throughout the West, have constantly led toward the pre-eminence of the type of power we can call 'government,' over all other types."[17]

And so Michel Foucault arrives at the fifth lecture, on 8 February 1978. He is suffering from the flu and announces that he "will be a little more muddled than usual today."[18] He returns to "the ugly word 'governmentality,'"[19] a "problematic and artificial" notion, "obscure," pertaining to an "insubstantial and vague domain," asking "Why attack the strong and the dense [the state and population] with the feeble, diffuse, and lacunar?"[20] Having spelled out the clinical symptoms and rhetorical signals that traditionally precede invention or creation (especially according to Romantic conventions), Michel Foucault launches the interrogation that places his present inquiry in the perspective of his previous work:

> Can we speak of something like a "governmentality," that would be to the State what techniques of segregation were to psychiatry, what techniques of discipline were to the penal system, what biopolitics was to medical institutions?[21]

A brief tour through historical dictionaries of the French language allows him to observe the multiplicity of what can be governed, but also to grasp the deep coherence of the term: "Those whom one governs are people."[22] The idea of a government of people is neither Greek nor Roman. Its origin is to be sought in the East, first in a pre-Christian context, then in the Christian East, under "the idea and organization of a type of pastoral power."[23]

---

15. Ibid., 106.
16. Ibid., 109.
17. Ibid., 108.
18. Ibid., 115.
19. Ibid.
20. Ibid., 116.
21. Ibid., 120.
22. Ibid., 122.
23. Ibid., 123.

The theme is found in Egypt, in Assyria, in Mesopotamia. It develops and intensifies with the Hebrews, but almost exclusively in order to define the relationship between God and his people. Comparing the Greek conception to the Hebrew one, Michel Foucault tries to define the specific traits of pastoral power. First,

> The shepherd's power is a power which is not exercised over a territory, it is a power that by definition is exercised over a flock; more exactly, over the flock in its movement; in the movement that causes it to go from one place to another. The shepherd's power is essentially exercised over a multiplicity in motion.[24]

Second, pastoral power is "entirely defined by its beneficence."[25] It is "a power of care," which, far from being characterized by "a striking display of strength and superiority," manifests itself "initially in its zeal, devotion, and endless application."[26] "The shepherd serves the flock."[27]

> Finally, the last feature, which confirms a certain number of things I have already brought up, is the idea that pastoral power is an individualizing power.[28]

Michel Foucault thus arrives at the paradox of the shepherd, summed up in the Latin phrase *omnes et singulatim*, all together and each one individually: "He does everything for the totality of his flock, but he does everything also for each sheep of the flock."[29]

> Here we are at the center of the challenge, of the moral and religious paradox of the shepherd, or what could be called the paradox of the shepherd: the sacrifice of one for all, and the sacrifice of all for one, which will be at the absolute heart of the Christian problematic of the pastorate.[30]

Too tired to continue, Michel Foucault briefly sums up the ideas that he will develop in the next lecture. Specifically:

> It was the Christian church that coagulated all these themes of pastoral power into precise mechanisms and definite institutions; it was the church

---

24. Ibid., 125.
25. Ibid., 126.
26. Ibid., 127.
27. Ibid., 128.
28. Ibid.
29. Ibid.
30. Ibid., 129.

that actually organized a pastoral power that was both specific and autonomous; it was the church that implanted its apparatuses within the Roman Empire, and which organized, at the heart of the Empire, a type of power which, I think, no other civilization had known.[31]

The editor of the 1977–1978 course calls Foucault's move in his fourth lecture, between "the history of apparatuses of security" and "the genealogy of the modern State," a theoretical coup de théatre, a profound turning point or a sensational twist to the plot.[32] The fevered fifth lecture seems to me to produce, in its own way, another coup de théatre, this one historical, with its sudden return to biblical sources in order to explain the premises of a "governmentality" that will be conceptualized only in the sixteenth century and not put into practice until the end of the eighteenth.

Already in the lecture of 1 February 1978 Michel Foucault had announced that he was going to try "to show how this governmentality was born, from an archaic model which was that of the Christian pastorate."[33] But it seems to me that on the evening of 8 February he gives this archeology a singular importance—or that this archeology had come to seem to him more important that he had previously realized. The proof is in the conclusion to the lecture, where the superlatives, oscillating between reproof and delight, are more abundant than usual in expressing the paradox that has just been put forth:

> It is that, of all civilizations, the Christian West has undoubtedly been, at the same time, the most creative, the most conquering, the most arrogant, and doubtless one of the most bloody. . . . The strangest form of power, the form of power that is most characteristic of the West, and that will also have the greatest and most durable fortune . . . this form of power so characteristic of the West, so unique, I think, in the entire history of civilizations, it was born, or at least it took its model, from the sheepfold, from politics seen as a matter of the sheepfold.[34]

---

31. Ibid., 129–130.
32. Michel Senellart, "Course Context," in Foucault, *Security, Territory, Population*, 379–80.
33. Foucault, *Security, Territory, Population*, 110.
34. Ibid., 130.

2. Pastorate

The opening moments of the sixth lecture, on 15 February 1978, mark a pause in the course's trajectory. Michel Foucault feels obliged to confront objections that have been raised, and that he has probably also raised to himself, in order to demonstrate that "the shepherd-flock relationship was not a good political model for the Greeks."[35] While acknowledging that this theme was present in Homeric literature (Agamemnon, the "shepherd of peoples") and in the Pythagorean tradition, he notes its extreme rarity in classical political vocabulary, with one major exception: Plato. Closely analyzing the text of *The Statesman*, Foucault shows that although Plato does raise the theme of the pastor as a figure for the king or magistrate, it is only in order to dismiss it, preferring the model of the weaver to that of the shepherd. The pastorate can be applied to the lesser activities of physicians, farmers, masters of gymnastics, and teachers, but "the royal art of prescribing cannot be defined on the basis of the pastorate."[36]

His intuition reinforced by this analysis, Michel Foucault now returns to the East, to the Hebrews, to Christianity:

> The real history of the pastorate, as the source of a specific type of power over men, the history of the pastorate as a model, as a matrix of procedures for the government of men, this history of the pastorate in the Western world really only begins with Christianity.[37]

More specifically, it begins with the institutionalization of a religion in the form of the church:

> A religion that thus lays claim to the daily government of men in their real life on the grounds of their salvation and on the scale of humanity; that is the church, and we have no other example of this in the history of societies.[38]

Of course this pastoral power did not remain unchanged between the third and the eighteenth century. But the battles, the revolts that broke out around this power starting in the thirteenth century, only served to reorganize and reinforce it:

> There have been anti-feudal revolutions; there has never been an anti-pastoral revolution. The pastorate has not yet experienced the process of profound revolution that would have definitively expelled it from history.[39]

---

35. Ibid., 136.
36. Ibid., 147.
37. Ibid., 147–48.
38. Ibid., 148.
39. Ibid., 150.

Nevertheless, Michel Foucault asserts, the history of this pastorate has yet to be written. The history of ecclesiastical institutions, of doctrines, of beliefs, of religious representations and practices, yes, these have been written; but not the history of pastoral power, even though it has been the subject of "a vast reflection."[40]

> This game of the government of some by others, of everyday government, of pastoral government, this was regarded for fifteen centuries as the science par excellence, the art of all arts, the knowledge of all knowledges.[41]

In contrast to the Hebrews, the Christian church as it becomes autonomous will make the pastoral theme all-encompassing, specific, the keystone of its organization. Apostles, bishops (as in Gregory the Great's *Pastoral Care*), and abbots (as in Benedict's Rule), following the model of Christ, are all pastors, though parish priests form a notable exception. Their sacramental and jurisdictional powers, in fact all religious power, is thus nothing other than pastoral power. Yet—an essential point, Michel Foucault stresses—in spite of their innumerable points of intersection, political power and pastoral power remained separate:

> Even when the same figures exercise pastoral power and political power, and God knows this has happened in the Christian West, even with church and state, church and political power, having every kind of alliance one could imagine, I think this specificity remained as an absolutely characteristic feature of the Christian West.[42]

The reason for this heterogeneity ("a big problem of history") remains for Foucault "an enigma."[43] He does not ignore all the mechanisms, such as the coronation of the kings of France and England, which could have allowed for transfers between one power and the other, even without abolishing the distinction between the king and the pastor, between "imperial sovereignty" and the "Christ-like pastorate."[44] Still, this was a distinctive trait of the West, differing, for example, from the Russian tradition, as Foucault illustrates with a 1846 letter from Nikolai Gogol exalting the czar as a "Christ-like sovereign," in a fusion, unthinkable in the West, of the figures of the pastor and the sovereign.[45]

---

40. Ibid.
41. Ibid., 151.
42. Ibid., 154–55.
43. Ibid., 155.
44. Ibid.
45. Ibid., 155–56.

PASTORATE 151

Opening the seventh lecture, on 22 February 1978, Michel Foucault announces his intention to "finish with the pastoral."[46] He reaffirms that the Christian pastorate, which "coincides with neither politics, nor pedagogy, nor rhetoric," is "the embryonic point of this governmentality whose entry into politics, at the end of the sixteenth and in the seventeenth and eighteenth centuries, marks the threshold of the modern state."[47] He tries to sketch out its contours beginning with the Greek and Latin Fathers of the church: John Chrysostom, Cyprian of Carthage, Ambrose of Milan, Gregory the Great, as well as, from the context of monastic communities, John Cassian, Jerome, and Benedict.

> Connection to salvation, connection to the law, connection to truth; the pastor guides toward salvation, he prescribes the law, he teaches the truth.[48]

This portrait, as Michel Foucault recognizes, is not particularly specific. What distinguishes the Christian pastorate from other forms of power is the subtlety and the complexity of those connections.

Thus, concerning salvation, Michel Foucault underlines the totally and "paradoxically distributive side of the Christian pastorate":[49] "To save the whole and to save each one," even at the risk of losing the whole flock to save one sheep. There follow four principles specific to Christianity: "the principle of analytic responsibility" (the pastor must account not only for all his sheep, but also for all the actions of all his sheep); "the principle of exhaustive and instantaneous transfer" (the pastor must immediately consider as his own action any action by any one of his sheep); "the principle of sacrificial reversal" (the pastor must be ready to lose his life and his soul for his sheep); "the principle of alternate correspondence" (the weaknesses of the flock are necessary for the pastor's merit, but the weaknesses of the pastor, because he repents of them in his humility, contribute to the edification and the salvation of the sheep).[50] "In short, a whole detailed economy of merits and faults between which, in the end, God will decide."[51]

The law does not define the pastor. It can even be said that he "is not fundamentally a man of the law."[52] The Christian pastorate is distinguished from the Greek city by having invented "the insistence on pure obedience, on obedience

---

46. Ibid., 163.
47. Ibid., 165.
48. Ibid., 167.
49. Ibid., 169.
50. Ibid., 169–72.
51. Ibid., 173.
52. Ibid.

III. MATERNAL GOVERNMENT

as a unitary conduct, a highly valued type of conduct, where the essence of its *raison d'être* lies in itself."[53] The pastor is a physician more than a judge, which creates between him and his sheep "a relationship of complete dependence," "a relationship of submission of one individual to another individual,"[54] applying as much to spiritual matters as to material everyday things. This taking charge and this complete dependence are pushed to the extreme in monastic life, to the point of absurdity, or even to the point where the order is against the law:

> The perfection of obedience consists in obeying an order, not because it is reasonable or because it entrusts you with an important task, but rather because it is absurd.[55]

Christian obedience is "a relationship of complete servitude,"[56] and one whose increase has no endpoint:

> For in Christian obedience, there is no end, for what does Christian obedience lead to? Quite simply to obedience.[57]

At most one can say that such obedience tends toward humility, that is, toward the renunciation of one's own will. While the "Greek *apatheia* guarantees mastery of oneself,"[58] Christian *apatheia* (detachment or equanimity) is an effacement of the will. This principle includes the pastor himself, who commands only "because he has been ordered to command."[59] Thus the qualifying test "is that he refuses the pastorate which is entrusted to him";[60] then, in turn, he must renounce this impulse, because it would express individual will.

> The pastor must experience his responsibility as a service, and a service that makes him the servant of his sheep.[61]

Concerning truth, the pastor must teach, first by the example of his own life, but also in an individualized manner that takes account of each one of his listeners. This teaching has less to do with general principles than with daily conduct. But it is not enough to teach the truth: the pastor must also direct consciences, give spiritual direction. Unlike antiquity, when spiritual direction was voluntary and circumstantial, under Christianity, direction of conscience is obligatory and

---

53. Ibid., 174.
54. Ibid., 175.
55. Ibid., 176.
56. Ibid., 177.
57. Ibid.
58. Ibid., 178.
59. Ibid., 179.
60. Ibid.
61. Ibid.

permanent. And the examination of conscience, far from reinforcing mastery of the self, only reinforces dependence on the spiritual director.

Michel Foucault thus concludes the seventh lecture:

> These new relationships of merits and faults, of absolute obedience, and of the production of hidden truths, these are what constitute, I think, the essential nature and the originality of Christianity specifically, and not salvation, not the law, and not the truth.[62]

The Christian pastorate traces a new type of individualization, "not by status, but by analytical identification,"[63] by the making of subjects and by subjection. This is why the pastorate, "one of the decisive moments in the history of power in Western societies," is a prelude to governmentality and at the same time to the "typical constitution of the modern Western subject."[64]

Despite his closing statement on 22 February ("We will now have finished with the pastorate"[65]), the eighth lecture, on 1 March 1978, finds Michel Foucault still grappling with the pastoral theme, since he dedicates this lecture to the crisis of the pastorate. He reveals, more than he summarizes, the implications of the preceding lectures: there is no Judeo-Christian morality; the relationship between religion and politics, in modern Western societies, has more to do with the interplay between pastorate and government than with that between church and state; the crucial figure is thus not the pope or the emperor but the minister. Foucault searches for the best translation of the expression by which Gregory of Nazianzus characterized the pastorate, *oikonomia psuchiôn* (literally "economy of souls"), and settles on the term "conduct."[66]

Foucault then comes to the crisis of the pastorate. He leaves aside the history of "external blockages,"[67] whether active or passive (paganism, reluctance concerning confession, witchcraft, dualist heresy, clashes with political power, and economic development), to concentrate on "some of the points of resistance, of the forms of attack and counter-attack that could appear *within* the field of the pastorate."[68]

> These are movements whose objective is a different form of conduct; that is to say, wanting to be led or conducted differently, by other conductors and by other shepherds, toward other objectives and toward

---

62. Ibid., 183.
63. Ibid., 184.
64. Ibid., 185.
65. Ibid.
66. Ibid., 194.
67. Ibid.
68. Ibid.

other forms of salvation, through other procedures and other methods. These are movements that also seek, possibly at any rate, to escape being conducted by others, which seek to define the way for each to conduct himself.[69]

But these rejections, these revolts, these resistances, should not be thought of as a subsequent reaction to a preceding pastorate:

> So we can say that you had an immediate and foundational correlation between conduct and counter-conduct.[70]

While each possesses its own specificity, these oppositions to the pastorate are almost always linked to other conflicts (between the bourgeoisie and feudalism, between men and women, between different cultural levels). They are also linked to the "great age of the pastorate" from the tenth and eleventh centuries to the sixteenth.[71]

Rejecting the terms "revolt" (too strong), "disobedience" (too weak)," and "dissidence" (too many misleading connotations), Michel Foucault justifies the use of "counter-conduct"[72] and announces his program more specifically:

> To identify what happened in the Middle Ages, to what extent these counter-conducts were able to question, work on, elaborate, erode the pastoral power . . . how an internal crisis of the pastorate was, for a long time, opened up in the Middle Ages by the development of counter-conducts.[73]

Michel Foucault recalls the relevant evolutions of the pastorate between the first centuries of Christianity and the high Middle Ages: radical distinction between clerics and laymen, definition of the sacramental power of priests, feudalization of the church, and introduction of the judicial model into pastoral practice. He specifies that antipastoral struggles could take the form of doctrinal conflicts, of individual or collective behaviors, of crisis-ridden groups, or of groups "oscillating from obedience to refusal and revolt."[74] At last he lays out the "five forms of counter-conduct developed by the Middle Ages":[75] asceticism, communities, mysticism, scripture, and eschatology.

---

69. Ibid., 194–95.
70. Ibid., 196.
71. Ibid., 197.
72. Ibid., 201.
73. Ibid., 202.
74. Ibid., 204.
75. Ibid.

Michel Foucault realizes that his first "form" will be the most surprising, since asceticism seems such an integral part of religious life. But he sees in asceticism a challenge to obedience. The ascetic poses a challenge to himself (an internal challenge) as the guide to his own asceticism; he poses a challenge to others (an external challenge) with whom he competes through his exploits; he strives toward an *apatheia* that is a mastery over himself; he identifies his tortured body with that of Christ. None of these traits is compatible with the pastorate. Foucault concludes that "Christianity is not an ascetic religion,"[76] and that asceticism, revived in the eleventh and twelfth centuries, turned against the structures of power: "Asceticism is a sort of exasperated and reversed obedience, turned into egoistic self-mastery."[77]

The second type of counter-conduct is the formation of communities, whose most learned members, such as John Wyclif and Jan Hus, challenge the power of any pastor in a state of mortal sin, arguing that the validity of his function depends on the quality of his conduct (one thinks of the earlier Patarines of Milan). Other doctrinal challenges manifested by these communities concern the sacramental powers of the priest: refusal of baptism, mistrust of confession, questioning of the real presence in the Eucharist. Through their organization, these communities tend to do away with the binary distinction between priests and laypeople and replace it with "the designation of the pastor by way of election and in a provisional manner"[78] or substitute for it a division between the elect and all others, and so render the intervention of the pastor pointless for both groups. The principle of equality is another way of undermining the pastorate ("each one is a pastor, each one is a priest, each one is a shepherd; that is to say, no one is"[79]), coupled with an absence of personal possessions, promises of reciprocal obedience, or the inversion of hierarchies:

> That is to say, while the Christian pastorate certainly says that, yes, the pastor must be the last of the servants of the community, one knows perfectly well—and one has had experience of this—that the last of the servants of the community will never become the pastor. But within these groups, to the contrary, you have systematic reversals of hierarchy. That is to say, they choose the most ignorant or poorest person, or someone with

---

76. Ibid., 207.
77. Ibid., 207–8.
78. Ibid., 210.
79. Ibid., 211.

the lowest reputation or honor, the most debauched, they choose the prostitute to become the leader of the group.[80]

The third counter-conduct is mysticism, "the privileged status of an experience that by definition escapes pastoral power."[81] Mysticism does not foster examination, or teaching, or even the idea of progress toward knowledge.

A fourth challenge comes from scripture, "because scripture is a text that speaks for itself, which has no need of pastoral relay."[82]

Finally, the fifth counter-conduct is eschatological belief: that God will return, and he will be the true shepherd. "The pastors are dismissed,"[83] all the more so since, according to Joachim of Fiore (d. 1202), the Third Age will be that of the Holy Spirit, which will fill everyone, imparting to them its spark.

> At heart, the problem is to know why, for example, political or economic problems like those that arose in the Middle Ages, such as the movements of urban revolt, the movements of peasant revolt, the conflicts between feudalism and the merchant bourgeoisie, how and why they were translated into a number of themes, of religious forms, of religious concerns that will finally result in the explosion of the Reformation, of the great religious crisis of the sixteenth century.[84]

Foucault proposes to see in pastoral power the pivot of these diverse movements, their "field of intelligibility," without which we risk falling back into "old conceptions of ideology."[85] He concludes: "There you have it. Forgive me for having taken too long, and next time, this is a promise, we won't speak any more about pastors."[86]

True to his word, Michel Foucault begins the ninth lecture, on 8 March 1978, like this:

> Today, I would finally like to pass from the pastoral care of souls to the political government of men.[87]

---

80. Ibid. Note that the published English translation omits part of this passage, where the translator's eye apparently skipped from the first "that is to say" (*c'est-à-dire*) to the second, thus leaving out the intervening text (many a medieval scribe made the same kind of mistake).
81. Ibid., 212.
82. Ibid., 213.
83. Ibid., 214.
84. Ibid., 215.
85. Ibid., 215–16.
86. Ibid., 216.
87. Ibid., 227.

I will leave Michel Foucault's thought as I found it, in the middle of a course, in the course of a career. I think we could not do better. Or rather, I know how we could do worse: by trying to apply historical tests to the philosophical discourse, whether to sap or to support it. For one thing, such an effort would display a singular arrogance in general and a taste for the ridiculous in particular. Few historians can hope to rival Michel Foucault, not just in the penetrating quality of his interpretations, but in the totality and the density of the astonishing historical knowledge he marshals. For another, the rare objections that might come to the medievalist's mind when reading Foucault's course are systematically swept away by the philosopher's careful statements. Let's take one example.

It is generally admitted that the papal administration was the initiator and model of secular administrations. At least from the time of the Gregorian reform, in the second half of the eleventh century, the ecclesiastical apparatus, its administrative machinery, and its procedures represent the origins of the apparatus, the administrative machinery, and the procedures of the modern state. The historical reason for this is simple. When the Roman Empire died away in the fifth century, it was the bishop of Rome who first picked up its remains, titles, attributes, and practices. At the turn of the sixth to the seventh centuries, Pope Gregory the Great, the son of a powerful senatorial family and a prefect (secular administrator) of Rome before his monastic conversion, was the living symbol of this "transfer of empire."

The "renewal of empire" advanced by Charlemagne in 800 never caught up from this late start. The power of emperors, kings, and princes always faced a papal power that not only enjoyed an unquestionably superior sacrality, but also drew its sovereignty from the same Roman imperial heritage (the possession of *imperium* not as a territory to dominate but as a sacralizing source of power), with the additional legitimacy afforded by priority in time and continuity in space. The emblematic confrontation between Pope Boniface VIII and King Philip IV of France, at the beginning of the fourteenth century, pitted against each other two monarchs both claiming sacral status. A king could occasionally gain the upper hand over a pope, but for the former, the battle, at least in that domain, was lost in advance.

On the other hand, kings had tried to reserve for themselves some of the shimmer of sacrality. The coronation rite, which made kings similar to consecrated bishops, is the most obvious manifestation of this in France and England. All romanticism aside, Gogol's letter of 1846—where he refers to the czar as "Christ-like sovereign," and which seemed to Michel Foucault, at the end of his lecture of 15 February 1978, to permit a distinction between Eastern and

Western traditions—could very well have been applied to King Louis IX of France, the eventual St. Louis (canonized in 1297). The claim that "the Western sovereign is Caesar and not Christ; the Western pastor is not Caesar, but Christ,"[88] here reaches its limits.

Or it would, if Michel Foucault had set out to offer a synthetic interpretation of medieval powers, when in fact his intention was to provide interpretive models that render intelligible the nature of power in the West from the eighteenth century onward. It would, if Foucault had not himself envisioned and described, in the same lecture of 15 February (on the page just before the quotation from Gogol), the reciprocal hybridization of powers typical of the two rival lights:

> First of all, obviously, there will be a series of conjunctions, supports, relays, a whole series of conflicts, on which I will not dwell and which you know well, such that the intertwining of pastoral and political power will in fact be a historical reality throughout the West.[89]

For the slice of his course that I have artificially carved out, the main advance that historians could offer on the perspectives opened up by Michel Foucault would be to proceed further in this direction, to look for the infiltrations, seepages, intersections, and confusions that could occur, intentionally or unintentionally, between the two main forms of power put forth by the philosopher.

It would be absurd for a historian to try to test whether or not Michel Foucault's thought works. His thought does not need to be tested in order to work. It works. It would be less arrogant, but still pointless, to try to demonstrate the truth of his proposals through illustrative historical vignettes, attempting to show that "in reality" everything happened just as he said it did. This would only diminish the drive of philosophical discourse while limiting historical inquiry to lying down on a Procrustean bed of theory.

By comparison, a more spontaneous approach—to climb aboard Foucault's thought as it speeds by and then to descend from it at a certain point, to borrow sometimes from him, sometimes from another—seems to me, paradoxically, a higher form of respect. If we distinguish (in the arbitrary, rigid manner of all such distinctions) between disciplinary fields, identified by their own histories, objectives, and practices, we do so not to authorize one profession to verify another or to force one to model itself on another. I do not believe in a hierarchy of disciplines, any more than of civilizations or historical periods. I believe in interdisciplinary dialogue, but only, as when comparing cultures or

---

88. Ibid., 156.
89. Ibid., 154.

eras, in the form of furtive and necessarily truncated tangents. This fortuitous, surreptitious, unfinished character seems to me necessary for a passing encounter that offers lasting inspiration.

Thus I leave Michel Foucault's thought, in order to better return to it by way of a detour through an autograph note written by Francis of Assisi.

3. A Note

Thirty years ago already! But the memory is still vivid. Rarely have I been so moved as I was while listening to the talk given by Attilio Bartoli Langeli on 15 October 1993, during a colloquium sponsored by the International Society of Franciscan Studies on the subject of "Brother Francis of Assisi." Moved by admiration for the Italian scholar, who demonstrated a perfect blend of critical and historical erudition, methodological caution, and interpretative audacity. Moved by emotion in encountering, thanks to his guidance, the visible, tangible traces of Francis of Assisi's internal conflict. Let's recall the facts.

The talk was entitled "Francis of Assisi's Writings: The Autograph of an *Illiteratus*."[90] In Italian, the organizers of the colloquium could play on the distinction between *Gli scritti da Francesco* and *Gli scritti di Francesco*—that is, between the autograph writings produced by Francis's own hand and the writings that Francis dictated (the latter were analyzed at the colloquium by Enrico Menestò).[91]

In his talk, Attilio Bartoli Langeli applied a rigorous, penetrating paleographic expertise to the only two autographs known to have been written by Francis of Assisi. One is a *chartula* conserved at the Sacro Convento of Assisi, a bit of goatskin parchment (132 × 100 mm) that bears (on the flesh side) the *Praises of the Most High God* and (on the hair side) the blessing to Brother Leo, framed by headings added later by its recipient. The other is a letter conserved in the archives of the cathedral of Spoleto, a fragment of goatskin parchment (130 × 60 mm) that has (only on the flesh side) the nineteen-line message addressed by Francis to this same Brother Leo (figure 1).

In fact, the dimensions of this latter document (the size of an iPhone) and the brevity of its message lead me to prefer the term "note" to that of "letter": a short word for a small object. We will focus only on the second of the two autographs. Figure 2 shows a reproduction of the note, accompanied by a transcription of the Latin as it was traditionally understood before Attilio Bartoli Langeli's intervention. Here is an English translation as it has usually been rendered:

> Brother Leo, health and peace from your Brother Francis. I say this to you, my son, like a mother, that I am putting everything we said on the road in this brief message and advice for you, and if, afterward, you must come to me for counsel, I advise you thus: In whatever way it seems better to you to please the Lord God and to follow his footprint and his poverty, do it with the blessing of the Lord God and my obedi-

---

90. Published as Attilio Bartoli Langeli, "Gli scritti da Francesco. L'autografia di un *illitteratus*," in *Frate Francesco d'Assisi. Atti del XXI Convegno internazionale, Assisi, 14–16 ottobre 1993* (Spoleto, 1994), 103–58.

91. Enrico Menestò, "Gli scritti di Francesco d'Assisi," in *Frate Francesco d'Assisi*, 163–81.

FIGURE 1. Framed autograph of Francis of Assisi's note to Brother Leo. ©Archives of the Cathedral of Spoleto. Used by permission.

III. MATERNAL GOVERNMENT

Frater Leo,
Frater Francisco tuo sa-
lutem et pacem. Ita dico tibi,
fili mei, sicut mater: quia
omnia verba, quae diximus
in via, breviter in hoc verba
dispono et consilio, et si
dopo tibi oportet propter
consilium venire ad me,
quia ita consilio tibi:
In quocumque modo melius
videtur tibi placere Domino
Deo et sequi vestigiam et paupertatem suam, faciatis
cum benedictione Domini
Dei et mea obedientia.
Et, si tibi est necessarium
animam tuam propter aliam
consolationem tuam et vis,
Leo, venire ad me, veni.

FIGURE 2. Text of Francis of Assisi's autograph note to Brother Leo, with traditional transcription.

ence. And if it is necessary for you to come to me, for your soul or for another consolation, and if you want, Leo, come.

In his study of this note, Attilio Bartoli Langeli offered two startling discoveries. First, he finally made the text of the sixth and seventh lines understandable, by proposing to read *et non oportet* ("and you must not") where others before him had read *et si dopo tibi oportet* ("and if afterward you must"). The older reading left the phrase strangely unfinished, hanging in suspense: "and if afterward you must come to me for counsel, since I counsel you this." Otherwise it would imply, as in the translation given above, that the conjunction "since" (*quia*) had to be omitted: "and if afterward you must come to me for counsel, I counsel you this."

Second, Attilio Bartoli Langeli showed that the last four lines of the note (*Et si tibi* . . .) are actually a later addition by Francis's hand. Taken together, the two discoveries suddenly make sense of each other. Francis begins by telling his faithful companion, Brother Leo, not to come see him. Then, repenting of this decision, he adds: If you want to come to me, then come!

Attilio Bartoli Langeli's profound revision sparked new interest in the Spoleto note among specialists. In 2000, Carlo Paolazzi offered a further deciphering. While paying homage to Bartoli Langeli's reconstruction, he suggested that the opposition between the two parts of the missive should not be pushed too far. From the beginning, Paolazzi suggested, Francis addressed Leo "like a mother," showing a loving kindness toward this son whom he understood so well. The concluding change of heart was thus "born of Francis's 'maternal' sensibility," his fear that Brother Leo might interpret "the invitation not to come" as a closing off, a definitive prohibition. Even if the initial counsel remained in force, Paolazzi concluded, Francis was still careful to assure Leo that the path to him remained open.[92]

Between them, Attilio Bartoli Langeli and Carlo Paolazzi have done the hard work. Thanks to their joint efforts, we now have a transcription of the Spoleto autograph that, it seems to me, marks an irreversible step forward on the essential points, even if certain details can still be revised. In its rough, literal quality, the note to Leo gives us one of the two most authentic surviving witnesses to Francis of Assisi. Other texts by Francis are almost all separated from us by the threefold barriers of a secretary's editing, of translation from Umbrian to Latin, and of the intervening hand of a later copyist. But the autograph guarantees that nothing comes between what Francis wanted to write in the thirteenth century and what we read today, eight centuries later. The autograph is that rare moment in the Middle Ages when the author and the scribe are one and the same, allowing the emergence of the modern figure of the writer—not one who dictates, but one who both composes and records, conceives as well as carries out the writing himself.

My own transcription of this note, shown in figure 3, combines the readings given by the two Italian scholars. I respect Francis's orthography, leave the original punctuation, and do not add capital letters. Clearly indicated abbreviations, however, are expanded.

It is enough to look at the reproduction of the Spoleto note to understand that Francis was a poor scribe. He tries, but suddenly the nib of his quill breaks. He sets down his letters well enough, separates them effectively, but they are coarse, shaky, uneven in size. He is clumsy. At least twice, in the seventh and eleventh lines, he makes a mistake, goes back, erases his incorrect letters, and

---

92. Carlo Paolazzi, "Per gli autografi di frate Francesco. Dubbi, verifiche e riconferme," *Archivum franciscanum historicum* 93 (2000): 3–28.

III. MATERNAL GOVERNMENT

f leo f francissco tuo sa-
lutem et pacem. ita dico tibi
fili mei sicut mater quia
omnia verba que disimus
in via, breviter in oc verbo
dispono et consilio, et non
oportet proter
consilium venire a me.
quia ita consilio tibi in
qocumque modo melius
videtur tibi placere domino
deo et sequi vestigia et paupertatem suam faciatis
cum beneditione domini
dei et mea obedientia
et si tibi est necesarium
animam tuam propter aliam
consolationem tuam et vis
revenire a me veni

FIGURE 3. Text of Francis of Assisi's autograph note to Brother Leo, with new transcription.

starts again. He tries, but he cannot quite keep his writing in straight horizontal lines, nor can he space out the lines evenly. The last four lines (his change of heart, according to Attilio Bartoli Langeli) are the worst; in a slightly lighter ink, they are rushed, cramped, chaotic, overflowing, curved like a bow. Francis is not a professional writer, not even semi-professional, in contrast to Leo (among others), whose hand we know from his headings on the Assisi *chartula*.

Still, however clumsy he may be, Francis knows how to form letters and words. He knows how to write. The way such statistics are compiled today, he would not be considered illiterate. By the standards of his own time, however, he is simple and unlettered (*illiteratus, idiota*), because he does not possess a perfect command of Latin. This was the crucial dividing line between the learned and everyone else, according to the way knowledge was defined in the Middle Ages.

We need to be clear on this point, to dispel the pious images that cling to Francis's memory and paint the Poverello as an innocent, as blissfully ignorant, as a happy fool. He was not just someone with an ardent spirituality. He also possessed an exceptional intelligence. He received a basic education at the school run by the church of San Giorgio in Assisi. Then, from his father, he learned the merchant's craft, its rules, its accounting practices, its tricks of the trade. As a young man, he showed himself to be a "capable shopkeeper." Today, he would enroll in a business school. He was hardly naïve. But he must have been more comfortable with numbers than with letters—more comfortable, for sure, with the Umbrian dialect of Assisi, maybe even with the French of the troubadours, than with the Latin of the clerics.

Italian was his language. His superb *Canticle of Brother Sun* inaugurates Italian literature. Yet for an inhabitant of the Italian peninsula in the thirteenth century, Latin was not entirely a foreign language, nor a dead one. There was still a certain permeability between the mother language (Latin) and the daughter (Italian). The vocabulary of Francis's note to Leo forms a kind of common denominator between Latin and romance languages. Most of the words are readily comprehensible to a modern speaker of French, Spanish, or Italian, even if he or she is not an accomplished Latinist. Here, in alphabetical order, are the fifty-four words used in the Spoleto note:

Ad, alius, anima, benedictio, bonus, breviter, consiliare, consilium, consolatio, cum, Deus, dicere, disponere, Dominus, ego, esse, et, facere, filius, Franciscus, frater, hic, in, ita, Leo, mater, meus, modum, necessarius, non, obedientia, omnis, oportet, paupertas, pax, placere, propter, qui, quia, quicumque, revenire, salus, sequi, si, sicut, suus, tu, tuus, velle, venire, verbum, vestigium, via, videri.

Many of these terms should be just as understandable to English-speakers (animate, benediction, bonus, brief, counsel, consolation, dispose, filial, fraternity, maternity, mode, necessary, obedience, pauper, please, salutation, sequel, verb, vestige), and anyone who has studied a bit of French, Spanish, or Italian can doubtless decipher the rest. The only obstacle might be a lingering fear of the sacred language, Latin, left over from the Middle Ages.

Francis's mistakes are happy accidents! They shatter the inhibitions of sacrality and shed the baggage of student complexes. He begins with a double mistake in declining the Latin forms of Leo's name and his own, because he is thinking in Italian. He puts one *s* too many in his own name, *Francissco* and one too few in *neces[s]arium*. In another Italianism, he has the possessive adjective in the dative form *tuo*, when Latin requires the nominative *tuus*. He renders *diximus* as *disimus* and shaves down *hoc* to *oc*. He forgets the *c* in *benedi[c]tione*, making it closer to Italian *benedizione*. His most amusing mistake is *venire a me*. In Italian, *venire a me* indeed means "come to me." In Latin, however, "to me" should be *ad me*, and *a me* actually means exactly the opposite, "away from me"!

These mistakes make us smile. They reassure us. But they must have dismayed the recipient of the note, Brother Leo, the young priest who regularly served as Francis's secretary. Francis was his admired and cherished master. For Leo, this note was a talisman, already a kind of relic. The disciple was filled with veneration, but the letter unnerved him. So Leo corrected his unlearned master himself. In his small, precise handwriting, he corrected *disimus* to *diximus*; added a discreet *h* (above the line) to make *hoc*; and twice added *d*, in the eighth and nineteenth lines, to make the correct *ad me* out of the faulty *a me*.

We feel as though we can grasp the sense of this unsteady writing, in such basic Latin, at first reading. But making a proper translation out of it is another matter. Real comprehension is not so simple. Let's sketch out the underlying difficulties, which stem neither from vocabulary nor from Latin grammar.

In the first lines, why does Francis address Leo "like a mother" (*sicut mater*) to her "son" (*fili*), but then issue an order in the form of a prohibition: "you must not" (*non oportet*)? The command is phrased gently, in the form of a "counsel" (*consilium*), but still it remains a fundamentally stark prohibition: do not come to me! An odd message for a mother to give . . .

Why, at the end of the first part, does "obedience" (*obedientia*) unexpectedly appear in a phrase that up to that point seems to be about an affectionate suggestion?

Why does Francis start by addressing the recipient (Leo) in the second person singular at the beginning of the first part (*tuo, tibi, tibi, tibi*), move to the second person plural at the end of the first part (*faciatis*), only to then return overwhelmingly to the singular in the second part (*tibi, tuam, tuam, vis, veni*)?

Why is it only in the last lines of the note, in the change of heart, that Francis seems to give in to his maternal affection for Leo by permitting him to come to him (*veni*), given that he claims to speak to his son "like a mother" right from the beginning of his message?

Finally, putting these questions together, why does Francis take up his quill to give, in so few words, two contradictory orders: do not come; come? What was the point of this note? And what is the point of trying to understand it?

4. Mother

Until now, in keeping with their focus on deciphering the script, specialists have commented mainly on the Spoleto note's vocabulary and grammar. It was obviously necessary to verify the form of the words and the syntax that linked them before turning to a new reading.

I propose to offer here a new interpretation of Francis of Assisi's note to Brother Leo, based on several semantic observations. The key to the entire text lies in two words: *sicut mater*. These really are the key, since they can close off meaning, or open it up.

> My son, I am speaking to you like a mother to her child . . .
> I say to you my son, and like a mother . . .
> I say this to you, my son, like a mother . . .

These are some of the translations that have been offered in the past. But if we translate *sicut mater* as "like a mother," we will misunderstand both parts of the note. Most importantly, we will fail to grasp the opposition between them, an opposition in both form and genre, paradoxical yet also deeply complementary.

Unlike Greek, Latin does not use articles. When we translate a text from Latin into English (and many other modern languages), we have to add either definite articles (*the*) or indefinite articles (*a*, *an*). Sometimes, however, the proper translation involves no article at all. Let's try this hypothesis with *sicut mater*. Francis does not speak to Leo "like a mother." He writes to him "as mother." *Da madre*, one would say in Italian. *Comme mère* or *en tant que mère* in French. This meaning of *sicut* is attested in four places in Francis's Latin writings—for instance, in this occurrence in the *Letter to the Whole Order*:

> Moreover I confess all my sins to the Lord God, Father, Son, and Holy Spirit, to the blessed ever Virgin Mary, and to all the saints in heaven and on earth, to Brother Elias, minister of our religion, as to my venerable lord [*sicut venerabili domino meo*], and to the priests of our Order and to all my other blessed brothers.[93]

The *sicut* here does not signal a comparison. That is, Francis does not confess to Elias *as if* he were confessing to his lord. He confesses to Elias, minister general of the Order of Lesser Brothers, because Elias really *is* his lord. In the same way, Francis does not write to Leo *as if* he were his mother, or as a good mother would. He writes to Leo inasmuch as Francis really *is* his mother.

---

93. *Scripta*, 218; *FAED*, 1:119.

III. MATERNAL GOVERNMENT

What is a mother for Francis? In his writings, as in the writings about him, the figure of the mother comes up often, but not as a metaphor for tender affection. At the heart of the brotherhood that Francis was usually reluctant to call an "order" (the *Letter to the Whole Order* is the unique exception to this aversion), "mother" was the only acceptable term for the one whom Francis preferred to call the "minister" or "servant," rather than the "superior." A mother is to a father what a minister is to an abbot. Motherhood is opposed to fatherhood as service is to domination, government to power. This opposition between "to govern" (*reggere*) and "to dominate" (*dominare*) is very old, since it was already expressed in Augustine's *The City of God*, which drew on a passage in Cicero's *The Republic*.

The Gospels provided justification for Francis's denial of fatherhood—"And call none your father upon earth; for you have only one Father, who is in heaven" (Matthew 23:9)—which may have been reinforced by a more personal factor: Francis had made himself into a new man by opposing the authoritarian, irritable, dominating figure of his own father, Pietro of Bernardone.

Motherhood is the incarnated metaphor of a government of service. Each brother must be a mother who "cherishes and nourishes" his brothers. The *Regula non bullata* and the *Regula bullata* both say this, and we have seen a nice example in the Rule for Hermitages, where the "mothers" serve their "sons." In the *Canticle of Brother Sun*, after "Sir brother Sun" and "sister Moon and the stars," and after the three elements "brother Wind," "sister Water," and "brother Fire," the fourth element is "our sister mother Earth, who sustains us and governs us."[94] We should fully appreciate the audacity of this reversal: it is no longer humans who dominate the Earth, but the Earth that governs humans. Government and motherhood are one.

In *The Beginning of the Order*, the *Legend of the Three Companions*, and the *Memorial*, we find echoes of an odd parable that is also contained in a collection of edifying stories gathered for the use of preachers by the English cleric Odo of Cheriton:

> When brother Francis was asked who would nourish his brothers since he was receiving everyone without distinction, he answered: "A king impregnated a woman in a woods; and she gave birth. When she had nourished her son for some time, she came to the king's door so that he could nourish his son henceforth. When they had been announced to the king, he answered, 'So many bad and useless people eat at my court, it is just that my son should be nourished among them.' Explaining this, Francis said that he was this woman whom the Lord had made fertile with his word

---

94. Jacques Dalarun, *The Canticle of Brother Sun: Francis of Assisi Reconciled*, trans. Philippe Yates (St. Bonaventure, NY, 2016), 2–3.

and who had brought forth spiritual sons. Given that the Lord nourishes so many unjust people, it is not surprising that he nourishes his own sons among the others.[95]

Odo of Cheriton's commentary stands on its own. Clare, for her part, fully grasped Francis's motherhood in his role as institutor of the community she formed with her sisters. She reveals this understanding in the astonishing "vision of the breast," where the woman nurses at the man's breast. Across Francis's entire dossier, the mother is a governor in the guise of a governess. The Franciscan mother is first and foremost an institutional figure.

It would seem that the link between motherhood and affection must be stronger and more binding nowadays than it was in the Middle Ages, since no one, so far as I know, has suggested that the first part of the Spoleto note might have an explicitly legal meaning. We have to make an effort to sever our mental link between motherhood and tenderness in order to see that the relationship between the mother and her son, between Francis and Leo, is also hierarchical. A strange hierarchy to be sure—a Franciscan hierarchy that rejects the idea of high and low, which indeed turns it upside down. But once this interpretive door is opened, we can see that the entire first part of the Spoleto note, in its first fifteen lines, is actually institutional and legal in nature. The law is expressed in Francis's elementary Latin vocabulary. It is this constellation of words, seemingly commonplace but holding juridical potential, that makes sense of the whole.

What is this *consilium* (advice) that shows up as a noun, flanked on both sides by the very rare verbal form *consilio* (I advise)? In the *Regula bullata* of 1223, *consilium* can refer to the advice of a wise man, and *consilia* (plural) can refer to conversations. In the *Letter to the Whole Order*, Francis associates divine *mandata* with *consilia*; for the brothers, the "commandments" (*mandata*) of God should be kept in the heart, and the *consilia* should be carried out perfectly. The two words are thus complementary, like the law and the rules that govern its application. Francis's usage is actually rather unusual. Ambrose of Milan had differentiated between divine "precepts" (*praecepta*) and *consilia* in the New Testament: the former applied to all Christians, the latter only to those who had chosen a consecrated religious life.[96] In Francis's *Letter to a Minister*, the term *consilium* implies a collective deliberation preceding a decision of the general chapter.

---

95. Michel Bihl, "S. Francisci parabola in sermonibus Odonis de Ceritona an. 1219 conscriptus," *Archivum franciscanum historicum* 22 (1929): 584–86.

96. Ambrose of Milan, "De viduis," in *Verginità et vedovanza: Tutte le opere di Sant'Ambrogio* ed. Franco Gori (Milan, 1989), 1: 244–318.

One thing is certain. In medieval usage, a *consilium* is not just a bit of friendly advice. It is at least a formal opinion, if not a prescription. A *consilium* can be a deliberation or its result, a resolution, decree, sentence, precept, or order. In my experience, its most common meaning in medieval Latin vocabulary seems to be "a decision resulting from collective deliberation." The term can also refer to a legal text (representing judicial expertise or as a product of jurisprudence) that informs a juridical act or a juridicial decision, revealing its formulation and the arguments behind it. At heart, for Francis a "counsel" (*consilium*) is to a mother what a "commandment" (*mandatum*) is to a father. It is a maternal order.

In the note to Leo, one of the occurrences of the verb *consilio* (I counsel) is followed by a prohibition, "you must not" (*non oportet*), and the other by a subjunctive expressing an order, "do" (*faciatis*). So these words have a real binding force, not just the tone of suggestions: "I counsel you" to not do something; "I counsel you" to do something. In following their mother's *consilium*, the brothers respect the "obedience" (*obediencia*) they owe her. A *consilium* thus implies the obligation to comply.

It is the legal and institutional character of this first part of the note that allows Francis as author to move from the specific case of Leo—"to you" (*tibi*, in the singular)—to a generally applicable *consilium*—"do" (*faciatis*, in the plural). The distancing of Leo—"you must not ... come to me" (*non oportet ... venire a me*)—merges the individual Leo into the community of brothers.

The verb *dispono* (I dispose) belongs to the same semantic field. A "disposition" (*dispositio* or *dispositum*) can be a normative legal text (a rule, an ordonnance, a law). And although the first meaning of "to dispose" (*disponere*) is to install, arrange, or organize, it can also mean to institute, prescribe, order, or promulgate. In the technical vocabulary of diplomatics (the rules of Latin document writing), the *dispositio* is the heart of an act (a charter, a diploma, a pontifical letter), the passage that contains the decision recorded in the document.

What did Francis "dispose"? He disposed "words" (*verba*) in a "word" (*verbum*). The former, in the plural, are the words spoken on the road, cast to the wind, in great number: "all the words" (*omnia verba*). The latter, in the singular, is evidently the present writing, "this word" (*oc verbo*), this note addressed to Leo. "Lend me your quill / to write a word," as the song says.[97] But the term can also indicate a decision, a judgment, a sentence, a precept, an order. In Francis's writings, "words" (*verba*) in the plural have a negative connotation, but the singular "word" (*verbum*) is positive. Thus in the *Admonitions*:

---

97. From the first verse of "Au clair de la lune" (Au clair de la lune / mon ami Pierrot / prête-moi ta plume / pour écrire un mot).

And they are put to death by the letter, the religious who do not want to follow the spirit of the divine scripture but rather wish only to know the words [*verba*] and to interpret them for others. And they are brought to life by the spirit of the divine scripture, those who do not attribute every letter they know, or wish to know, to their body, but who, by word [*verbo*] and example, return it to the most high Lord God to whom every good belongs.[98]

In the note to Leo, the long-winded words (*omnia verba*) are thus gathered "concisely" or "briefly" (*breviter*) into a single writing (*in oc verbo*), which is disposed—put in order, fixed, as well as promulgated—and so assumes the quality of a disposition. Francis moves from speaking to writing, from prolixity to brevity, from a discussion as equals—"we said" (*disimus*)—to a unilateral decision—"I dispose" (*dispono*). All of this to tell Leo that he must not come! But what is writing—what is a letter in particular—if not an ambivalent measure of distance? We are distant from each other, so we write to bring ourselves closer together: a love letter, a letter of friendship, a letter of introduction, a letter offering employment, a letter sending best wishes for the new year. Or I do not want to speak to you or to see you anymore, so I send you a break-up letter, a letter of dismissal, a letter of resignation.

Finally, let's not forget the use of Latin. The two men could have understood each other perfectly well in Umbrian. Such a choice would have allowed Francis to avoid a number of barbarisms and gaffes. For the *Canticle of Brother Sun*, composed at San Damiano, and for the poem addressed to the sisters of San Damiano, "Listen, Little Poor Ones," he used the vernacular—the *lingua madre*, the "mother tongue," the language of women, the language of the heart. Yet "as mother," Francis chose the language of the father. The usage of Latin in and of itself already implies the institutional dimension of Francis's note to Leo.

Then comes the change of heart. In contrast to Carlo Paolazzi, I see a clear opposition between the two unequal parts of the note, linked to the nature of each part. The first part is primarily juridical. Because it has an institutional force, it moves naturally from singular forms of address to plural; from the individual to the community. The second part returns to the individual and opens up another semantic field, the spiritual. Paolazzi sees the final change of heart as born of Francis's maternal sensibility. This position seems difficult to maintain, however, since the maternal title, *sicut mater*, comes at the beginning of the first part of the note, not in the second.

---

98. *Scripta*, 360 (chap. 7); *FAED*, 1:132 (cf. 2 Corinthians 3).

Still, I agree with Carlo Paolazzi on the underlying point. There is an obvious temptation to read the added passage as a psychological leap, but above all it is essential that we understand it as a move to draw together the note's two parts. Francis of Assisi's two opposing statements (do not come, come) are simply the two duties of the good shepherd, balancing between institutional norm and spiritual direction, between care for the flock and concern for the sheep. The final change of heart in the Spoleto note is not a moment of remorse, but of fulfillment. It is not a sudden eruption of a last-minute maternal sentiment, but the logic of maternal government pushed to its conclusion.

"It is not fitting" (*non oportet*) that Leo should come back, should close the distance, should speak again, should restart the endless discussions. But what if it were suddenly "necessary" (*necesarium*) for him to do so? Better yet: what if it were necessary for his soul? Leo could not legitimately return for a new *consilium*—the *consilium* was already set in stone, the disposition had been given once and for all. But if his soul should thirst for another kind of speech, a "consolation" (*consolationem*): in that case, come!

> I am the good shepherd and I know my sheep and my sheep know me. As the Father knows me, and I know the Father and I lay down my life for my sheep. (John 10:14–15)

> What man of you, if he has a hundred sheep, and if he shall lose one of them, would not leave the ninety-nine in the desert, and go after the one which was lost, until he finds it? And when he has found it, lay it upon his shoulders, rejoicing? And coming home, call together his friends and neighbors, saying to them, "Rejoice with me, because I have found my sheep that was lost?" (Luke 15:4–7)

The eternal story of the sheepfold, as Michel Foucault would have said . . .

5. Word by Word

So we have the hypothesis and the general keys for interpretation. Let's now take up the commentary and proceed phrase by phrase, word by word, to sketch out a translation. Only a scrupulous translation can tell us whether an edition is correct, whether a hypothesis is tenable. This exercise might seem tedious, but it is a question of intellectual honesty.

> To Brother Leo your brother Francis, greetings and peace [*f Leo f francissco tuo salutem et pacem*].

Francis's first Italianism already appears in the proper names. In correct Latin, he should have written *f. Leoni f. Franciscus tuus*, but instead he inverts the grammatical cases (dative and nominative). The term *salus* conveys several meanings at once in Latin, because it expresses greetings (like "salutations" in English), good health (like "salubrious"), as well as the "salvation" of the soul. It doesn't mean just one of these things, but all three together. It is a greeting of peace. Elsewhere in his writings Francis often instructs that it be given, or uses it himself.

> Thus I say to you, my son, as mother, that all the words which we said on the road, briefly, in this word, I dispose them; and I counsel [*ita dico tibi fili mei sicut mater quia omnia verba que disimus in via, breviter in oc verbo dispono et consilio*]

Let's take the charming expression, so simple in Latin: "all the words which we said on the road" (*omnia verba que disimus in via*). The discussion is a free exchange, without hierarchy, between two men, two equals, until Francis affirms his legislative role: "briefly, in this word, I dispose them" (*breviter in oc verbo dispono*). The circumstantial description "on the road" (*in via*) is there as a reminder that itinerancy is the fundamental way of life for Francis and his companions. They are a group of men wandering the earth, pilgrims and strangers, a little flock migrating between pastures, with Francis as its pastor. Michel Foucault's words come to mind:

> The shepherd's power is a power which is not exercised over a territory, it is a power that by definition is exercised over a flock; more exactly, over the flock in its movement; in the movement that causes it to go from one place to another. The shepherd's power is essentially exercised over a multiplicity in motion.[99]

---

99. Foucault, *Security, Territory, Population*, 125.

III. MATERNAL GOVERNMENT

A miniscule flock for a tiny shepherd; as always, Francis of Assisi enacts the church in miniature. We have already commented on the essential points for the rest of the phrase: *sicut mater* should be translated without adding an article ("as mother"); "I dispose" (*dispono*) has the sense of giving a disposition, of putting into a form that carries normative value.

Yet we have to linger over the end of the phrase in order to understand the nature (verb or noun?) and function of *consilio*. The first option would be to see *consilio* as a noun: "all the words . . . , I dispose them in this word and counsel." This choice is tempting, because it would reinforce the idea that the note itself constitutes a *consilium* in the legal sense, a judgment. But putting a second, complementary noun after the verb (*in oc verbo dispono et consilio*) is really not part of Francis of Assisi's Latin repertoire.

In the second option, *consilio* would be another verb in the main clause, a sort of reiteration of *dispono*: "in this word, I dispose and counsel them." *Consiliare* is a rare form. More common would be the deponent verb *consiliari*, but *consiliare* is much closer to the Italian *consigliare*. Francis was certainly capable of employing *consilio* as a verb. The proof is in the next phrase: "thus I counsel you" (*ita consilio tibi*), where treating *consilio* as a noun would not make sense. But the meaning resulting from this option would be unconvincing: What would Francis be counseling? The words he had already said?

Thus I opt for a third solution, which, as far as I know, has never before been proposed: *dispono* governs the clause that precedes it ("the words . . . , in this word, I dispose them"), while *consilio* governs what follows, in fact delivering not merely a counsel but an opinion in the strong sense of the word, somewhere between a suggestion and an injunction. This solution implies the punctuation "I dispose them; and I counsel:"

> —and you must not come to me to take counsel, since I counsel you thus [*et non oportet proter consilium venire a me. quia ita consilio tibi*]

The presence of the *et* in *et non oportet* poses a problem. After "and I counsel" (*et consilio*), we expect "that you must not come" (*non oportet*). The systematic use of *et* at the beginning of phrases, however, is one of the most characteristic markers of the "humble style," which Francis customarily employs. For the learned in the Middle Ages, the humble style, lauded long before by Gregory the Great, was often an affectation of humility. But for the unlearned Francis, this simplistic level of writing was not a stylistic effect. It was not a choice, but a necessity; not a studied rhetorical device, but a level of language. Moreover, in medieval Latin manuscripts, *et* very often stands in for punctuation. Diverted from its main meaning, the preposition no longer acts as a coordinating conjunction, but rather becomes a pause signaling the beginning of another phrase.

The text of the Spoleto note does have rudimentary punctuation. Thus a comma follows the first *consilio*, at the end of the preceding phrase. Unlike our modern usage, medieval punctuation does not divide up a phrase's syntax. Instead, it signals vocal inflexions or suspensions. It is not grammatical but musical. The medieval writer who put a comma after *consilio* (Francis, or Leo completing Francis's work) was thus indicating that a pause (vocal and mental) should precede *et non oportet*. This does not get us very far in deciding the substance of the question.

Between *non* and *oportet*, Francis first wrote *dopor*, which he then erased; he probably intended to say "after [*dopo*] you have received this advice, you do not need to come back again." He committed his delicious Italianism with *venire a me*, which Leo corrected by adding a superscript *d* to the *a* (to make the correct Latin word *ad*). The note's recipient also filled in the missing letter to complete *proter* as *propter* (for, in order to).

The verb *oportet*, employed three times elsewhere in Francis's writings, expresses a necessity with a strong sense of obligation (used here in the negative). Yet Leo is not forbidden to come to Francis absolutely; he is forbidden to come *proter consilium*. To translate these two words as "to receive a counsel" or "to [ask for] some advice" would be to transform the juridical into the anecdotal. Again in this case there is no need to add an article in modern English; it is "for counsel" in a general sense, "because of counsel," that Leo is not to come. That is, he is not to come for anything pertaining to the arrangements of institutional life that the mother issues and makes explicit to her sons in the functional decrees making up her "counsels."

The reason for the prohibition is quickly given: "since I counsel you thus" (*quia ita consilio tibi*). *Quia* here retains its classical sense of a conjunction signaling causal subordination ("since"), indeed of a coordinating conjunction ("for" meaning "because"), whereas in its earlier occurrence (*dico tibi* . . . *quia*) it had the very common medieval sense of a conjunction that introduces the completing subordinate clause ("I say to you . . . that"). Leo no longer has to come for an oral opinion, precisely because Francis is going to state this opinion in writing.

We have seen that the *et* at the beginning of the phrase raises a first problem. A second stems from the fact that this phrase, introduced by "and I counsel" (*et consilio*), itself ends by announcing another counsel: "thus I counsel you" (*ita consilio tibi*). In fact, these two problems are actually one, and they have a single solution. The phrase that follows immediately after "and I counsel" (*et consilio*) is not actually the contents of that counsel. It is an interjection, containing a last warning from Francis at the moment of delivering his verdict (which we will mark off with dashes): "I counsel—and you must not come to me for counsel, since I counsel you thus—": at this climactic point the two "I counsel's" merge. The "counsel" itself will follow.

> In whatever manner seems to you best to please the Lord God and to follow his footsteps and his poverty, do this, with the blessing of the Lord God and my obedience [*in qocumque modo melius videtur tibi placere domino deo et sequi vestigia et paupertatem suam faciatis cum beneditione domini dei et mea obedientia*].

Here at last we arrive at the heart of Francis's message! The phrase is complex. We have to read it slowly, one section at a time.

> In whatever manner seems to you best to please the Lord God [*in qocumque modo melius videtur tibi placere domino deo*]

The verb "seems" (*videtur*) was first written *visodetur*, then corrected by Francis. The pronoun "to you" (*tibi*) was added above the line, abbreviated as a *t* with a superscript *i*. The place where this addition is to be inserted, between *videtur* and *placere*, is indicated by a double bar, which yields "seems to you to please" (*videtur tibi placere*). The question is to know who made the addition. Giulia Ammannati has suggested that the pronoun *tibi* might have been added by Leo;[100] with this manipulation, the young secretary would have tried to give himself a sort of unwarranted authority over the community of brothers, setting himself up as their collective conscience, invested with the role of determining what was best for them, and, consequently, what they should do.

A conspiracy theory is always seductive. But we must guard against it. I reject this interpretation for two reasons. For one thing, such a manipulation hardly seems compatible with what we know about Leo's practice as a witness to Francis, in particular in the *Assisi Compilation*. The former secretary certainly felt himself appointed as guardian of the memory of Francis's life, but he saw himself precisely as a scrupulously exact repository of this memory—as a zealous guardian, not a manipulator. When Leo's memory inevitably did transform his recollections—for instance, concerning the role of clerics and lay brothers at the Portiuncula—he still acted in good faith, manipulated by his memory rather than manipulating it. At the time of his writing, twenty years later, Leo's day-to-day reality was superimposed on his recollections of Francis's life. But above all, he never ever claimed the spotlight for himself, never made himself the star. Never did he give himself any role other than to be in his master's shadow. Leo's sole ambition was to be the "little sheep," not the shepherd. Moreover, from a

---

100. Giulia Ammannati, "La lettera autografa di Francesco d'Assisi a frate Leone," in *Il linguaggio della biblioteca. Scritti in onore di Diego Maltese*, ed. M. Guerrini (Florence, 1994), 73–87.

paleographical point of view, Attilio Bartoli Langeli thinks that the addition is in Francis's hand.[101] And after having carefully examined all the *t*'s in the note, I happily concur in this opinion.

Why then did Francis, as author, insert this *tibi* after the fact? "Do what seems best to please the Lord God" would have set up an ambiguous command, opening the door to endless debates: Who can say what is pleasing to God? The addition of *tibi* sealed off the opening while diving into the dilemma: it is up to you to decide; that is, it is not up to you alone, Leo, to decide for all the brothers; rather it is up to each one of you to decide for himself. To my mind, this added *tibi* should be interpreted in accordance with an expression that is found three times in the *Assisi Compilation*, precisely at the heart of Leo's recollections: "in the person of all the brothers" (*in persona omnium fratrum*). A provincial minister is worried about preserving his books. Although he is alone with Francis, he becomes "you" in the plural when Francis addresses him directly, because in the founder's eyes he suddenly represents a collective person:

> Seeing how disturbed he was, the blessed Francis said to him, with intensity of spirit, as if he represented the totality of brothers [*in persona omnium fratrum*]: "You, Lesser Brothers, want to be regarded and called by all as observers of the holy Gospel, but in your deeds you want to have a nest egg stashed away!"[102]

In addressing Leo "in the person of all the brothers," and all the brothers in the person of Leo, what lesson did Francis want to teach?

Commentators on the Spoleto note usually imagine it as Francis's response to a tormented brother. The hypothesis is constructed by means of analogy: we know, in fact, that Francis's other autograph, the Assisi *chartula* that preserves the *Praises of the Most High God* and the blessing to Leo ("May the Lord bless you, Brother Leo"), was given by Francis to his secretary in order to free him from a grave spiritual temptation. The episode, concerning an anonymous brother whom we can recognize as Leo, is recounted by Thomas of Celano in the *Memorial*:

> While the saint was secluded in a cell on Mount La Verna, one of his companions was yearning with great desire to have an encouraging writing taken from the words of our Lord, written briefly by St. Francis with his own hand. He believed that by this means he would be set free from a serious temptation which oppressed him, not in the flesh but in the spirit, or at least he could bear it more easily. Growing weary with this desire, he

---

101. Attilio Bartoli Langeli, *Gli autografi di frate Francesco e di frate Leone* (Turnhout, 2000).
102. *FF*, 1640 (chap. 102); *FAED*, 2:206.

feared to express it to the most holy father. But what man did not tell him, *the Spirit revealed* to him (I Corinthians 2:10). One day, St. Francis called this brother and said, "Bring me a sheet and ink, because I want to write down the words of the Lord and his praises upon which I have *meditated in my heart* (Psalms 77:1)." As soon as what he had asked for was brought to him, he wrote down with his own hand the *Praises of the Lord* and the words he wanted and, at the end, a blessing of that brother, saying: "Take this sheet for yourself and guard it carefully to your dying day." Immediately, the whole temptation was put to flight. The letter was preserved, and it later worked wonders.[103]

The note to Brother Leo is also addressed to a man—the same one, in fact—in deep distress. The young brother wants to be sure of doing the right thing, according to Francis's "counsel." But the general rule is not enough for him. He needs constant personal reassurance: reassurance about what he should do; even more, reassurance about Francis's affection for him. Far from offering his friend an exceptional place in the community, Francis gives him the only teaching that can free him from his personal torment, by reminding him of how ordinary his situation is in the eyes of the institution: what goes for him goes for all, what goes for all goes for him.

Thus his master offers Leo the opportunity to understand that the very fact that he believes himself set apart proves that he is just like everyone else, because it is at the moment when each one feels himself different that he shares the common condition and experiences it most intimately. Everyone is like everyone else: according to René Girard, this is the ultimate lesson taught by the greatest literary works, the "novelistic truth" against the "romantic lie."[104] Or, to use Jean Genet's words, Francis guides Leo toward

> that precious point where the human being would be led back to his most irreducible quality: his solitude in being exactly equivalent to any other.[105]

But in so doing, Francis acknowledges in Leo (and, through him, in all the brothers) a dizzying capacity to examine freely and to choose: to assess what is able "to please the Lord God." The exact manner matters little: "in whatever manner" (*in qocumque modo*). Each one is the judge, in his own conscience, not of how to act in a manner pleasing to himself, but of how to act in a man-

---

103. *FF*, 490 (chap. 20); *FAED*, 2:280.

104. René Girard, *Deceit, Desire and the Novel: Self and Other in Literary Structure*, trans. Yvonne Freccero (Baltimore, 1965).

105. Jean Genet, "The Studio of Alberto Giacometti," in *The Selected Writings of Jean Genet*, ed. and introduced by Edmund White (Hopewell, NJ, 1995), 316.

ner that it seems to him will be pleasing to God. There is perfect agreement, in the community, on the goal to be attained, and on the freedom for each one to choose the manner of achieving it.

> . . . to please the Lord God and to follow his footsteps and his poverty, do this, with the blessing of the Lord God and my obedience [*placere domino deo et sequi vestigia et paupertatem suam faciatis cum beneditione domini dei et mea obedientia*].

This "Lord God" (*Domino Deo*) is at once "God" (*Deo*) generally, and Christ (*Domino*) more specifically. Not that *Dominus* may not be used to address the Trinity or the Father, but in light of what follows, "to please God" would not be adequate. It says either too much or too little. We need here some points of reference, and such historical points of comparison do exist. It is necessary "to follow his footsteps" (*sequi vestigia*), the footsteps of the Lord, of the Son, of God made flesh, echoing Peter's first epistle (2:21), "that you should follow his footsteps," and St. Jerome's ascetic adage "to follow naked the naked Christ." Poverty is the very essence of this following of Christ. The pairing of the verbs "to please . . . and to follow" (*placere . . . et sequi*) continues into a doubling of their objects: "his footsteps and his poverty" (*vestigia et paupertatem suam*), if we understand that the possessive adjective *suam*, which agrees with *paupertatem* due to its proximity, applies equally to *vestigia*.

Taken together, the sequence creates a kind of narrowing or focusing of the field. To please God is to follow in the footsteps of his incarnation; and what epitomizes this fall of God to earth, mirroring Adam's fall but bearing the promise of redemption, is the loss of everything, poverty. The Incarnation is the most radical of denudings, of dispossessions, of renunciations of power, because it is the renunciation of omnipotence. Having dreamed of climbing the social ladder and thrilled to pretensions of prestige, Francis felt the Incarnation as a physical fall, from heaven to earth, from the Most High to the Most Low, a salvific descent. The free choice that is left to the brothers, to each brother, is oriented and given magnetic force by the message of the Gospel, the example of Christ, and the Franciscan value that follows from it: poverty.

If Leo and the brothers follow Christ in the very essence of his nature and of his human experience, poverty, then they will naturally gain the approval and favor of the Lord God who had shown the way—"with the blessing of the Lord God" (*cum beneditione Domini Dei*)—and they will have fulfilled the obedience that they promised Francis according to the terms of the Rule—"and my obedience" (*et mea obedientia*). Such is Francis's last wish for Leo, who becomes, at the end of the first part of the note, the representative of all the brothers.

III. MATERNAL GOVERNMENT

A brief insertion of Francis's writing within Clare of Assisi's Form of Life is usually called the *Last Wish*. What "counsel" (*consilium*) does he give the women there? To live in poverty.[106] In the *Regula non bullata*, he had laid down this precept: "Let all the brothers devote themselves to following the humility and poverty of our Lord Jesus Christ."[107] There is only one rule, and it applies to all: to Leo and his brothers, to Francis, to Clare and her sisters. It all comes down to poverty.

A potential space for democracy (because, in the end, it is only ever a question of that) comes not so much, as we too often think, from the development of scrupulous procedures of designation, representation, debate, or voting, or even from popular pressure that would guarantee democracy its universal basis. The possible arrival of democracy (necessarily a permanent and internal invention) emerges from a sort of call from the void to the summit, a void through the pursuit of humility. The pastor is always on the verge of resignation. Government is a power resigned in advance.

---

106. *Scripta*, 382; *CAED*, 118.
107. *Scripta*, 256 (chap. 9); *FAED*, 1:70.

6. Resumption

Sicut mater. It's hard for us to admit that a maternal figure can express more than just sentiment or an overflowing tenderness, that it can also stand as an institutional metaphor. To sharpen my interpretive reversal for the original draft of the Spoleto note, from maternal affection to maternal government, let's throw caution to the wind and transpose into masculine terms the juridical disposition that Francis wanted to express in the feminine:

> To Brother Leo your father Francis, greetings and strength. I tell you thus, my son, as father, that all the words which we said on the road, I order them, briefly, in this decree; and I prescribe—and you are forbidden to come to me for prescriptions concerning the Order, since I prescribe for you thus: in whatever manner seems to you best to please the Lord God and to follow his footsteps and his poverty, do this, with the blessing of the Lord God and in the obedience that you owe me!

Producing this imagined version lets us appreciate just how inconceivable it really is. No sooner do we see it, than we have to tear it up in our minds. But this nonsensical translation has the merit of demonstrating, through its very absurdity, that a father figure would hardly give free rein to his power only so that in the end he could order "do what you think best." The heart of Francis's message is evangelical poverty. Motherhood is the institutional application of this poverty, a representation of the "renunciation of power," to use the title of Michael Cusato's majestic work.[108] It is a poverty that decidedly transcends gender, because here is the full citation of the *Last Wish* addressed by Francis to Clare's sisters:

> I, little brother Francis, wish to follow the life and poverty of our most high Lord Jesus Christ and of his most holy Mother and *to persevere* in this *until the end* (Matthew 10:22). And I ask you, my ladies, and I give you counsel to always live in this most holy life and poverty. And be very careful that you never depart from this in any way, through the teachings or counsel of anyone.[109]

Mary's appearance here may be related to the fact that this text was addressed to women. But from the outset, "little brother Francis" and the sisters alike must follow Mary and Christ, a Christ shorn of his omnipotence to become a man. This destitution, this denuding, this dispossession, this shedding

---

108. Michael F. Cusato, "La renonciation au pouvoir chez les frères mineurs au XIIIe siècle," Ph.D. diss. (Université Paris-IV, 1991).
109. *Scripta*, 382; *CAED*, 118.

of all wealth and dominance cannot be extolled with thundering paternal power, because that would directly contradict the intended message. At the most (that is, at the least), there is nothing but to become a mother, to become a woman as Christ became a man, to offer counsel that directs each one to use his or her own best judgment.

In the Spoleto note, Francis sets Leo, and through him all the brothers, face to face with God and their own freedom. The final order is given in the name of obedience even while removing obedience as an external constraint, since the same result can be reached by the exercise of internal free will, which in turn reinforces the subject's adherence to the original order.

But doesn't the leader's retreat run the risk of bordering on abandonment? Might not respect for each person's freedom lead to the abdication of all responsibility toward others? So Francis recommences. More than an expression of remorse or even of repentance, the note's last four lines are really a resumption: Francis resumes the course of his writing; he restarts, and he recaptures Leo in a net whose mesh is finer than that of institutional snares: the government of the soul.

> And if it is necessary to you, and if you wish, that your soul return to me for another consolation of yours, come [*et si tibi est necesarium animam tuam propter aliam consolationem tuam et vis revenire a me veni*]!

The *v* of *revenire* ("return"), according to Attilio Bartoli Langeli, may have covered up the *Tau*-cross that Francis would have used as a kind of signature at the bottom of the first draft of his note. The writer's Italianism (*a me*) is again corrected by the addition of a superscript *d* in Leo's hand (*ad me*).

If the final change of heart of the Spoleto note rests on an opposition in terms of genre (institutional direction versus spiritual welcome), there is still no fundamental contradiction. Once again, Francis's vocabulary proves this point. He does not open his last phrase with a conjunction signaling strong or weak opposition (*sed, tamen, autem, vero* . . .), but with a simple *et* ("and"). The grammatical term for this is "parataxis"; the two phrases are set one next to the other without syntactical hierarchy. Both are equally true.

Concerning the internal construction of the phrase, Carlo Paolazzi's hypothesis might seem grammatically far-fetched; following the impersonal verb construction "it is necessary" (*est necesarium*), the accusative "your soul" (*animam tuam*) would be the subject of "return" (*revenire*), the verb in the infinitive clause. I believe this hypothesis is not only grammatically well-founded, but spiritually profound.

The subject is no longer Leo, the brother who is a member of the community of brothers, but Leo's soul, Leo's person in the sense that cannot be reduced to any common identity. This is always the implication of the word "soul" in Francis's writings. Because what makes everyone just like everyone else is the fact that everyone is unique—"entirely defined by its beneficence," "a power of care," "pastoral power is an individualizing power," as Michel Foucault suggests.[110]

In the last four lines of the Spoleto note, the second person singular (*tibi, tuam, tuam, vis, veni*) appears with notably greater frequency than in the fifteen preceding lines (*tuo, tibi, tibi, tibi*). In Francis's other writings, the soul's reservation (what we would call the conscience clause) is the only possible justification for withholding obedience. Leo may thus legitimately, indeed legally, feel the necessity for his soul to return to Francis.

For what reason? "For another consolation of yours" (*propter aliam consolationem tuam*). The adjective "another" poses a problem at first reading, because up to now it has not been a question of "consolation," but of "counsel." And the rule that has just been laid down remains inviolable: Brother Leo must not return "for counsel," for whatever counsel it might be, for this one or any other. But his soul may return for "consolation" (*consolationem*). The adjective "another" does not, in my opinion, distinguish this consolation from an earlier one; rather it indicates that "consolation" is of a different nature than "counsel." Leo's soul may not return for the same reason (counsel), but "for another" reason (consolation).

Grammatically speaking, "and if you wish" (*et vis*) is on the same level as "and if it is necessary to you": "if it is necessary to you and if you wish that your soul return." But in the Latin phrasing, "and if you wish" comes after the infinitive clause that it cogoverns. Concerning this proposition as well—whether to come or not to come—Leo, in the final analysis, is the sole judge. In strict parallel with his treatment of the community at large, Francis leaves it up to Leo in the end. Finally, shedding his own will, he can only let fall, as one lets fall a last bag of ballast, the single word "come" (*veni*).

In Thomas of Celano's *Memorial*, Francis sketches the portrait of the ideal minister general:

> He must be a man, he says, of very austere life, of great discernment, and of praiseworthy reputation. A man without personal affection, lest by loving some more than others, he creates scandal for all. A man to whom the ardor of holy prayer is a friend, who can devote certain hours to his soul and others to the flock entrusted to him. In early morning he must put first the sacrament of the mass, and with prolonged devotion commend

---

110. Foucault, *Security, Territory, Population*, 126–28.

himself and his flock to divine protection. After prayer, he says, let him resolve to be plucked in public by all, to respond to all, and provide for all with meekness.[111]

The shepherd becomes a mother hen; the flock becomes a brood. The hagiographic passage retraces the double movement of the Spoleto note. Francis begins by refusing to give in to his personal affection for Leo, but in the end he allows himself to be "plucked" by him, as he must be by each of his brothers. It is a Franciscan reversal, an evangelical reversal, a pastoral reversal that did not escape Michel Foucault:

> But, inversely, the pastor must experience his responsibility as a service, and a service that makes him the servant of his sheep.[112]

Let's retrace the steps of our deciphering and bring together the two parts of the Spoleto note in our English translation:

> To Brother Leo your brother Francis, greetings and peace. Thus I say to you, my son, as mother, that all the words which we said on the road, briefly, in this word, I dispose them; and I counsel—and you must not come to me to take counsel, since I counsel you thus—: in whatever manner seems to you best to please the Lord God and to follow his footsteps and his poverty, do this, with the blessing of the Lord God and my obedience! And if it is necessary to you that your soul return to me for another consolation of yours, and if you wish, come!

Is there a divide, a tear, between the two parts of the note? At the risk of playing with words (though what else have we been doing?), I would say there is no tear, but rather an visible tension and a deep coherence. This tension, to me, is at the center of what is sometimes called "the drama of Francis of Assisi."

Where does it come from? From his evangelical choice? Certainly not. The Gospel is Francis's joy, not his drama. The tension comes from the community itself. Nothing could be simpler than to live alone in the poverty of Christ and of his mother, and so many people live this life involuntarily. It is a truism to say that voluntary poverty is a privilege of the rich. The joy comes from the choice to lighten one's load. Poverty is no longer a lack, but a lightness. It no longer weighs down, but raises up.

To live the Gospel in a little group, in an almost informal manner, with a few very close companions, this is the golden age of any brotherhood. But the

---

111. *FF*, 605 (chap. 139); *FAED*, 2:365.
112. Foucault, *Security, Territory, Population*, 179.

desire to follow Christ leads back to the world. According to the first legend by Thomas of Celano, in the days after Innocent III approved his form of life, Francis

> chose not *to live for himself* alone, but for the One *who died for all* (2 Corinthians 5:15). He knew that he was sent for this: to win for God souls which the devil was trying to snatch away.[113]

The anguish arises from sheer numbers. Hence we see, following Michel Foucault, the role of demographic expansion and so of "the emergence of the problem of population" in the implementation of governmental techniques.[114] To reconcile poverty with settling down, simplicity with success, renunciation of power with organizational efficiency, ignorance with preaching, the individual with the collectivity, is to square the circle. From this quandary is born the question of government.

How to escape it? Shed the prerogatives of the superior and leave it up to each one's judgment? Fine. But these judgments may diverge, and then the communitarian principle is jeopardized. A majority that veers off from the original project may prevail, and the spiritual father be thrown into crisis by his sons. The change of heart of the Spoleto note bears the tangible traces of indecision.

The same tension opposes and unites the Rule and the *Testament*. What else is Francis's *Testament*, dictated in the last days of his life, if not a repentance of the Rule, a desire to hammer home *in extremis* the prescriptions from which he fears the brothers may stray?

> And let the brothers not say: "this is another Rule." Because this is a remembrance, an admonition, an exhortation, and my testament, which I, little brother Francis, make for you, my blessed brothers, that we might observe in a more catholic manner the Rule we have promised the Lord. And let the minister general and all the other ministers and custodes be bound by obedience not to add to or take away from these words. And let them always have this writing with them together with the Rule. And in all the chapters which they hold, when they read the Rule, let them also read these words. And to all my brothers, clerical and lay, I strictly forbid them, through obedience, to place any gloss upon the Rule or upon these words, saying they should be understood in this way. But as the Lord has given me to speak and write the Rule and these words simply and purely,

---

113. *FF*, 310 (chap. 14); *FAED*, 1:214.
114. Foucault, *Security, Territory, Population*, 104.

may you understand them simply and purely and without gloss, and observe them and implement them in a holy manner until the end.[115]

The Rule is not enough, hence the need for the *Testament*. But the *Testament* claims to have no other goal than to cause the Rule to be better observed. By such an "admonition," Francis in fact glosses the Rule, even as he forbids the leaders of the order to dare to gloss his *Testament*! Neither of these reference texts is supposed to be glossed; but doesn't leaving two reference texts instead of one guarantee that not only glosses but disputes will arise, in a never-ending battle between legality and legitimacy?

The autograph note to Brother Leo cannot be dated precisely, but I cannot help reading it as intimately related to Francis's resignation as minister general, to his enigmatic stepping-down on 29 September 1220. The founder ceased to be the superior that he had never wanted to be, yet he remained the spiritual director, the brother par excellence, the point of reference. He renounced power and gained authority. He transcended the institutional by means of the spiritual. He left, but remained. Remorse, repentance, or resumption? Wasn't effacing himself (as I have already suggested) a way of more subtly retaking the order in hand?

We have already cited two other writings by Francis that particularly clarify the Spoleto note: the Rule for Hermitages, for the ties between mother and sons, and the *Last Wish* addressed to Clare's sisters, for the absolute centrality of poverty in following Christ and Mary. Here is chapter 3 of the *Admonitions*, "On Perfect Obedience," which expresses more fully the irresolvable dilemma between obedience and the soul's reservation:

> The Lord says in the Gospel: *Whoever does not renounce all that he possesses cannot be my disciple* (Luke 14:33); and *Whoever wishes to save his life must lose it* (Luke 9:24). The person who offers himself totally to obedience in the hands of his prelate abandons all that he possesses and loses his body. And whatever he does and says which he knows is not contrary to his will is true obedience, provided that what he does is good. And if a subject should sometimes see that some things might be better and more useful for his soul than what the prelate commands, let him willingly sacrifice such things to God and earnestly strive to fulfill those of the prelate. For this is loving obedience, because it pleases God and neighbor. But if the prelate prescribes to the subject something contrary to his soul, even though he may not obey him, let him not, however, abandon him. And if

---

115. *Scripta*, 402; *FAED*, 1:127.

he then suffers persecution from others, let him love them all the more for the sake of God. For whoever chooses persecution rather than wish to be separated from his brothers truly remains in perfect obedience, because he lays down his soul for his brothers. In fact, there are many religious who, under the pretext of seeing things better than those which their prelates command, look back, and return to the vomit of their own will. These people are murderers and, because of their bad examples, they cause many to lose their souls.[116]

---

116. *Scripta*, 356; *FAED*, 1:130.

7. Bonds

We have explored the meaning of the Spoleto note, letter by letter and in light of its intertextual relationship with other Franciscan writings. It remains to place it in its historical context.

Francis is an "evangelical man," a man of the Gospels. He seems to continually collapse time in order to draw directly from the deep wellspring of the New Testament. The Gospels repeatedly testify to the argumentative dialogues by which Christ sent each person back to his or her own judgment. Concerning the good shepherd, must he not assume the care of his flock and at the same time be capable of abandoning it in an instant if one of his lambs wanders off? The shepherd Francis called Leo a "lamb of God." The Spoleto note's change of heart is the naked expression, in its vividly austere implementation, of what Michel Foucault called "the paradox of the shepherd":

> Here we are at the center of the challenge, of the moral and religious paradox of the shepherd, or what could be called the paradox of the shepherd: the sacrifice of one for all, and the sacrifice of all for one, which will be at the absolute heart of the Christian problematic of the pastorate.[117]

But creating this shortcut between Christ and Francis risks decontextualizing the latter. Rather than a historical figure, the Poverello can easily become transhistorical, then ahistorical. As André Vauchez has aptly reminded us, Francis was a man of the twelfth century.[118] Although he died at the end of the first quarter of the thirteenth century (where we tend to think of him), he was really the superlative expression of the evangelical ideal of the century of his birth. With the notable exception of the Cistercians, many monastic creations or reforms of the turn of the eleventh to the twelfth centuries bore as a badge of honor (as we have seen) their rejection of the Benedictine title of abbot, a rejection that Francis pushed to its limits.

A saint does not fit neatly within the arbitrarily divided and deforming framework of religious history. The twelfth century that saw the birth, in 1181, of Pietro of Bernardone's son, was also a specific social system and a particular culture. If this fact is forgotten, studies of Francis risk becoming a disembodied discourse, whether of atemporal evangelism, undifferentiated mysticism, or anachronistic psychology. The late twelfth century was the apex of feudalism, and, consequently, the beginning of its end, the very moment when the great apparatuses—church, orders, states, communes—began their rise. To be sure,

---

117. Foucault, *Security, Territory, Population*, 129.
118. André Vauchez, "François d'Assise entre littéralisme évangélique et renouveau spirituel," in *Frate Francesco d'Assisi*, 185–98.

these great machines did not abolish (not all at once, far from it) interpersonal relationships; they channeled and absorbed them more than they surpassed them. They redeployed them in the service of an empire, which, as a result, empirically increased its influence.

The genesis of the Franciscan brotherhood represents a startling acceleration, like a film on fast forward, of these slower political and social evolutions.

At the beginning, a small group of men from Assisi gathered around Francis; they were a penitential company, a quasi-family with the hue of spiritual siblings, the evangelical version (and thus the con-version) of the groups of young men aspiring to knighthood that were so effectively highlighted for northwestern France by Georges Duby,[119] and whose riotous rituals animated the cities of central Italy as well.

These men came to Francis, who received them into obedience. The bond between one man and another—homage—was immediate, physical. It rested on shared faith, on reciprocal fidelity, and on the firm expectation of a benefit to be received: salvation. The minimal Franciscan organization (of which the Rule for Hermitages represents both a utopian expression and a nostalgic longing) resulted from a basic transfer of familial relations, even if there is no *paterfamilias*, only a mother, and that office is held by each in turn.

Then staggering success raised the number of brothers into the thousands, between three and five thousand, according to the sources, by the beginning of the 1220s. Many brothers now knew Francis only by name, from afar, and he could not know them all himself. Hence we see the strange confession of Thomas of Celano in the *Life of the Blessed Francis*:

> Alas, we poor ones who have thus lost you, worthy father, model of all beneficence and humility! It is by a just judgment that we have lost you, you whom we did not take care to know when we had you![120]

Marc Bloch rightly noted, in his *Feudal Society*, that when "human contact" lessened, the bonds of vassalage weakened.[121] To save a wayward sheep, it would now not have been enough for Francis to abandon ninety-nine others to their fate. It was no longer physically possible for the mother to give herself to all her sons. At times even the companions of the early days must have felt neglected. Thus the story of brother Riccerio, once again told by Thomas of Celano in the *Life of the Blessed Francis*:

---

119. Georges Duby, "Youth in Aristocratic Society: Northwestern France in the Twelfth Century," in *The Chivalrous Society*, trans. Cynthia Postan (Berkeley, CA, 1981), 112–22.

120. *FF*, 328 (chap. 19); *FAED*, 1:229.

121. Marc Bloch, *Feudal Society*, trans. L. A. Manyon (Chicago, 1961), 1:236–38.

A certain brother named Riccerio, noble by birth but more noble in character, full of love of God and disdain for himself, was led by a spirit of piety and an unfailing will to seek out and fully obtain, if he could, the favor of the holy father Francis; but he feared greatly that the holy Francis would detest him, out of some secret judgment, and thus he would be kept apart from the favor of his affection. That brother, since he was fearful, thought that any person the holy man Francis loved with profound charity was also worthy to merit divine favor. On the other hand, he thought that someone to whom he did not show himself kindly and pleasant would incur the wrath of the supreme Judge.[122]

Francis discerned Riccerio's secret trouble and said to him:

"Let no temptation disturb you, son, let no thought torment you, because you are most dear to me; know that, among those I cherish most, you are worthy of my love and my familiarity. Have no fear to come to me whenever you like, knowing you are welcome, and let our familiarity make you eloquent."[123]

But for every brother such as Riccerio who was consoled, how many others felt worried or, conversely, indifferent? Overextended by his success, the founder had a vision related in the *Legend of the Three Companions*:

He saw a hen, small and black, with feathered legs and the feet of a domestic dove. She had so many chicks that she was unable to gather them all under her wings, and so they wandered around her in circles. Waking from sleep, he began to think about this vision. Immediately, he understood by means of the Holy Spirit that it was he who was symbolized by the hen. "I am that hen," he said, "short in stature, and dark by nature. I must be simple like a dove and fly up to heaven on the feathered strokes of virtue. The Lord in his mercy has given and will give to me many sons, whom I will not be able to protect with my own strength. I must therefore commend them to the holy church so that she may protect and guide them under the shadow of her wings."[124]

Thus the bond is made between Francis, once more a mother, and our "holy mother the Roman Church." The word "religion" is etymologically tied to the Latin verbs *ligare* and *religare*, meaning to "bind" or "unite." The inclusion of this "lesser" religion in the larger church was a major preoccupation for Francis. It

---

122. *FF*, 324 (chap. 18); *FAED*, 1:226.
123. *FF*, 324 (chap. 18); *FAED*, 1:229.
124. *FF*, 1436 (chap. 16); *FAED*, 2:105.

was important for him that this bound-together group of men be just as tightly bound to the church. The idea of Francis as a dreamy innocent manipulated by the papacy is absurd; it was he who initiated a dependence that was not only voluntary but ardently desired by him.

At the very beginning of the Franciscan brotherhood, in 1209, Francis went deliberately to place himself under the direct authority of Pope Innocent III. The "religion" and then the Order of the Lesser Brothers were firmly anchored to the apostolic See. Hence we have the openings of the two Rules, that of 1221 and that of 1223, both of which are subsequent to Francis's resignation of his responsibilities:

> This is the life that Brother Francis petitioned the lord pope to grant and confirm for him. And he did grant and confirm it for him and for his brothers present and to come. Let Brother Francis and whoever will be the head of this religion promise obedience and reverence to the Lord Pope Innocent and his successors. And let the other brothers be bound to obey Brother Francis and his successors.[125]

> The rule and life of the Lesser Brothers is this: to observe the holy Gospel of our Lord Jesus Christ, by living in obedience, without anything of one's own, and in chastity. Brother Francis promises obedience and reverence to the Lord Pope Honorius and to his canonically elected successors and to the Roman Church. And let the other brothers be bound to obey Brother Francis and his successors.[126]

The 1221 Rule affirms that the initiative for this inclusion came from Francis; the grant and confirmation were received from Pope Innocent III. As "head of this religion," Francis promised obedience to the pope, and all the brothers in turn were held to obey Francis. The Rule of 1223 confirms this disposition and, in a formulation close to Stephen of Muret's *Book on Doctrine* ("There is no other rule than the Gospel of Christ"), recalls that the unique point of reference for the life of the Lesser Brothers is "the holy Gospel of our Lord Jesus Christ."[127]

Chapter 2 of the 1221 *Regula non bullata* envisioned that the ministers would receive new recruits, who would owe them obedience. But Jordan of Giano's *Chronicle* reveals that up to 1219 the reception of new brothers remained the prerogative of Francis alone. So at the beginning the community worked and

---

125. *Scripta*, 242; *FAED*, 1:63.
126. *Scripta*, 322; *FAED*, 1:100.
127. *Scripta*, 322; *FAED*, 1:100.

meshed with the church through interlocking interpersonal relationships that pivoted around Francis.

At the end of the founder's life, the system had become more complex and better publicized, but his prerogatives had not changed. In the secular world, one would have said that the brothers were Francis's men and that he was their lord. Here, they are his sons and he is their mother. No matter: the bond between individuals, guaranteed by faith, is at the center of the Franciscan religion, just as it is at the heart of the feudal system. But it is used to build an order, just as the channeled feudalism of this period contributed to the tightening hold of princes and kings over lords and, more paradoxically, of the pope himself over princes and kings.

Let's return to two centuries earlier, to before 9 June 1021, the moment when the ideology of fealty found detailed expression in the famous letter written by Fulbert, bishop of Chartres, to Duke William of Aquitaine. This might seem to take us a long way in space and time from the Assisi that saw Francis's birth near the end of 1181. But Fulbert's successor, Yves of Chartres, integrated this letter into his canon law collection, the *Panormia*, and from there it passed into Gratian's twelfth-century *Decretum*, where the name Fulbert was deformed as "Philibert."

The "Letter of Philibert" occupies a prime place in title 6, book 2 of the *Books of Fiefs*, the famous collection of customary feudal law gathered in northern Italy during the twelfth century. One of the first great glossators to use both the *Books of Fiefs* and the *Letter of Philibert* was Pillius, when he began teaching at Modena in 1182. From the first decades of the thirteenth century on, Fulbert of Chartres's letter stands as the principle reference for oaths of fealty, where such evidence survives, in Italy as well as in southern France. Alfons Becker details the way Fulbert's letter was used by the Roman See:

> The oaths of fealty [sworn to the pope] for which we have the texts, from the oaths of the Normans of Italy in 1059 to that of King John of England in 1213, all contained the core of the *Forma fidelitatis* of Fulbert of Chartres, with additional mention of the characteristic duties of Roman vassalage.[128]

There is no question, obviously, of claiming that Francis of Assisi was implementing the *Books of Fiefs*. But this merchant's son, driven by social ambition, had been imbued with chivalric ideology and courtly culture. As Jean-Claude

---

128. Alfons Becker, "Politique féodale de la papauté à l'égard des rois et des princes (XIe–XIIe siècles)," in *Chiesa e mondo feudale nei secoli X–XII* (Milan, 1995), 432.

Maire Vigueur has stressed, the knightly elites of the Italian cities, in the era when communes were directed by consuls and then *podestà*, possessed real legal competence.[129] Moreover, Francis, who must have spent a good fifteen years of his life in writing his brotherhood's Rule with the help of the Roman curia's experts in canon law, had undeniable experience with legal texts.

Here is the conclusion from Fulbert of Chartres's letter to Duke William:

> So it remains that . . . [the vassal] should faithfully give his lord counsel and aid if he wishes to seem worthy of his benefice and to acquit himself of the fealty he has sworn. The lord should give the same to his vassal . . . If he did not do so, he would be justly judged to be of bad faith, just as the vassal would be found perfidious or perjured if he was shown to have failed to fulfill his obligations in doing them or in consenting to them.[130]

The system described in this way is founded on fealty sworn by the vassal and supported by the "benefice" received from the lord, which enlisted the vassal as surely as his oath. The bond between the two men was asymmetrical, but it still created a reciprocal obligation: "The lord should give the same to his vassal." Thus the lord as much as the vassal owes "counsel and aid," or he risks being held perfidious and perjured. As Pierre Toubert emphasizes in his *Structures du Latium*, oaths played a crucial role in the region around Rome and in the territories of the Patrimony of St. Peter, at the origin of the papal state:

> In the establishment of bonds between men, the oath always constituted the essential element in our region. On this point, Roman legal traditions and church ideology joined perfectly. The former promoted the importance of consensual declarations in concluding contracts. The latter arranged its conception of ideal relations between men or communities around faith [*fides*].[131]

Let's now transpose this doctrine of fidelity to two centuries later. Francis is Leo's mother, a "lord" who does not want the title. When the young Leo joined the fraternity, he had been received by Francis personally; Leo gave himself to him, in his hands, and made himself Francis's "vassal" in promising him obedience. From then on, they owed each other, both of them, "counsel and aid." The Spoleto note, in its two sections, reflects these two promises. Francis first

---

129. Jean-Claude Maire Vigueur, *Cavaliers et citoyens: guerre, conflits et société dans l'Italie communale, XIIe–XIIIe siècles* (Paris, 2003).
130. Frederick Behrends, ed., *The Letters and Poems of Fulbert of Chartres* (Oxford, 1976), 93.
131. Pierre Toubert, *Les structures du Latium médiéval. Le Latium méridional et la Sabine du IXe à la fin du XIIe siècle* (Rome, 1973), **2**:1141.

gives his "counsel." He thinks he has discharged his duty, but then understands that he has failed in one of his obligations. He resumes—quickly, I think—and then offers the spiritual form of "aid" referred to as "consolation."

The parallel between the two systems, feudal and religious, is not exact. In the former one swears, in the latter one promises—on one hand fealty, on the other obedience—and both sets of values are much older than either feudalism or the new orders. Yet entrance into vassalage and entrance into religion both create a hierarchical link (whatever Francis might say, he is indeed considered by the pope as "head of this religion") and at the same time a society of equals united by reciprocal exchange. This also creates the conditions of "governmentality," because Olivier Guyotjeannin's profound reflection applies to both worlds, the feudal and the religious: "Aid and counsel, which goes well beyond the feudal field, is the privileged site for the art of government."[132]

In the secular realm, just as in the church, the usage—in fact, the diversion—of interpersonal ties allowed the construction of an institution that integrated and ultimately transcended them. In *The Beginning of the Order*, Brother John recounts the inclusion of the lesser (Franciscan) religion in the greater church. Francis goes first to find Cardinal Hugolino, bishop of Ostia, the future Pope Gregory IX:

> Seeing [Francis], the cardinal received him with joy and said: "I offer myself to you for counsel, aid, and protection as you wish, and I want you to remember me in your prayers.[133]

Francis then obtains Honorius III's agreement that Hugolino should become cardinal protector of his "religion":

> After this, having received this commission from the lord pope, the lord bishop of Ostia, raising his hand to protect the brothers, sent letters to many bishops where the brothers had experienced hardships, so that they would not be opposed to the brothers, but rather give them counsel and aid in preaching and living in their provinces, as good and religious men approved by the church.[134]

The exchange of "counsel and aid" thus applies from the top to the bottom of the feudal and ecclesiastical pyramid. It cements it.

---

132. Olivier Guyotjeannin, "1060–1285," in *Le Moyen Âge. Le roi, l'Église, les grands, le peuple, 481–1514*, ed. Philippe Contamine (Paris, 2002), 275.
133. *FF*, 1346 (chap. 10); *FAED*, 2:55.
134. *FF*, 1348 (chap. 11); *FAED*, 2:56–57.

In his *Testament*, Francis recalls the beginnings of the brotherhood:

> And after the Lord gave me [*dedit mihi*] some brothers, no one showed me what I had to do, but the Most High himself revealed to me [*revelavit mihi*] that I should live according to the form of the Holy Gospel. And I had this written down simply and in a few words and the lord pope confirmed it for me.[135]

If Francis of Assisi cannot leave Leo without an answer and without seeing him again, if he cannot abandon to their fate the men who had given themselves to him, if he cannot entirely follow through with his resignation, it is because the words of Christ according to the Gospel of John (17: 6–8) run over and over again through is mind:

> I have manifested your name to the men whom, from this world, you have given me [*dedisti mihi*]. They were yours, and you gave them to me [*mihi eos dedisti*], and they have kept your word. Now they know that all that you have given me [*dedisti mihi*], comes from you. Because the words that you have given me [*dedisti mihi*], I have given to them. And they have received them, and they know truly that I came out from you, and they have believed that you sent me.

These "givings" of men must have resonated with the feudal background to create unbreakable obligations in Francis's mind. The change of heart of the Spoleto note carries the echoes of these bonds as well.

---

135. *Scripta*, 396; *FAED*, 1:125.

Afterword

Francis's note to Leo is like a preliminary sketch that allows us to examine "the embryonic point of this governmentality" whose history Michel Foucault proposed to bring to light.[1] There are multiple points of contact and reciprocal illumination between Foucault's course of 1977–1978, especially the lectures delivered between 8 February and 1 March 1978, and Francis's autograph note. It would be tedious to enumerate and comment on all of them. Most are readily apparent and speak for themselves. I will concentrate instead on only the most intriguing.

When he proposed to identify "some of the points of resistance, of the forms of attack and counter-attack that could appear within the field of the pastorate," Michel Foucault warned that there is "an immediate and foundational correlation between conduct and counter-conduct."[2]

In light of the experiments described in the second part of this little book, which sought to put unworthiness in power, and in view of the Franciscan experience of maternal government, I tend to think that "counter-conducts" are even more essential to the pastorate than Foucault imagined; that the pastorate begins with an original transgression that borders on an original sin

---

1. Michel Foucault, *Security, Territory, Population: Lectures at the Collège de France, 1977–1978*, ed. Michel Senellart, general eds. François Ewald and Alessandro Fontana, trans. Graham Burchell, English series ed. Arnold I. Davidson (New York, 2007), 165.

2. Ibid., 194, 196.

and allows the pastor to emerge from the flock and become its head; or, more exactly, that it isolates a group of people and transforms them into a flock through the emergence of the shepherd. The pastor issues the rule precisely because he has transgressed the law.

At the heart of the vast panorama that Michel Foucault sketches from antiquity to modernity, an unforeseen effect of his unfolding thought is the way, almost against his will, the central and decisive place of the Middle Ages is revealed. This treasure trove moves me to offer three reflections, concerning three encounters.

On the social level, there was an encounter between the Christian pastorate and the feudal system, where the latter played the role of catalyst for pastoral potential. In a well-known article, Jacques Le Goff affirms that "there is nothing specifically Christian in the feudal-vassalic ritual."[3] Perhaps this is true. But whatever the different genealogies of these two systems of organization, the religious and the secular, each individual and the entire social body experienced them within an overall ideological coherence, reinforced by the permeability and interchangeability of their vocabularies: faith, faithful, fidelity, fealty, between the hands, benefice, *militia*, service, ministry, concord, counsel and aid, charity . . . the structural coherence of medieval society lies in this productive ambiguity.

On the governmental level, Francis of Assisi's note to Leo signals another hybridity, between pastorate and motherhood, between pastoral power and maternal government. Here again the perspective is neither genealogical nor archeological, and I would carefully refrain from suggesting any point of fusion between patriarchy and matriarchy. Francis's government was strictly a male affair.

But the confrontation between Clare of Assisi's experience, explored in the first part of this book, and Francis's experience, which drives the third part, suggests that the governing position implies, to a more or less explicit degree and in a more or less pronounced manner, a reversal of gender. The mother abbess must become the father, while, as Caroline Bynum has shown, the father abbot, following Christ, must also be the mother in order to fulfill completely his pastoral paternity.[4] The "complete" pastor must take responsibility for the totality of his parental status. Even God. On her deathbed, Clare murmured to her soul:

---

3. Jacques Le Goff, "The Symbolic Ritual of Vassalage," in *Time, Work, and Culture in the Middle Ages*, trans. Arthur Goldhammer (Chicago, 1980), 284.

4. Caroline Walker Bynum, *Jesus as Mother: Studies in the Spirituality of the High Middle Ages* (Berkeley, 1982).

Go in peace, because you will have a good escort, for he who created you has first made you holy. After he created you, he put in you the Holy Spirit, and he has always watched over you as the mother watches over her son whom she loves.[5]

In his relationship to Brother Leo, Francis is completely pastor and completely mother. As pastor, he moves, guides, goes out to search, then returns. As mother, he settles, governs, disposes, waits, welcomes. The pastor "does everything for the totality of his flock, but he does everything also for each sheep of the flock"[6]: exactly the same goes for the mother hen for all of her brood and for each of her chicks.

A third encounter lies on the level of chronology. According to Michel Foucault, the Old Testament put in place certain pastoral elements that assumed their full significance only with the New Testament:

> The real history of the pastorate, as the source of a specific type of power over men, the history of the pastorate as a model, as a matrix of procedures for the government of men, this history of the pastorate in the Western world really only begins with Christianity.[7]

We could say, by analogy, that the church fathers of the first Christian centuries prepared the pastoral material, which came to the fore and took full effect only with the eleventh-century Gregorian reform.

The reign of Emperor Louis the Pious seems, in this light, like a kind of ninth-century dress rehearsal. Telling signs point in this direction: the diffusion of the Benedictine Rule under the authority of the emperor and through the efforts of Benedict of Aniane; the writing of "mirrors of princes"—the *Royal Way* by Smaragdus of Saint-Mihiel for Louis before his accession to the imperial title, *On the Royal Office* by Jonas of Orléans for Louis's son Pepin I of Aquitaine—which tried to inject the pastoral model into royal government; the public penances of the emperor in 822 and 833. Let's remember that among the four principles that construct the Christian pastorate as described by Michel Foucault is "the principle of alternate correspondence"[8]: if the weaknesses of the flock are necessary for the pastor's merit, the weaknesses of the pastor, because he repents of them in his humility, contribute to the edification and salvation of the sheep. At the instigation of the bishops and

---

5. *Legenda S. Clarae*, 196 (chap. 29); *CAED*, 317.
6. Foucault, *Security, Territory, Population*, 128.
7. Ibid., 147–48.
8. Ibid., 171.

with the active complicity of his sons, Louis the Pious's imperial power was indeed eroded by the injection of the pastoral model.

What the ninth century tried to accomplish through insinuation, the eleventh achieved through confrontation. The Gregorian reform was a battle for the liberty of the church against secular powers, accompanied by the diffusion of a heightened awareness of individual guilt and of the search for salvation for all and for each one. *Omnes et singulatim.* A selection of citations from Michel Foucault on the pastorate could easily be used to characterize the ecclesiastical reforms of the eleventh and twelfth centuries. Yet Foucault uttered not a word about these reforms during his 1977–1978 course.

As with the pastorate, we can say of the Gregorian reform that it represents "one of the decisive moments in the history of power in Western societies," a prelude to governmentality and to the "typical constitution of the modern Western subject."[9] Like the pastorate, these reforms created an "individualizing power," since they proposed to save "all together and each one."[10] Hence the claim to "daily government," of the entire human being, body and soul:

> A religion that thus lays claim to the daily government of men in their real life on the grounds of their salvation and on the scale of humanity; that is the church, and we have no other example of this in the history of societies.[11]

Obligatory and permanent, the Christian direction of conscience strengthens the dependence of the directed on the director. This interiorization of the exercise of power ultimately goes beyond even the axiom that Michel Foucault took to be essential to the pastorate:

> The perfection of obedience consists in obeying an order, not because it is reasonable or because it entrusts you with an important task, but rather because it is absurd.
>
> For in Christian obedience, there is no end, for what does Christian obedience lead to? Quite simply to obedience.[12]

In fact, Francis's note to Leo marks a sort of sublimation of this obedience to the pastor: such a sublimated obedience no longer consists of obeying an order that has been given, absurd or not, but rather of obeying an order that does not even have to be given. From empire to influence, from domination to enfolding: this could be the subtitle of the Gregorian reform, as of the pastorate.

---

9. Ibid., 185.
10. Ibid., 128.
11. Ibid., 148.
12. Ibid., 176–77.

Medieval historians thus have much to contribute to the history of governmentality. Their contributions are all the more necessary, because in most studies that propose such an archeology, even the most fascinating and the most profound, the medieval period remains undervalued, when it is not skipped over entirely. Drawing on their classical training and too-readily accepting the myth the Renaissance happily forged for itself, many authors link ancient thought directly to modern with no attention to the possibility of medieval continuity. This possibility of continuity positions the Middle Ages as neither an era of amnesia nor a clean slate, but rather as a period of radical re-composition of classical traditions; of reversal; of *metanoia* (conversion, change of heart) of realities, words, and signs. In the current state of scholarly affairs, it is far from clear that the supposed transparency between our way of thinking and that of "classical" antiquity does full justice to the specificity of the Middle Ages as a historical period.

The medieval period—not only at its two extremities, the patristic and scholastic eras, but across the central Middle Ages of feudalism and the reform of the church—can teach us something about the manner in which we are governed today. Governmentality—this strange exercise of power that we now recognize, following Michel Foucault, as constituting the Western mode of politics, this power that enfolds more than it overawes, that abases itself to embrace more fully—finds one of its foundations in an ideologically dominant medieval church in the West, which, since it neither wished nor was able to rely on force of arms, had to resort to the force of conviction. Even earlier, it finds its principle foundation in the figure whom Marcel Gauchet calls a "messiah turned upside down": "Christ, or the figure of an apparent defeat which is in reality a victory."[13] Governmentality boils down to an oxymoron: the power of weakness.

This is also why it raises suspicion. Faced with a power based on strength, we can either surrender or resist. But we fear what may lurk behind a claim of weakness, and for good reason. The social function of historical inquiry is to turn suspicion into vigilance, by disassembling the inner workings of complex developments. It would be pointless (in vain, a "vanity" in every sense of the word) to hold in general distrust the shared inheritance that governmentality has ultimately left to us: democracy.

The pastorate intrinsically and unalterably bears the imprint of charisma; only the charisma of the shepherd transforms the group into a flock. But, from the Rule of Grandmont to the note of Francis to Leo, it is readily apparent that the principle of the pastorate—government of some by others, obedience of all to each one—also carries within itself the antidote to charisma: a "lesser"

---

13. Gauchet, *La Condition historique. Entretiens avec François Azouvi et Sylvain Piron* (Paris, 2003), 102–3.

government of humility, as the exercise of a power resigned in advance. The danger is obvious: charisma that is misused, charisma that refuses to relinquish its hold on power. The remedy is just as clear: constant vigilance, through law and custom, to ensure that the charismatic temptation (which comes from the flock even more than from the shepherd) is tempered by an awareness of shared responsibility. The "society of the spectacle," long ago denounced by Guy Debord,[14] arises only when actors consent to become spectators, when the resignation of the governors gives way to the abdication of the governed.

I would like to be clear to the very end. I am not claiming, by means of a facile reversal or a cute historical coup de théâtre, that the Middle Ages "invented" democracy, any more than they invented capitalism. I am not offering any kind of plea for "Christian democracy." Rather I am saying that the lesson of the Middle Ages, on this subject, is that there is no such thing as a single, ideal form of democracy, a disembodied Athenian model whose recurrent epiphanies can be traced, in a Hegelian manner, across the centuries.

Medieval communitarian experiences teach us that democracy is continuously reinvented, that in every instance, every day, it is "original." The truth of this statement is borne out not only by the variety of ways in which medieval communitarian institutions were constructed, but also by the wide range of contemporary regimes that we merge, artificially, into the single idea of democracy. From this observation we can draw a last lesson. Since it is invented from within, this democracy of a thousand faces can neither be exported nor imported. It is created not by imposing constraints, even those overflowing with good intentions, but by removing them; by releasing pressure, not by applying it: if you believe something is good for you and for others, do it.

To conclude, I would like to return to the paradox of Christian society, the paradox with which this little essay, woven together from the sources, began, and without which governmentality would never have found its place. This paradox energized the Western Middle Ages, and the sources gathered here have revealed it in a kind of explosive outburst. Christian society functioned in a dynamic disequilibrium, a critical mode, due to the fundamental imbalance between the foundations of its social order and the evangelical message that held the place of its ideology. "Christianity," Nietzsche lamented, "has taken the part of all that is weak, low, failed."[15]

I will borrow a final citation from Michel Foucault to shed light on the paradoxical driving force of Christian society in the Western Middle Ages: "Scripture

---

14. Guy Debord, *The Society of the Spectacle*, trans. Donald Nicholson-Smith, rev. ed. (New York, 1995).

15. Friedrich Nietzsche, *The Anti-Christ, Ecce Homo, Twilight of the Idols, and Other Writings*, ed. Aaron Ridley and Judith Norman, trans. Judith Norman (Cambridge, UK, 2005), 5.

is a text that speaks for itself, which has no need of pastoral relay."[16] It is a text, by the same token, that cannot be silenced, that distils doubts that cannot be eradicated, and that gradually calls into question the moments of equilibrium that may be reached but are never really secured.

The dossiers that we have worked through in order to sharpen our question have centered on figures widely recognized for their exceptional spirituality: Clare of Assisi, Benedict of Nursia, Robert of Arbrissel, Peter Abelard, Stephen of Muret, Dominic, Francis . . . but my treatment has hardly been spiritual in nature. This dimension is certainly not absent from the sources studied here. But it has not been my intention to write a book of spirituality, nor even a book of religious history. This has been a work about society, where ideological, political, and social history meet.

Over the last sixty years or so, historians have succeeded in making religious history an autonomous field of study. Their efforts have given respectability to the field. It seems to me that the task passed on to the next generation is to build on these remarkable successes by offering the reconciliation necessary for a full understanding of the Middle Ages. The radical division between sacred and profane, between religious history and secular history, is the product of the nineteenth-century university, the French university most of all.

We have to find our way back to understanding a time when these two registers, although certainly distinct, were lived in a coherence to which we have for too long lost the key. It falls now to medieval historians, I think, to do for medieval society what Michel Zink and Barbara Newman have done for medieval literature by stitching sacred and profane literatures back together, rejecting the way they have been artificially torn apart.[17] A younger and highly talented generation of historians is already setting itself to this task.

In one of his last interviews, Georges Duby remarked:

> There is no border between the visible and invisible worlds, no demarcation between what is sacred and what pertains to the temporal. We have to free ourselves from religious history as it has been practiced up to now. We have to place churchmen back inside the group, and thus better see what binds them to laymen in an inextricable manner, and try to rethink the place, the role, the function of what we call religion within the general field of social organization.[18]

---

16. Foucault, *Security, Territory, Population*, 213.

17. Michel Zink, *Poésie et conversion au Moyen Âge* (Paris, 2003); Barbara Newman, *Medieval Crossover: Reading the Secular against the Sacred* (Notre Dame, IN, 2013).

18. Georges Duby, "À la recherche du Moyen Âge," interview with Michel Pierre, *Magazine littéraire*, November 1996, 100.

I have tried to answer this call with its exact opposite: to rethink "social organization" at the heart "of what we call religion." Between the social and the religious, which one frames the other? A question like this leads nowhere. Religion binds, society joins. Human beings are doubly entangled at the place where they meet. What intrigues me, what interests me far more, across the sources and in the deepest part of people's lives, are the innumerable adjustments, the repeated accommodations, made between the social order and the message of the Gospels; eternal new beginnings at work in the tiny spaces of everyday life, which, one way or another, allow each and every one of us to move forward.

Bibliography

This bibliography includes sources and studies used for the original French edition of this book, plus a number of sources and studies specifically consulted for the English translation. Secondary sources are listed in English translation when such translations exist. Please see also the "Additional Bibliography from the Translator's Introduction," which follows.

Primary Sources

Adalbéron of Laon. *Poème au roi Robert.* Edited by Claude Carozzi. Paris, 1979.
Alfani, Battista. *Vita et leggenda della seraphica vergine sancta Chiara distinta in capitoli.* Edited by Giovanni Boccali. Assisi, 2004.
Ambrose of Milan. "De viduis." In *Verginità et vedovanza: Tutte le opere di Sant'Ambrogio,* edited by Franco Gori, 1:244–318. Milan, 1989.
———. *Commentary of Saint Ambrose on Twelve Psalms.* Translated by Ide M. Ní Riain. Dublin, 2000.
———. *Explanatio psalmorum XII.* Edited by Michael Petschening. Vienna, 1919.
Armstrong, Regis J., ed. and trans. *The Lady. Clare of Assisi: Early Documents.* New York, 2006.
Armstrong, Regis J., J. A. Wayne Hellmann, and William J. Short, eds. and trans. *Francis of Assisi: Early Documents.* Vol. 1: *The Saint.* New York, 1999.
———, eds. and trans. *Francis of Assisi: Early Documents.* Vol. 2: *The Founder.* New York, 2000.
Augustine of Hippo. "Sermon 340." In *Patrologiae latinae cursus completus,* edited by Jean-Paul Migne, vol. 38, cols. 1482–84.
———. *De civitate Dei.* Edited by Bernhard Dombart and Alfons Kalb. Turnhout, 1955.
Aymon. "Vita Willihelmi abbatis Hirsaugiensis." In *Monumenta Germaniae historica* (*Scriptores,* 12), edited by Wilhelm Wattenbach, 209–25. Hannover, 1856.
Baird, Joseph L., Giuseppe Baglivi, and John Robert Kane, trans. *The Chronicle of Salimbene de Adam.* Binghamton, NY, 1986.
Becquet, Jean, ed. *Scriptores ordinis Grandimontensis.* Turnhout, 1968.
Behrends, Frederick, ed. *The Letters and Poems of Fulbert of Chartres.* Oxford, 1976.
Benedict of Aniane. *Concordia regularum.* Edited by Pierre Bonnerue. Turnhout, 1999.
Benedict of Nursia. *Regula. Editio altera emendata.* Edited by Rudolf Hanslik. Vienna, 1977.
———. *The Rule of Saint Benedict, in Latin and English.* Edited and translated by Justin McCann. London, 1952.

BIBLIOGRAPHY

Bernard of Clairvaux. "Liber de gradibus humilitatis et superbiae." In *Sancti Bernardi opera*, edited by Jean Leclercq and Henri Rochais, 3:13–59. Rome, 1963.

Biblia sacra iuxta vulgatam versionem. Edited by Robert Weber and Roger Gryson. Stuttgart, 1994.

Bienvenu, Jean-Marc, Robert Favreau, and Georges Pon, eds. *Grand Cartulaire de Fontevraud (Pancarta et cartularium abbatissae et ordinis Fontis Ebraudi)*. Poitiers, 2000–2005.

Bigaroni, Marino, ed. *Compilatio Assisiensis dagli scritti di fra Leone e compagni su S. Francesco d'Assisi. Dal Ms. 1046 di Perugia. II edizione integrale riveduta e corretta con versione italiana a fronte e varianti*. Assisi, 1992.

Bihl, Michel. "S. Francisci parabola in sermonibus Odonis de Ceritona an. 1219 conscriptus." *Archivum franciscanum historicum* 22 (1929): 584–86.

Boccali, Giovanni. "Testamento e benedizione di S. Chiara. Nuovo codice latino." *Archivum franciscanum historicum* 82 (1989): 282–92.

Boccali, Giovanni, ed. "La *Cum omnis vera religio* del cardinale Ugolino." *Frate Francesco* 78 (2008): 456–76.

———, ed. *Legenda latina sanctae Clarae virginis Assisiensis*. Assisi, 2001.

———, ed. *Legende minores latine sancte Clare virginis Assisiensis*. Assisi, 2008.

———, ed. *Santa Chiara di Assisi. I primi documenti ufficiali: Lettera di annunzio della sua morte, Processo e Bolla di canonizzazione*. Assisi, 2002.

Boehmer, Heinrich, ed. *Chronica fratris Jordani*. Paris, 1908.

Bonaventure. "Legenda maior S. Francisci." In *Legendae S. Francisci Assisiensis saeculis XIII et XIV conscriptae*, 555–652. Quaracchi [Florence], 1926–1941.

Brémond, Antoine, ed. *Bullarium Ordinis Fratrum praedicatorum*, vol. 1. Rome, 1729.

Cenci, Cesare, and Romain G. Mailleux, eds. *Constitutiones generales Ordinis Fratrum minorum*, vol. 1 (Saeculum XIII). Grottaferrata [Rome], 2007.

Cesarius of Arles. *Œuvres monastiques. Œuvres pour les moniales*. Edited by Joël Courreau and Adalbert de Vogüe. Paris, 1988.

Cicero. *De re publica*. Edited by Konrat Ziegler. Liepzig, 1969.

Clare of Assisi. *Écrits*. Edited by Marie-France Becker, Jean-François Godet, and Thaddée Matura. Paris, 1985; new ed. 2003.

———. *Lettere ad Agnese. La visione dello specchio*. Edited by Giovanni Pozzi and Beatrice Rima. Milan, 1999.

Constitutiones primaevae s. ordinis Praedicatorum. Fiesole, 1962.

Coste, Jean. *Boniface VIII en procès. Articles d'accusation et dépositions des témoins (1303–1311)*. Preface by André Vauchez. Rome, 1995.

Dalarun, Jacques, ed. *François d'Assise. Écrits, Vies, témoignages*. Preface by André Vauchez. Paris, 2010.

———, ed. *The Rediscovered Life of St. Francis of Assisi, by Thomas of Celano*. Translated by Timothy J. Johnson. St. Bonaventure, NY, 2016.

Dalarun, Jacques, Geneviève Giordanengo, Armelle Le Huërou, Jean Longère, Dominique Poirel, and Bruce L. Venarde, eds. *Les Deux Vies de Robert d'Arbrissel. Légendes, écrits et témoignages—The Two Lives of Robert of Arbrissel: Legends, Writings, and Testimonies*. Turnhout, 2006.

Dalarun, Jacques, and Armelle Le Huërou, eds. and trans. *Claire d'Assise: Écrits, Vies, documents*. Paris, 2013.

Desbonnets, Théophile, ed. "Legenda trium sociorum." *Archivum franciscanum historicum* 67 (1974): 89–144.
de Vogüé, Adalbert, ed. *La Règle du Maître*, 2 vols. Paris, 1964.
"Dictatus papae." In *Das Register Gregors VII*, edited by Erich Caspar, 202–8. Berlin, 1920–23.
Di Fonzo, Lorenzo, ed. "L'Anonimo Perugino tra le fonti francescane del sec. XIII. Rapporti letterari e testo critico." *Miscellanea francescana* 72 (1972): 435–65.
Du Cange, Charles Du Fresne. *Glossarium mediae et infimae latinitatis*. Re-edition, Paris, 1937–38.
Dudo of Saint-Quentin. *De moribus et actis primorum Normanniae ducum*. Edited by Jules Lair. Caen, 1865.
———. *History of the Normans*. Translated by Eric Christiansen. Woodbridge, UK, 1998.
Eberle, Luke, ed. and trans. *The Rule of the Master*. Kalamazoo, MI, 1977.
Eusebius of Caesarea. *De vita Constantini*. Edited by Bruno Bleckmann. Turnhout, 2007.
Federazione S. Chiara di Assisi delle Clarisse di Umbria-Sardegna. *Chiara di Assisi e le sue fonti legislative. Sinossi cromatica*. Padua, 2003.
Field, Sean L., ed. and trans. *The Writings of Agnes of Harcourt: The Life of Isabelle of France and the Letter on Louis IX and Longchamp*. Notre Dame, IN, 2003.
Foreville, Raymonde, and Gillian Keir, eds. *The Book of St Gilbert*. Oxford, 1987.
Friedberg, Emil, ed. *Corpus iuris canonici*, vol. 2. Leipzig, 1881.
Godet, Jean-François, and Georges Mailleux, eds. *Corpus des sources franciscaines*. Vol. 5: *Opuscula sancti Francisci. Scripta sanctae Clarae. Concordances, Index, Listes de fréquence, Tables comparatives*. Louvain, 1976.
Gogol, Nikolai. *Œuvres complètes*. Paris, 1967.
Gregory IX. "Die Bulle 'Quo elongati' Papst Gregors IX." Edited by Herbert Grundmann, in *Archivum franciscanum historicum* 54 (1961): 20–25.
Gregory the Great. *Dialogorum libri IV*. Edited by Adalbert de Vogüé. Paris, 1978–1980.
———. *Dialogues*. Translated by Odo John Zimmerman. Washington, DC, 1959.
———. *Homeliae in Evangelia*. Edited by Raymond Étaix. Turnhout, 1999.
———. *Pastoral Care*. Translated by Henry Davis. New York, 1978.
———. *Le Pastoralet. Traduction médiévale française de la Regula Pastoralis*. Edited by Martine Pagan. Paris, 2007.
———. *Registrum epistularum*. Edited by Dag Norberg. Turnhout, 1982.
Gregory of Nazianzus. *Select Orations*. Translated by Martha Pollard Vinson. Washington, DC, 2003.
Hallinger, Kassius, ed. *Consuetudines cluniacensium antiquiores cum redactionibus derivatis*. Siegburg, 1983.
Homer. *The Iliad*. Translated by Augustus Taber Murray, revised by William F. Wyatt. Cambridge, MA, 1999.
———. *The Odyssey*. Translated by Augustus Taber Murray, revised by George E. Dimock. Cambridge, MA, 1995.
Honorius III. "Letter of 1 March 1219" ("Reformatio ordinis Grandimontis in regno Francorum"). In *Bullarium, diplomatum et privilegiorum sanctorum Romanorum pontificum*, 3rd ed, edited by Luigi Tomassetti, 350–55. Turin, 1858.
Jerome. *Lettres*. Edited by Jérôme Labourt. Paris, 1949–1963.

Jonas of Orléans. *Le Métier de roi (De institutione regia)*. Edited by Alain Dubreucq. Paris, 1995.
Jordan of Giano, Thomas of Eccleston, Salimbene degli Adami. *XIIIth Century Chronicles*. Translated by Placid Hermann, introduced by Marie-Thérèse Laureilhe. Chicago, 1961.
Jordan of Saxony. *Libellus de principiis ordinis praedicatorum*. Edited by D. H.-C. Scheeben, in *Monumenta historica sancti patris nostri Dominici*. Monumenta ordinis fratrum praedicatorum historica, vol. 16: 25–86. Rome, 1935.
———. *On the Beginnings of the Order of Preachers*. Edited and translated by Simon Tugwell. Chicago, 1982.
Joseph, Stephen, and Peter Van Dijk, eds. *Sources of the Modern Roman Liturgy: The Ordinals by Haymo of Faversham and Related Documents (1243–1307)*. Leiden, 1963.
Lactantius. *De mortibus persecutorum*. Edited by J. L. Creed. Oxford, 1984.
Leander of Seville. "Regula." In *Patrologiae latinae cursus completus*, edited by Jean-Paul Migne, vol. 72, cols. 873–94.
Lehmann, Karl. *Das langobardische Lehnrecht (Handschriften, Textenwicklung, ältester Text und Vulgattext nebst den capitula extraordinaria)*. Göttingen, 1896.
Lehmann, Paul, and Johannes Stroux, eds. *Mittellateinisches Wörterbuch bis zum ausgehenden 13. Jahrhundert*. Munich, 1967–2009.
Luscombe, David, ed. and trans. *The Letter Collection of Peter Abelard and Heloise*. Oxford, 2013.
McLaughlin, T. P. "Abelard's Rule for Religious Women." *Mediaeval Studies* 18 (1956): 242–92.
Menestò, Enrico, and Stefano Brufani, eds. *Fontes francescani*. Assisi, 1995.
Mews, Constant. *The Lost Love Letters of Heloise and Abelard: Perceptions of a Dialogue in Twelfth-Century France*. New York, 1999.
Mommsen, Theodor, and Paul M. Meyer, eds. *Theodosiani libri XVI cum constitutionibus Sirmondianis*. Berlin, 1904–1905.
Muckle, J. T., ed. "Abelard's Letter of Consolation to a Friend (*Historia Calamitatum*)." *Mediaeval Studies* 12 (1950): 175–213.
———. "The Letter of Heloise on Religious Life and Abelard's First Reply." *Mediaeval Studies* 17 (1955): 240–81.
———. "The Personal Letters between Abelard and Heloise." *Medieval Studies* 15 (1953): 47–94.
Muret, Stephen. *Maxims of Stephen of Muret*. Preface by Jean Bequet, translated by Deborah Van Doel, introduction by Carole Hutchison, edited by Maureen M. O'Brien. Kalamazoo, MI, 2002.
Newman, Barbara, ed. and trans. *Making Love in the Twelfth Century: "Letters of Two Lovers" in Context*. Philadelphia, 2016.
Niccolò Machiavelli. *The Prince*. Translated by Harvey C. Mansfield, 2nd ed. Chicago, 1998.
Niermeyer, Jan F., C. Van de Kieft, and J. W. J. Burgers, eds. *Mediae latinitatis lexicon minus. Lexique latin médiéval—Medieval Latin Dictionary—Mittellateinisches Wörterbuch*. Leiden and Boston, 2002.
Oliger, Livarius, ed. *Expositio quatuor magistrorum super Regulam fratrum minorum (1241–1242)*. Rome, 1950.

Omaechevarría, Ignacio, ed. *Escritos de Santa Clara y documentos complementarios*. Madrid, 1970; new ed., 1999.

Pagan, Martine. "Les Légendes françaises de Claire d'Assise (XIIIe-XVIe siècle) III. Édition et commentaire du manuscrit 663 de la bibliothèque de l'Institut de France." *Études franciscaines* n. s. 8 (2015): 5–25.

Paolazzi, Carlo, ed. *Francesco d'Assisi, Scritti / Francisci Assisiensis, Scripta*. Grottaferrata [Rome], 2009.

Peregrini de Bononia. "Chronicon abbreviatum de successione Ministrorum Generalium." In *Tractatus fr. Thomae vulgo dicti de Eccleston*, edited by Andrew G. Little, 141–45. Paris, 1909.

Peter Abelard. *Letters IX–XIV: An Edition with an Introduction*. Edited by E. R Smits. Groningen, 1983.

———. *Sic et non: A Critical Edition*. Edited by Blanche B. Boyer and Richard McKeon. Chicago, 1976.

Peter Lombard. *Sententiae in IV libris distinctae*. Edited by Ignatius Brady. Grottaferrata [Rome], 1971–81.

Piron, Sylvain, ed. and trans. *Lettres des deux amants attribuées à Héloïse et Abélard*. Paris, 2005.

Plato. *The Being of the Beautiful: Plato's Theaetetus, Sophist, and Statesman*. Translated by Seth Benardete. Chicago, 1984.

Radice, Betty, and Michael T. Clanchy, eds. and trans. *The Letters of Abelard and Heloise*. London, 2003.

Roscelin de Compiègne. "Epistola XIV, Quae est Roscelini ad P. Abaelardum." In *Patrologiae latinae cursus completus*, edited by Jean-Paul Migne, vol. 178, cols. 357–72.

Salimbene de Adam. *Cronica*, 2 vols. Edited by Giuseppe Scalia. Turnhout, 1998–1999.

Sbaralea, J.-H., ed. *Bullarium franciscanum Romanorum pontificum constitutiones, epistolas ac diplomata continens*, vol. 1. Rome, 1759.

Schlageter, Johannes. "Die Chronica des Bruders Jordan von Giano. Einführung und kritische Edition nach den bischer bekannten Handschriften." *Archivum franciscanum historicum* 104 (2011): 3–63.

Smaragdus of Saint-Mihiel. "Via regia." In *Patrologiae latinae cursus completus*, edited by Jean-Paul Migne, vol. 102, cols. 931–70.

Thomas of Celano. *Memoriale. Editio critico-synoptica duarum redactionum ad fidem codicum manuscriptorum*. Edited by Felice Accrocca and Aleksander Horowski. Rome, 2011.

———. "Vita prima S. Francisci." In *Legendae S. Francisci Assisiensis saeculis XIII et XIV conscriptae*, 1–117. Quaracchi [Florence], 1926–1941.

Thomas of Eccleston. *Tractatus fr. Thomae vulgo dicti de Eccleston de adventu fratrum minorum in Angliam*. Edited by A. G. Little. Paris, 1909.

Tugwell, Simon, ed. and trans. *Early Dominicans: Selected Writings*. Mahwah, NJ, 1982.

Urban III. "Letters of 14 and 15 July 1186." In *Patrologiae latinae cursus completus*, edited by Jean-Paul Migne, vol. 202, cols. 1415–18.

Vernarde, Bruce L., ed. and trans. *Robert of Arbrissel: A Medieval Religious Life*. Washington, DC, 2003.

Waddell, Chrysogonus, ed. *The Paraclete Statutes "Institutiones nostrae." Troyes, Bibliothèque Municipale Ms 802, ff. 89r–90v: Introduction, Edition, Commentary.* Trappist, KY, 1987.
Wadding, Luke, ed. *Annales Minorum seu Trium Ordinum a S. Francisco institutorum*, 3rd ed. Quaracchi [Florence], 1931.
Walz, Angelo, ed. *Acta canonizationis sancti Dominici*. In *Monumenta historica sancti patris nostri Dominici*, 2:89–194. Rome, 1935.
William Durand. *Rationale Book Four: On the Mass and Each Action Pertaining to it*. Edited and translated by Timothy M. Thibodeau. Turnhout, 2013.
Yves of Chartres. "Panormia." In *Patrologiae latinae cursus completus*, edited by Jean-Paul Migne, vol. 161, cols. 1037–1344.
Ziolkowski, Jan M., ed. and trans. *Letters of Peter Abelard: Beyond the Personal*. Washington, DC, 2008.

Secondary Sources

Accrocca, Felice. "Le durezze di fratello Francesco. L'*Epistola ad fratrem Leonem*." *Vita Minorum* 3 (1997): 243–60.
Agamben, Giorgio. *The Signature of All Things: On Method*. Translated by Luca d'Isanto with Kevin Attell. New York, 2009.
———. *State of Exception*. Translated by Kevin Attell. Chicago, 2005.
Alberzoni, Maria Pia. *Chiara e il papato*. Milan, 1995.
Althusser, Louis. "Ideology and Ideological State Apparatuses (Notes Towards an Investigation)." In *Lenin and Philosophy and Other Essays*, translated by Ben Brewster, 127–86. New York and London, 1971.
———. *Positions (1964–1975)*. Paris, 1976.
Ammannati, Giulia. "La lettera autografa di Francesco d'Assisi a frate Leone." In *Il linguaggio della biblioteca. Scritti in onore di Diego Maltese*, edited by Mauro Guerrini, 73–87. Florence, 1994.
Andenna, Cristina. "Dall'esempio alla santità. Stefano di Thiers e Stefano di Obazine: Modelli di vita o fondatori di ordini?" In *Das Eigene und das Ganze. Zum Individuellen im mittelalterlichen Religiosentum*, edited by Gert Melville and Markus Schürer, 177–224. Munster, 2002.
Andenna, Cristina, and Gert Melville, eds. *Regulae—Consuetudines—Statuta. Studi sulle fonti normative degli Ordini religiosi nei secoli centrali del Medioevo*. Munster, 2005.
Andenna, Giancarlo, Mirko Breitenstein, and Gert Melville, eds. *Charisma und religiöse Gemeinschaften im Mittelalter*. Munster, 2005.
Arendt, Hannah. *The Origins of Totalitarianism*, 3 vols. New York, 1968.
Austin, John L. *How to Do Things with Words: The William James Lectures Delivered at Harvard University in 1955*. Oxford, 1962.
Barone, Giulia. *Da frate Elia agli Spirituali*. Preface by Jacques Dalarun. Milan, 1999.
Barret, Sébastien, and Gert Melville, eds. *Oboedientia. Zu Formen und Grenzen von Macht und Unterordnung im mittelalterlichen Relgiosentum*. Munster, 2005.
Barthélemy, Dominique. *L'an mil et la paix de Dieu. La France chrétienne et féodale, 980–1060*. Paris, 1999.

Bartoli, Marco. "Analisi storica et interpretazione psicanalitica di una visione di s. Chiara d'Assisi." *Archivum franciscanum historicum* 73 (1980): 449–72.
———. *Clare of Assisi*. Translated by Frances Teresa. Quincy, IL, 1993.
Bartoli Langeli, Attilio. "Ancora sugli autografi di frate Francesco." In *"Verba Domini mei." Gli "opuscula" di Francesco d'Assisi a 25 anni dalla edizione di Kajetan Esser, OFM*, edited by Alvaro Cacciotti, 89–95. Rome, 2003.
———. *Gli autografi di frate Francesco e di frate Leone*. Turnhout, 2000.
———. "Gli scritti da Francesco. L'autografia di un *illitteratus*." In *Frate Francesco d'Assisi*, 103–58. Spoleto, 1994.
———. "Il patto di Assisi: Ritorno sulla *Carta Pacis* del 1210." *Franciscan Studies* 65 (2007): 1–8.
———. "La realtà sociale assisana e il patto del 1210." In *Assisi al tempo di san Francesco*, 271–336. Assisi, 1978.
———. "La *Solet annuere* come documento." In *La Regola di frate Francesco. Eredità e sfida*, edited by Pietro Maranesi and Felice Accrocca, 57–94. Padua, 2012.
Battais, Lise. "La courtoisie de François d'Assise. Influence de la littérature courtoise sur la première génération franciscaine." *Mélanges de l'École française de Rome. Moyen Âge* 109 (1997): 131–60.
Becker, Alfons. "Form und Materie. Bemerkungen zu Fulberts von Chartres *De forma fidelitatis* im Lehnrecht des Mittelalters und der frühen Neuzeit." *Historisches Jahrbuch* 102 (1982): 325–61.
———. "Politique féodale de la papauté à l'égard des rois et des princes (XIe–XIIe siècles)." In *Chiesa e mondo feudale nei secoli X–XII*, 411–49. Milan, 1995.
Becquet, Jean. *Études grandmontaines*. Ussel, 1998.
———. "Grandmont (Ordre et abbaye de)." In *Dictionnaire d'histoire et de géographie ecclésiastiques*, vol. 21, cols. 1129–40. Paris, 1986.
Berman, Constance H. "Distinguishing between the Humble Peasant Lay Brother and Sister, and the Converted Knight in Medieval Southern France." In *Religious and Laity in Western Europe, 1000–1400: Interaction, Negotiation and Power*, edited by Emilia Jamroziak and Janet Burton, 263–83. Turnhout, 2006.
Bienvenu, Jean-Marc. *L'Étonnant Fondateur de Fontevraud, Robert d'Arbrissel*. Paris, 1981.
Bloch, Marc. *Feudal Society*, 2 vols. Translated by L. A. Manyon. Chicago, 1961.
Bobin, Christian. *The Secret of Francis of Assisi: A Meditation*. Translated by Michael H. Kohn. Boston, 1999.
Boucheron, Patrick. "Signes et formes du pouvoir." In *Le Moyen Âge en lumière. Manuscrits enluminés des bibliothèques de France*, edited by Jacques Dalarun, 172–204. Paris, 2002.
Bougerol, Jacques-Guy. "Il reclutamento sociale delle clarisse di Assisi." *Mélanges de l'École française de Rome. Moyen Âge-Temps modernes* 89 (1977): 629–32.
Bourgain, Pascale, and Marie-Clotilde Hubert. *Le Latin médiéval*. Turnhout, 2005.
Boynton, Susan, and Isabelle Cochelin, eds. *From Dead of Night to the End of Day: The Medieval Customs of Cluny*. Turnhout, 2005.
Brown, Peter. *Authority and the Sacred: Aspects of the Christianisation of the Roman World*. Princeton, NJ, 1997.
———. *Power and Persuasion in Late Antiquity: Towards a Christian Empire*. Madison, WI, 1992.

Butz, Reinhardt, and Jörg Oberste, eds. *Studia monastica: Beiträge zum klösterlichen Leben im Mittelalter*. Munster, 2004.

Bynum, Caroline Walker. *Holy Feast and Holy Fast: The Religious Significance of Food to Medieval Women*. Berkeley, CA, 1987.

———. *Jesus as Mother: Studies in the Spirituality of the High Middle Ages*. Berkeley, CA, 1982.

Cacciotti, Alvaro, and Maria Melli, eds. *Francesco a Roma dal signor Papa*. Milan, 2008.

———, eds. *La grazia del lavoro*. Milan, 2010.

Cammarosano, Paolo. *Italia medievale. Struttura e geografia delle fonti scritte*. Rome, 1991.

Cannetti, Luigi. *L'invenzione della memoria. Il culto e l'immagine di Domenico nella storia dei primi frati Predicatori (1221–1260)*. Spoleto, 1996.

Charageat, Martine, and Corinne Leveleux-Teixeira, eds. *Consulter, délibérer, décider. Donner son avis au Moyen Âge*. Toulouse, 2010.

Châtillon, Jean. "Nudum Christum nudus sequere. Note sur les origines et la signification du thème de la nudité spirituelle dans les écrits de saint Bonaventure." In *S. Bonaventura, 1274–1974*, 719–72. Grottaferrata [Rome], 1974.

Constable, Giles. "Nudus nudum Christum sequi and Parallel Formulas in the XIIth Century: A Supplementary Dossier." In *Continuity and Discontinuity in Church History: Essays Presented to G. H. Williams on the Occasion of his 65th Birthday*, edited by F. Forrester Church and Timothy George, 83–91. Leiden, 1979.

———. *The Reformation of the Twelfth Century*. Cambridge, UK, 1996.

———. *Three Studies in Medieval Religious and Social Thought. The Interpretation of Mary and Martha. The Ideal of the Imitation of Christ. The Orders of Society*. Cambridge, UK, 1995.

Creytens, Raymond. "Costituzioni domenicane." In *Dizionario degli Istituti di perfezione*, vol. 3, cols. 183–98. Rome, 1976.

Cusato, Michael F. "*Commercium*: From the Profane to the Sacred." In *Francis of Assisi: History, Hagiography and Hermeneutics*, ed. Jay Hammond, 179–209. Hyde Park, IL, 2004; reedited in Cusato, *Early Franciscan Movement*, 377–405.

———. *The Early Franciscan Movement (1205–1239): History, Sources, and Hermeneutics*. Preface by André Vauchez. Spoleto, 2009.

———. "Francis of Assisi, Deacon? An Examination of the Claims of the Earliest Franciscan Sources, 1229–1235." In *Defenders and Critics of Franciscan Life: Essays in Honor of John V. Fleming*, ed. Michael F. Cusato and Guy Geltner, 9–39. Leiden, 2009; reedited in Cusato, *Early Franciscan Movement*, 283–315.

———. "Joachim of Fiore's *Epistola universis Christi fidelibus*: An Influence on Francis of Assisi's *Epistola ad fideles*?" *Franciscan Studies* 61 (2003): 253–78; reedited in Cusato, *Early Franciscan Movement*, 129–52.

———. "La renonciation au pouvoir chez les frères mineurs au XIIIe siècle." PhD dissertation, Université Paris-IV, 1991.

———. "Talking about Ourselves: The Shift in Franciscan Writing from Hagiography to History (1235–1247)," *Franciscan Studies* 58 (2000): 37–75; reedited in Cusato, *Early Franciscan Movement*, 339–75.

Cygler, Florent. *Das Generalkapitel im hohen Mittelalter. Cisterzienser, Prämonstratenser, Kartäuser und Cluniazenser*. Munster, 2002.

———. "Schriftlichkeit und Funktionalität: das Beispiel der dominikanischen Konstitutionen." In *Pragmatische Dimensionen mittelalterlicher Schriftkultur*, edited by Christel Meier-Staubach, 77–90. Munich, 2002.

Cygler, Florent, and Gert Melville. "Augustinusregel und dominikanische Konstitutionen aus der Sicht Humberts de Romanis." In *Regula sancti Augustini. Normative Grundlage differenter Verbände im Mittelalter*, edited by Gert Melville and Anne Müller, 419–54. Paring, Germany, 2002.

———. "Nouvelles approches historiographiques des ordres religieux en Allemagne. Le groupe de recherche de Dresde sur les structures institutionnelles des ordres religieux au Moyen Âge." *Revue Mabillon* n. s. 12 (2001): 314–21.

Dagron, Gilbert. *Emperor and Priest. The Imperial Office in Byzantium*. Translated by Jean Birrell. Cambridge, UK, 2003.

Dahan, Gilbert. *L'exégèse chrétienne de la Bible en Occident médiéval, XIIe–XIVe siècles*. Paris, 1999.

Dalarun, Jacques. "Abbon et le temps." In *Abbon, un abbé de l'an mil*, edited by Annie Dufour and Gillette Labory, 439–45. Turnhout, 2008.

———. *The Canticle of Brother Sun: Francis of Assisi Reconciled*. Translated by Philippe Yates. St. Bonaventure, NY, 2016.

———. "Dieu changea de sexe, pour ainsi dire." *La religion faite femme (XIe–XVe siècles)*. Munster, 2008.

———. "D'un testament à l'autre. Le charisme franciscain en peu de mots." In *Institution und Charisma. Festschrift für Gert Melville zum 65. Geburtstag*, edited by Franz J. Felten, Annette Kehnel, and Stefan Weinfurter, 503–11. Cologne, Weimar, Vienna, 2009.

———. "François d'Assise et la quête du Graal." *Romania* 127 (2009): 147–67.

———. *Francis of Assisi and the Feminine*. St. Bonaventure, NY, 2006.

———. *Francis of Assisi and Power*. Foreword by Michael F. Cusato. St. Bonaventure, NY, 2007.

———. *L'Impossible Sainteté. La vie retrouvée de Robert d'Arbrissel (v. 1045–1116), fondateur de Fontevraud*. Preface by Pierre Toubert. 1985; new ed., Paris, 2007.

———. "La Madeleine dans l'Ouest de la France au tournant des XIe et XIIe siècles." *Mélanges de l'École française de Rome. Moyen Âge* 104 (1992): 71–119.

———. *The Misadventure of Francis of Assisi*. St. Bonaventure, NY, 2002.

———. "Nouveaux aperçus sur Abélard, Héloïse et le Paraclet." *Francia. Forschungen zur westeuropäischen Geschichte* 32 (2005): 19–66.

———. "Le plus ancien témoin manuscrit de la *Vita beati Francisci* de Thomas de Celano." In *"Arbor ramosa." Studi per Antonio Rigon da allievi, amici, colleghi*, edited by Luciano Bertazzo, Donato Gallo, Raimondo Michetti, and Andrea Tilatti, 129–51. Padua, 2011.

———. "Les plus anciens statuts de Fontevraud." In *Robert d'Arbrissel et la vie religieuse dans l'Ouest de la France*. Edited by Jacques Dalarun, 139–72. Turnhout, 2004.

———. *Robert of Arbrissel: Sex, Sin, and Salvation in the Middle Ages*. Translated and introduced by Bruce L. Venarde, with a new preface by the author. Washington, DC, 2006.

———. *Vers une résolution de la question franciscaine. La "Légende ombrienne" de Thomas de Celano*. Paris, 2007.

Dalarun, Jacques, Courtney Hull, Edgar Magana, Robert Mayer, Geoffrey Omondi-Muga, and Juliane Ostergaard. "Francis's Autograph to Brother Leo: A New Reading." *The Cord* 57 (2007): 329–35.

Dalarun, Jacques, ed. *Le Moyen Âge en lumière. Manuscrits enluminés des bibliothèques de France.* Paris, 2002.

———, ed. *Robert d'Arbrissel et la vie religieuse dans l'Ouest de la France.* Turnhout, 2004.

Débax, Hélène. "Le conseil dans les cours seigneuriales du Languedoc et de la Catalogne (XIe–XIIe siècles). In *Consulter, délibérer, décider. Donner son avis au Moyen Âge*, edited by Martine Charageat and Corinne Leveleux-Teixeira, 109–28. Toulouse, 2010.

———. "Le serrement des mains." *Le Moyen Âge* 113 (2007): 9–23.

Debord, Guy. *The Society of the Spectacle*, rev. ed. Translated by Donald Nicholson-Smith. New York, 1995.

Delmas-Goyon, François. *Saint François d'Assise, le frère de toute créature*. Paris, 2008.

Desbonnets, Théophile. *De l'intuition à l'institution: Les Franciscains*. Paris, 1983.

Duby, Georges. "À la recherche du Moyen Âge." Interview with Michel Pierre. *Magazine littéraire*, November 1996, 98–103.

———. *The Legend of Bouvines: War, Religion, and Culture in the Middle Ages.* Translated by Catherine Tihanyi. Berkeley, CA, 1990.

———. *The Three Orders: Feudal Society Imagined.* Translated by Arthur Goldhammer. Chicago, 1980.

———. *William Marshal: The Flower of Chivalry.* Translated by Richard Howard. New York, 1985.

———. *Women of the Twelfth Century, Volume 1: Eleanor of Aquitaine and Six Others.* Translated by Jean Birrell. Chicago, 1997.

———. "Youth in Aristocratic Society: Northwestern France in the Twelfth Century." In *The Chivalrous Society*, translated by Cynthia Postan, 112–22. Berkeley, CA, 1981.

Dunbabin, Jean. "Government." In *The Cambridge History of Medieval Political Thought, c. 350–1450*, edited by James H. Burns, 477–519. Cambridge, UK, 1997.

Eddé, Dominique. *The Crime of Jean Genet*. Translated by Andrew Rubens and Ros Schwartz. Chicago, 2016.

Elia da Cortona tra realtà e mito. Atti dell'Incontro di studio, Cortona, 12–13 luglio 2013. Spoleto, 2014.

Évangile et évangélisme (XIIe–XIIIe-siècles). Cahiers de Fanjeaux, 34. Toulouse and Fanjeaux, 1999.

Felskau, Christian-Frederik. *Agnes von Böhmen und die Klosteranlage der Klarissen und Franziskaner in Prag. Leben und Institution, Legende und Verehrung.* Nordhausen, 2008.

Flood, David. *Daily Labor of the Early Franciscans.* St. Bonaventure, NY, 2010.

———. *Francis of Assisi and the Franciscan Movement.* Quezon City, Philippines, 1989.

———. "Regula melius observare." In *"Verba Domini mei." Gli "opuscula" di Francesco d'Assisi a 25 anni dalla edizione di Kajetan Esser, OFM*, edited by Alvaro Cacciotti, 329–61. Rome, 2002.

———. *Work for Every One: Francis of Assisi and the Ethic of Service.* Quezon City, Philippines, 1997.

Fortini, Arnaldo. *Nova vita di San Francesco*. Assisi, 1959.
Foucault, Michel. *Abnormal: Lectures at the Collège de France, 1974–1975*. Translated by Graham Burchell. Edited by Valerio Marchetti and Antonella Salomoni. General Editors, François Ewald and Alessandro Fontana. English Series Editor, Arnold I. Davidson. New York, 2003.
——. *The Birth of Biopolitics: Lectures at the Collège de France, 1978–79*. Translated by Graham Burchell. Edited by Michel Senellart. General Editors, François Ewald and Alessandro Fontana. English Series Editor, Arnold I. Davidson. New York, 2008.
——. *The Courage of Truth. The Government of Self and Others II: Lectures at the Collège de France, 1983–1984*. Translated by Graham Burchell. Edited by Frédéric Gros. General Editors, François Ewald and Alessandro Fontana. English Series Editor, Arnold I. Davidson. New York, 2012.
——. *Discipline and Punish: The Birth of the Prison*. Translated by Alan Sheridan. New York, 1977.
——. *The Government of Self and Others: Lectures at the Collège de France, 1982–1983*. Translated by Graham Burchell. Edited by Frédéric Gros. General Editors, François Ewald and Alessandro Fontana. English Series Editor, Arnold I. Davidson. New York, 2011.
——. *The Hermeneutics of the Subject: Lectures at the Collège de France, 1981–1982*. Translated by Graham Burchell. Edited by Frédéric Gros. General Editors, François Ewald and Alessandro Fontana. English Series Editor, Arnold I. Davidson. New York, 2005.
——. *History of Madness*. Translated by Jonathan Murphy. Edited by Jean Khalfa. New York, 2006.
——. *The History of Sexuality, vol. 1: An Introduction*. Translated by Robert Hurley. New York, 1990.
——. *Lectures on the Will to Know: Lectures at the Collège de France, 1970–1971*. Translated by Graham Burchell. Edited by Daniel Defert. General Editors, François Ewald and Alessandro Fontana. English Series Editor, Arnold I. Davidson. New York, 2013.
——. "*Omnes et singulatim*: Toward a Critique of Political Reason." In *The Essential Work of Michel Foucault, 1954–1984*, vol. 3: *Power*. Edited by James D. Faubion. Translated by Robert Hurley, 298–325. New York, 2001.
——. *Psychiatric Power: Lectures at the Collège de France, 1972–1973*. Translated by Graham Burchell. Edited by Jacques LaGrange. General Editors, François Ewald and Alessandro Fontana. English Series Editor, Arnold I. Davidson. New York, 2006.
——. *Security, Territory, Population: Lectures at the Collège de France, 1977–1978*. Translated by Graham Burchell. Edited by Michel Senellart. General Editors, François Ewald and Alessandro Fontana. English Series Editor, Arnold I. Davidson. New York, 2007.
——. "*Society Must Be Defended*": *Lectures at the Collège de France, 1975–1976*. Translated by David Macey. Edited by Mauro Bertani. General Editors, François Ewald and Alessandro Fontana. English Series Editor, Arnold I. Davidson. New York, 2003.

Foucault, Michel, ed. *I, Pierre Riviere, Having Slaughtered My Mother, My Sister, and My Brother . . . : A Case of Parricide in the 19th Century.* Translated by Frank Jellinek. New York, 1975.

Foulon, Jean-Hervé. *Église et réforme au Moyen Âge. Papauté, milieux réformateurs et ecclésiologie dans les Pays de la Loire au tournant des XIe–XIIe siècles.* Preface by Jacques Dalarun. Brussels, 2008.

Ganshof, François-Louis. *Feudalism.* Translated by Philip Grierson. Toronto, 1996.

Garzena, Cristiana. *"Terra fidelis manet." "Humilitas" e "servitium" nel 'Cantico di frate Sole.'* Florence, 1997.

Gauchet, Marcel. *La Condition historique. Entretiens avec François Azouvi et Sylvain Piron.* Paris, 2003.

———. *The Disenchantment of the World: A Political History of Religion.* Translated by Oscar Burge. Princeton, NJ, 1997.

Géhin, Paul, ed. *Lire le manuscrit médiéval. Observer et décrire.* Paris, 2005.

Genet, Jean. "The Studio of Alberto Giacometti." In *The Selected Writings of Jean Genet,* edited and introduced by Edmund White, 309–29. Hopewell, NJ, 1995.

Giordanengo, Gérard. "Epistola Philiberti. Note sur l'influence du droit féodal savant dans la pratique du Dauphiné médiéval." *Mélanges d'archéologie et d'histoire* 82 (1970): 809–53.

———. "État et droit féodal en France (XIIe–XIVe siècles)." In *L'État moderne: le droit, l'espace et les formes de l'État,* edited by Noël Coulet and Jean-Philippe Genet, 61–83. Paris, 1990.

Girard, René. *Deceit, Desire and the Novel: Self and Other in Literary Structure.* Translated by Yvonne Freccero. Baltimore, 1965.

Godet, Jean-François. "Le rôle de la prédication dans l'évolution de l'Ordre des Frères mineurs d'après les écrits de saint François." *Franziskanische Studien* 59 (1977): 53–64.

Godet-Calogeras, Jean-François. "Francis of Assisi's Resignation: An Historical and Philological Probe." In *Charisma und religiöse Gemeinschaften im Mittelalter,* edited by Giancarlo Andenna, Mirko Bretenstein, and Gert Melville, 281–300. Munster, 2005.

Grégoire, Réginald. "L'adage ascétique *Nudum Christum nudus sequi.*" In *Studi storici in onore di O. Bertolini,* 1:395–408. Pisa, 1972.

Guida, Marco. *Una leggenda in cerca d'autore. La "Vita di santa Chiara d'Assisi." Studio delle fonti e sinossi intertestuale.* Preface by Jacques Dalarun. Brussels, 2010.

Guillot, Olivier, Albert Rigaudière, and Yves Sassier. *Pouvoirs et institutions dans la France médiévale.* Paris, 1994.

Guyotjeannin, Olivier. "1060–1285." In *Le Moyen Âge. Le roi, l'Église, les grands, le people, 481–1514,* edited by Philippe Contamine, 171–284. Paris, 2002.

Hinnebusch, William A. *The History of the Dominican Order.* New York, 1966–1973.

Hutchison, Carole A. *The Hermit Monks of Grandmont.* Kalamazoo, MI, 1989.

Iogna-Prat, Dominique. *Order and Exclusion: Cluny and Christendom Face Heresy, Judaism, and Islam (1000–1150).* Translated by Graham Robert Edwards. Foreword by Barbara H. Rosenwein. Ithaca, NY, 2003.

Jansen, Katherine Ludwig. *The Making of the Magdalene: Preaching and Popular Devotion in the Later Middle Ages.* Princeton, NJ, 2000.

Jenal, Georg. "*Caput autem mulieris vir* (I Kor 11, 3). Praxis und Begründung des Doppelklosters im Briefkorpus Abaelard-Heloise." *Archiv für Kulturgeschichte* 76 (1994): 285–304.
Johnson, Timothy J. "Lost in Sacred Space: Textual Hermeneutics, Liturgical Worship, and Celano's *Legenda ad Usum Chori*." *Franciscan Studies* 59 (2001): 109–31.
———. "Meraviglie di pietre e spazi. La dimensione teologica delle narrazioni sui miracoli in Tommaso da Celano e Bonaventura da Bagnoregio." In *Paradoxien der Legitimation. Ergebnisse einer deutsch-italienisch-französischen Villa Vigoni-Konferenz sur Macht im Mittelalter*, edited by Annette Kehnel and Cristina Andenna, with Cécile Caby and Gert Melville, 479–96. Florence, 2010.
Jordan, William Chester. *Louis IX and the Challenge of the Crusade. A Study in Rulership*. Princeton, NJ, 1979.
Kantorowicz, Ernst. *Laudes regiae: A Study in Liturgical Acclamations and Medieval Ruler Worship*. Berkeley, CA, 1946.
Kehnel, Annette. "The Narrative Tradition of the Medieval Franciscan Friars on the British Isles. Introduction to the Sources." *Franciscan Studies* 63 (2005): 461–530.
Kuntzmann, Raymond. *Typologie biblique. De quelques figures vives*. Paris, 2002.
Landini, Lawrence C. *The Causes of the Clericalization of the Order of Friars Minor, 1209–1260, in the Light of Early Franciscan Sources*. Chicago, 1968.
Larigauderie-Beijeaud, Martine. *De l'ermitage à la seigneurie. L'espace économique et social de Grandmont, XIIe–XVIIIe siècle*. Amiens, 2009.
Le Goff, Jacques. *Saint Louis*. Translated by Gareth Evan Gollrad. Notre Dame, IN, 2009.
———. "The Symbolic Ritual of Vassalage." In *Time, Work, and Culture in the Middle Ages*, translated by Arthur Goldhammer, 237–87. Chicago, 1980.
Le Jan, Régine. "Le royaume des Francs de 481 à 888." In *Le Moyen Âge. Le roi, l'Église, les grands, le people, 481–1514*, edited by Philippe Contamine, 11–111. Paris, 2002.
Lobrichon, Guy. *Héloïse. L'amour et le savoir*. Paris, 2005.
Lopez, Elizabeth. "Frères et sœurs extérieurs dans les couvents des Ordres mendiants." In *Les Mouvances laïques des Ordres religieux*, edited by Nicole Bouter, 117–33. Saint-Étienne, 1996.
Lubac, Henri de. *Medieval Exegesis: The Four Senses of Scripture*, 3 vols. Translated by Mark Sebenc and Edward M. Macierowski. Grand Rapids, MI, 1998–2009.
Maccarone, Michele. *Il sovrano "Vicarius Dei" nell'alto Medioevo*. Leyden, 1959.
———. *"Vicarius Christi." Storia del titolo papale*. Rome, 1952.
Magnani, Eliana. "Le pauvre, le Christ et le moine: la correspondance de rôles et les cérémonies du *mandatum* à travers les coutumiers clunisiens du XIe siècle." In *Les clercs, les fidèles et les saints en Bourgogne médiévale*, edited by Vincent Tabbagh, 11–26. Dijon, 2005.
Magnou-Nortier, Élisabeth. *Foi et fidélité. Recherches sur l'évolution des liens personnels chez les Francs du VIIe au IXe siècle*. Toulouse, 1976.
Maire Vigueur, Jean-Claude. *Cavaliers et citoyens. Guerre, conflits et société dans l'Italie communale, XIIe-XIIIe siècles*. Paris, 2003.

———. "Comuni e signorie in Umbria, Marche e Lazio." In *Storia d'Italia*, 7/2. *Comuni e signorie nell'Italia nordorientale e centrale: Lazio, Umbria e Marche, Lucca*, edited by Giuseppe Galasso, 321–606. Turin, 1987.

Mapelli, Francesca J. *L'amministrazione francescana di Inghilterra e Francia. Personale di governo e strutture dell'Ordine fino al Concilio di Vienne (1311)*. Preface by Giulia Barone. Rome, 2003.

Marini, Alfonso. *Agnese di Boemia*. Rome, 1991.

———. "Dalla *sequela* alla *conformitas*. Una ricerca su fonti francescane." *Franciscana. Bollettino della Società internazionale di studi francescani* 7 (2005): 69–87.

———. "*Vestigia Christi sequi* o *imitatio Christi*. Due differenti modi di intendere la vita evangelica di Francesco d'Assisi." *Collectanea franciscana* 64 (1994): 89–119.

Marx, Karl, and Friedrich Engels. "The German Ideology: Part I." In *The Marx-Engels Reader*, 2nd ed., translated by Robert C. Tucker, 156–200. New York, 1978.

Mayeur, Jean-Marie, Charles Pietri, Luce Pietri, André Vauchez, and Marc Venard, eds. *Histoire du christianisme des origines à nos jours*. Paris, 1990–2000.

Mazel, Florian. *La noblesse et l'Église en Provence, fin X^e–début XIVe siècle. L'exemple des familles d'Agoult-Simiane, de Baux et de Marseille*. Paris, 2002.

Melville, Gert. "Der geteilte Franziskus. Beobachtungen zum institutionellen Umgang mit Charisma." In *Kunst, Macht und Institution. Studien zur philosophischen Anthropologie, soziologischen Theorie und Kultursoziologie der Moderne*, edited by Joachim Fischer and Hans Joas, 347–63. Frankfurt and New York, 2003.

———. "Il Francesco diviso. Sulla istituzionalizzazione di un carismatico." In *"Omnia religione moventur." Culti, carismi ed istituzioni ecclesiastiche. Studi in onore di Cosimo Damiano Fonseca*, edited by Pierantonio Piatti and Raffaela Tortorelli, 33–54. Galatina, Italy, 2006.

———. "*In solitudine ac paupertate*. Stephans von Muret Evangelium vor Franz von Assisi." In *In proposito paupertatis. Studien zum Armutsverständnis bei den mittelalterlichen Bettelorden*, edited by Gert Melville and Annette Kehnel, 7–30. Munster, 2001.

———. "Unitas e diversitas. L'Europa medievale dei chiostri e degli ordini." In *Europa in costruzione. La forza delle identità, la ricerca di unità (secoli IX–XIII)*, edited by Giorgio Gracco, Jacques Le Goff, Hagen Keller, and Gherardo Ortalli, 357–84. Bologna, 2006.

———. "Von der *Regula regularum* zur Stephansregel. Der normative Sonderweg der Grandmontenser bei der Auffächerung der *Vita religiosa* im 12. Jahrhundert." In *Vom Kloster zum Klosterverband*, edited by Hagen Keller and Franz Neiske, 342–63. Munich, 1997.

Melville, Gert, and Annette Kehnel, eds. *In proposito paupertatis. Studien zum Armutsverständnis bei den mittelalterlichen Bettelorden*. Munster, 2001.

———, eds. *Mittelalterliche Orden und Klöster im Vergleich. Methodische Ansätze und Perspektiven*. Munster, 2007.

Melville, Gert, and Jörg Oberste, eds. *Die Bettelorden im Aufbau. Beiträge zu Institutionalisierungsprozessen im mittelalterlichen religiosentum*. Munster, 1999.

Melville, Gert, and Markus Schürer, eds. *Das Eigen und das Ganze. Zum Individuellen im mittelalterlichen Religiosentum*. Munster, 2002.

Menant, François. *Campagnes lombardes du Moyen Âge. L'économie et la société rurales dans la région de Bergame, de Crémone et de Brescia du Xe au XIIIe siècle*. Rome, 1993.
Menestò, Enrico. "Gli scritti di Francesco d'Assisi." In *Frate Francesco d'Assisi*, 163–81. Spoleto, 1994.
Merlo, Grado G. *In the Name of Saint Francis: History of the Friars Minor and Franciscanism until the Early Sixteenth Century*. Translated by Raphael Bonnano. St. Bonaventure, NY, 2009.
———. "Storia di frate Francesco e dell'Ordine dei Minori." In *Francesco d'Assisi e il primo secolo di storia francescana*, 3–32. Turin, 1997.
Mews, Constant J. *Abelard and Heloise*. Oxford, 2005.
Miccoli, Giovanni. *Francesco d'Assisi e l'Ordine dei minori*. Milan, 1999.
———. *Francesco d'Assisi. Realtà e memoria di un'esperienza cristiana*. Turin, 1991.
———. "Gli scritti di Francesco." In *Francesco d'Assisi e il primo secolo di storia francescana*, 35–69. Turin, 1997.
Michetti, Raimondo. *Francesco d'Assisi et il paradosso della minoritas. La "Vita beati Francisci" di Tommaso da Celano*. Rome, 2004.
Modéran, Yves. *L'Empire romain tardif, 235–395*. Paris, 2003.
Monti, Dominic. "The Friars Minor: An Order in the Church." *Franciscan Studies* 61 (2003): 235–52.
Morsel, Joseph. *L'Aristocratie médiévale. La domination sociale en Occident (V^e–XVe siècle)*. Paris, 2004.
Moulin, Léo. "*Sanior et maior pars*. Note sur l'évolution des techniques électorales dans les Ordres religieux du VIe au XIIIe siècle." *Revue historique de droit français et étranger* 36 (1958): 368–97, 491–529.
———. *La vie quotidienne des religieux au Moyen Âge, X^e–XVe siècle*. Paris, 1978.
Muzerelle, Denis. *Vocabulaire codicologique. Répertoire méthodique des termes relatifs aux manuscrits, édition hypertextuelle*. Paris, 2003. http://vocabulaire.irht.cnrs.fr.
Nault, François. *Le Lavement des pieds. Un asacrement*. Montreal, 2010.
Newman, Barbara. *Medieval Crossover: Reading the Secular against the Sacred*. Notre Dame, IN, 2013.
Nguyên-Van-Khanh, Norbert. *Le Christ dans la pensée de saint François d'Assise d'après ses écrits*. Paris, 1989.
Nietzsche, Friedrich. *The Anti-Christ, Ecce Homo, Twilight of the Idols, and Other Writings*. Edited by Aaron Ridley and Judith Norman. Translated by Judith Norman. Cambridge, UK, 2005.
Oudart, Hervé. *Robert d'Arbrissel, ermite et prédicateur*. Spoleto, 2010.
Paolazzi, Carlo. "Della vera, caritativa e perfetta obbedienza. L'Ammonizione III di frate Francesco." In *Pietate e studio. Miscellanea di studi in onore di p. Lino Mocatti*, edited by Domenico Gobbi, 187–202. Trento, 2006.
———. *Francesco per Chiara*. Milan, 1993.
———. "Per gli autografi di frate Francesco. Dubbi, verifiche e riconferme." *Archivum franciscanum historicum* 93 (2000): 3–28.
———. *Studi sugli "Scritti" di frate Francesco*. Grottaferrata [Rome], 2006.
Paravicini Bagliani, Agostino. *Boniface VIII, un pape hérétqiue?* Paris, 2003.
Parkes, Malcolm. *Pause and Effect: An Introduction to the History of Punctuation in the West*. Aldershot, UK, 1992.

Pellegrini, Luigi. *L'incontro tra due 'invenzioni' medievali: università e Ordini mendicanti.* Naples, 2003.

Pinto-Mathieu, Elisabeth. *Marie-Madeleine dans la littérature du Moyen Âge.* Paris, 1997.

Podlech, Adalbert. "Repräsentation." In *Geschichtliche Grundbegriffe: Historisches Lexikon zur politisch-sozialen Sprache in Deutschland*, edited by Otto Brunner, Werner Conze and Reinhart Koselleck, 5:509–47. Stuttgart, 1984. French translation as "La représentation: une histoire du concept." *Trivium* 16 (2014): 1–48. http://journals.openedition.org/trivium/4781.

Pratesi, Alessandro. *Genesi e forme del documento medievale.* Re-edition, Rome, 1987.

Raimbault, Ginette, and Caroline Eliacheff. *Les Indomptables. Figures de l'anorexie.* Paris, 1991.

Rava, Eleonora, and Filippo Sedda. "Sulle tracce dell'autore della *Legenda ad usum chori*. Analisi lessicografica e ipotesi di attribuzione." *Archivum Latinitatis Medii Aevi* 69 (2011): 107–75.

La représentation dans la tradition du ius civile en Occident. Actes des "Entretiens Volterra" de Rome, 2–3 juin 1995. In *Mélanges de l'École française de Rome. Moyen Âge* 114 (2002): 7–169.

Ricoeur, Paul. *Memory, History, Forgetting.* Translated by Kathleen Blamey and David Pellauer. Chicago, 2004.

Robson, Michael, and Jens Röhrkasten, eds. *Franciscan Organisation in the Mendicant Context: Formal and Informal Structures of the Friars' Lives and Ministry in the Middle Ages.* Munster, 2010.

Rosier-Catach, Irène. *La Parole efficace. Signe, rituel, sacré.* Preface by Alain de Libera. Paris, 2004.

Rusconi, Roberto. "*Clerici secundum alios clericos*: Francesco d'Assisi e l'istituzione ecclesiastica." In *Frate Francesco d'Assisi*, 71–90. Spoleto, 1994.

———. *Francesco d'Assisi nelle fonti e negli scritti.* Milan, 2002.

Sartre, Jean-Paul. *Saint Genet. Actor and Martyr.* Translated by Bernard Frechtman. Reprint edition, Minneapolis, MN, 2012.

Saxer, Victor. *Le culte de Marie Madeleine en Occident des origines à la fin du Moyen Âge.* Preface by Henri Irénée Marrou. Auxerre, France, 1959.

Schäfer, Thomas. *Die Fusswaschung im monastischen Brauchtum und in der lateinischen Liturgie, liturgiegeschichtliche Untersuchung.* Berlin, 1956.

Sedda, Filippo. "La *Legenda ad usum chori* e il codice assisano 338." *Franciscana* 12 (2010): 43–84.

Showalter, Dennis E. "The Business of Salvation: Authority and Representation in the Thirteenth-Century Dominican Order." *Catholic Historical Review* 58 (1973): 556–74.

Stock, Brian. *The Implications of Literacy: Written Language and Models of Interpretations in the Eleventh and Twelfth Centuries.* Princeton, NJ, 1983.

Todeschini, Giacomo. *Franciscan Wealth: From Voluntary Poverty to Market Society.* St. Bonaventure, NY, 2009.

———. *Visibilmente crudeli. Malviventi, persone sospette e gente qualunque dal Medioevo all'età moderna.* Bologna, 2007.

Toubert, Pierre. *Les structures du Latium médiéval. Le Latium méridional et la Sabine du IXe à la fin du XIIe siècle*, 2 vols. Rome, 1973.

Tugwell, Simon. "Notes on the Life of St Dominic." *Archivum fratrum praedicatorum* 66 (1996): 5–200.
———. *Saint Dominic*. Strasbourg, 1995.
Turcan, Robert. *Constantin en son temps. Le baptême ou la pourpre?* Dijon, 2006.
Uribe, Fernando. *Introducción a las hagiografías de san Francisco y santa Clara de Asís (siglos XIII y XIV)*. Murcia, 1999; new ed., 2010.
Van Dijk, Stephen J. P., and Joan Hazelden Walker. *The Origins of the Modern Liturgy. The Liturgy of the Papal Court and the Franciscan Order in the Thirteenth Century*. Westminster, MD, 1960.
Vauchez, André. "Les Écrits de saint François: une réponse à la contestation hérétique?" In *"Verba Domini mei." Gli "opuscula" di Francesco d'Assisi a 25 anni dalla edizione di Kajetan Esser, OFM*. Edited by Alvaro Cacciotti, 427–37. Rome, 2002.
———. *Francis of Assisi: The Life and Afterlife of a Medieval Saint*. Translated by Michael F. Cusato. New Haven, CT, 2013.
———. "François d'Assise entre littéralisme évangélique et renouveau spirituel." In *Frate Francesco d'Assisi*, 185–98. Spoleto, 1994.
Vauchez, André, and Cécile Caby, eds. *L'histoire des moines, chanoines et religieux au Moyen Âge. Guide de recherche et documents*. Tunhout, 2003.
Ventrone, Paola, and Laura Gaffuri, eds. "Immagini, culti, liturgie: le connotazioni politiche del messaggio religioso—Images, cultes, liturgies: les connotations politiques du message religieux." *Annali di storia moderna e contemporanea* 16 (2010): 107–481. https://books.openedition.org/psorbonne/17025?lang=en.
Veyne, Paul. *When Our World Became Christian, 312–394*. Translated by Janet Lloyd. Cambridge, UK, 2010.
Weber, Max. *Economy and Society*. Edited by Guenther Roth and Claus Wittich. Translated by Ephraim Fischoff et al. Berkeley, CA, 1978.
———. *The Protestant Ethic and the Spirit of Capitalism and Other Writings*. Edited, translated, and introduced by Peter Baehr and Gordon Wells. Hammondsworth, UK, 2002.
Wheeler, Bonnie, ed. *Listening to Heloise: The Voice of a Twelfth-Century Woman*. New York, 2000.
Wilkinson, Maire M. "Laïcs et convers de l'Ordre de Grandmont au XIIe siècle: la création et la destruction d'une fraternité." In *Les Mouvances laïques des Ordres religieux*, edited by Nicole Bouter, 35–50. Saint-Étienne, 1996.
Zimmerman, Michel, ed. *"Auctor et auctoritas." Invention et conformisme dan l'écriture médiévale*. Paris, 2001.
Zink, Michel. *Poésie et conversion au Moyen Âge*. Paris, 2003.

Additional Bibliography from the Translator's Introduction

Accrocca, Felice. "Da Tommaso a Tommaso. La *Vita beati patris nostri Francisci* nel panorama dell'agiografia francescana," *Frate Francesco* 83 (2017): 229–49.
———. "*Nolo carnifex fieri*. Ancora su Francesco d'Assisi et il governo." In *L'épaisseur du temps*, edited by Field, Guida, and Poirel, 147–58.
Alberzoni, Maria Pia. *Clare of Assisi and the Poor Sisters in the Thirteenth Century*. St. Bonaventure, NY, 2004.

BIBLIOGRAPHY

Bériou, Nicole. *Religion et communication. Un autre regard sur la prédication au Moyen Âge*. Geneva, 2018.

Bériou, Nicole, Jacques Dalarun, and Dominique Poirel, eds. *Le manuscrit franciscain retrouvé*. Paris, 2021.

Bériou, Nicole, and Bernard Hodel, eds. and trans. *Saint Dominique de l'ordre des frères prêcheurs. Témoignages écrits fin XIIe—XIVe siècle*. Paris, 2019.

Bianchi, Nunzio. "Sulla Vita beati patris nostri Francisci di Tommaso da Celano." *Quaderni di storia* 87 (2018): 307–32.

Blastic, Michael W., Jay M. Hammond, and J. A. Wayne Hellmann, eds. *The Writings of Clare of Assisi: Letters, Form of Life, Testament and Blessing*. St. Bonaventure, NY, 2011.

Bösch, Paul. "Die *Vita brevior* des Franziskus von Assisi und ihre entfernten verwandten." *Archivum franciscanum historicum* 111 (2018): 3–32.

———. "Die *Vita brevior* und drei Verslegenden als Spiegel verschollener Franziskusviten." *Archivum franciscanum historicum* 110 (2017): 125–94.

Carney, Margaret. *Light of Assisi: The Story of Saint Clare*. Cincinnati, 2021.

Cusato, Michael F. "The Minorite Vocation of the *Fratres laici* in the Franciscan Order (13th–Early 14th Centuries)." *Archivum franciscanum historicum* 112 (2019): 21–124.

Da Silva Gonçalves, Gustavo. "Uma nova história de Francisco de Assis? Possibilidades de pesquisas a partir de uma recente descoberta (*Vita beati patris nostri Francisci*, de Tomás de Celano)." *Ars historica* 15 (2017): 43–61.

Dalarun, Jacques. "L'avis des autres." *Critique, Giorgio Agamben*, 836–837 (2017): 109–21.

———. *Claire de Rimini. Entre sainteté et hérésie*. Paris, 1999.

———. "Codicologie et histoire des textes. La *Vita beati patris nostri Francisci* et ses miracles." *Archivum franciscanum historicum* 114 (2021): 557–84.

———. "Du procès de canonisation à la Légende latine de Claire d'Assise." *Memini. Travaux et documents* 24 (2018). https://journals.openedition.org/memini/1044.

———. *François d'Assise en questions*. Paris, 2016.

———. "*Lapsus linguae*." *La légende de Claire de Rimini*. Spoleto, 1994.

———. *Modèle monastique. Un laboratoire de la modernité*. Paris, 2019.

———. "The New Francis in the *Rediscovered Life* (*Vita brevior*) of Thomas of Celano." In *Ordo et sanctitas: The Franciscan Spiritual Journey in Theology and Hagiography. Essays in Honor of J. A. Wayne Hellmann, O. F. M. Conv.*, edited by Michael F. Cusato, Timothy J. Johnson, and Steven J. McMichael, 32–46. Leiden, 2017.

———. "Une nouvelle source pour la Légende des trois compagnons de François d'Assise." In *Fleur de clergie. Mélanges en l'honneur de Jean-Yves Tilliette*, edited by Olivier Collet, Yasmina Foehr-Janssens, and Jean-Claude Mühlethaler, 849–70. Geneva, 2019.

———. "Pour poursuivre le dialogue sur la *Vie retrouvée* de Thomas de Celano." *Collectanea franciscana* 86 (2016): 759–63.

———. "Le premier chapitre général. Bologna, 1220." In *Domenico e Bologna. Genesi e sviluppo dell'Ordine dei Frati Predicatori*. Forthcoming.

———. "The Rediscovered Manuscript: A Story of Friendship." *Franciscan Studies* 74 (2016): 231–38, 259–62.

———. "Résilience de la mémoire. Le procès de canonisation de Clare d'Assise et ses marges." *Frate Francesco* 78 (2012): 317–36.

———. "Risposte a quattro domande di Luigi Pellegrini." *Fogli. Rivista dell'Associazione Biblioteca Salita dei Frati di Lugano* 38 (2017): 17–18.

———. "La ritrovata *Vita beatissimi patris nostri Francisci* (*Vita brevior*) di Tommaso da Celano." *Fogli. Rivista dell'Associazione Biblioteca Salita dei Frati di Lugano* 38 (2017): 1–12.

———. "Robert d'Arbrissel et les femmes." *Annales. Économies, sociétés, civilisations* 29 (1984): 1140–60.

———. *Robert d'Arbrissel, fondateur de Fontevraud*. Paris, 1986; 2nd ed. 2007.

———. *La sainte et la cité. Micheline de Pesaro († 1356), tertiaire franciscaine*. Rome, 1992.

———. "Thome Celanensis *Vita beati patris nostri Francisci* (*Vita brevior*). Présentation et édition critique." *Analecta Bollandiana* 133 (2015): 23–86.

———. "Une *Vie* inédite de François d'Assise par Thomas de Celano." *Académie des Inscriptions & Belles-Lettres. Comptes rendus des séances de l'année 2015, janvier–février*, 2016, 57–69.

———. "La *Vie retrouvée* en questions." *Frate Francesco* 83 (2017): 250–90.

Dalarun, Jacques, Thierry Buquet, Gilles Kagan, Guy Lanoë, Claudia Rabel, and Véronique Trémault. *La lettre volée. Le manuscrit 193 de la Bibliothèque municipale de Vendôme*. Ædilis, publications scientifiques, 1. Paris, 2003. http://lettrevolee.irht.cnrs.fr.

Dalarun, Jacques, Sean L. Field, and Valerio Cappozzo. *A Female Apostle in Medieval Italy: The Life of Clare of Rimini*. Philadelphia, 2023.

Dóci, Viliam Štefan, and Gianni Festa, eds. *Fra trionfi et sconfitte: La "Politica della santità" dell'Ordine dei Predicatori*. Rome, 2021.

Field, Sean L. "New Light on the 1230s: History, Hagiography, and Thomas of Celano's *The Life of Our Blessed Father Francis*." *Franciscan Studies* 74 (2016): 239–47.

———. "La *Vita beati patris nostri Francisci* au cœur d'un triptyque franciscain." In *Le manuscrit franciscain retrouvé*, edited by Nicole Bériou, Jacques Dalarun, and Dominique Poirel, 297–313. Paris, 2021.

Field, Sean L., Marco Guida, and Dominique Poirel, eds. *L'épaisseur du temps. Mélanges offerts à Jacques Dalarun*. Turnhout, 2021.

Guida, Marco. "Da Bartolomeo da Spoleto a Battista da Perugia: i processi di canonizzazione di Chiara d'Assisi." In *L'épaisseur du temps*, edited by Field, Guida, and Poirel, 213–34.

———. "Dalla *Vita beati Francisci* alla *Vita brevior* di Tommaso da Celano: per un confronto sinottico." *Frate Francesco* 83 (2017): 191–220.

Horowski, Aleksander. "Intorno alla *Vita ritrovata di san Francesco* edita da Jacques Dalarun." *Collectanea franciscana* 86 (2016): 269–89.

Johnson, Timothy J. "In the Workshop of a Theologian: The *Life of Our Blessed Father Francis* by Thomas of Celano." *Franciscan Studies* 74 (2016): 249–58.

Knox, Lezlie, and David B. Couturier, eds., *Franciscan Women: Female Identities and Religious Culture, Medieval and Beyond*. St. Bonaventure, NY, 2020.

Knox, Lezlie S. *Creating Clare of Assisi: Female Franciscan Identities in Later Medieval Italy*. Leiden, 2008.

Kumka, Emil, ed. *Tommaso da Celano, agiografo di san Francesco. Atti del Convegno internazionale, Roma, 29 gennaio 2016.* Rome, 2016.

Maggioni, Giovanni Paolo. "L'edizione critica della *Vita beati patris nostri Francisci* di Tommaso da Celano." *Frate Francesco* 83 (2017): 181–90.

Melville, Gert. "The Dominican *Constitutiones.*" In *A Companion to Medieval Rules and Customaries,* edited by Krijn Pansters, 253–81. Leiden, 2020.

Mooney, Catherine M. *Clare of Assisi and the Thirteenth-Century Church: Religious Women, Rules, and Resistance.* Philadelphia, 2016.

Mueller, Joan, ed., *A Companion to Clare of Assisi: Life, Writings, and Spirituality.* Leiden, 2010.

———. *The Privilege of Poverty: Clare of Assisi, Agnes of Prague, and the Struggle for a Franciscan Rule for Women.* University Park, PA, 2006.

Pellegrini, Luigi. "Considerazzioni sulla *Vita brevior* ritrovata." *Fogli. Rivista dell'Associazione Biblioteca Salita dei Frati di Lugano* 38 (2017): 13–16.

Piron, Sylvain. "François d'Assise et les créatures: le témoignage de la *Vita brevior.*" In *La restauration de la création. Quelle place pour les animaux?*, edited by Michele Cutino, Isabel Iribarren, and Françoise Vinel, 231–41. Leiden, 2018.

———. *Généalogie de la morale économique.* Brussels, 2020.

Poirel, Dominique. "Un écrit inédit de François d'Assise? L'homélie sur le *Pater* de Paris, Bibl. nat. de France, nal 3245." *Académie des Inscriptions & Belles-Lettres. Comptes rendus des séances de l'année 2016, janvier–mars,* 2017, 415–85.

Postec, Amandine. "Un nouveau témoin des sermons d'Antoine de Padue." *Il Santo* 56 (2016): 231–42.

Roest, Bert. "The Franciscan School System: Re-Assessing the Early Evidence (ca. 1220–1260)." In *Franciscan Organisation in the Mendicant Context: Formal and Informal Structures of the Friars' Lives and Ministry in the Middle Ages,* edited by Michael Robson and Jens Röhrkasten, 269–96. Berlin, 2010.

———. *Order and Disorder: The Poor Clares between Foundation and Reform.* Leiden, 2013.

Sedda, Filippo. "Vita brevior o breviatio liturgica?" *Frate Francesco* 83 (2017): 221–28.

Şenocak, Neslihan. *The Poor and the Perfect: The Rise of Learning in the Franciscan Order, 1209–1310.* Ithaca, NY, 2012.

Thompson, Augustine. *Dominican Brothers. Conversi, Lay, and Cooperator Friars.* Chicago, 2017.

———. *Francis of Assisi: A New Biography.* Ithaca, NY, 2012.

Index

Abelard. *See* Peter Abelard
Achilles, 45
Agamben, Giorgio, 73
Agamemnon, 149
Agnellus of Pisa, 122, 132
Agnes (Clare of Assisi's sister), 14, 23, 43
Agnes of Oportulo, 8–9, 13, 24–25, 32, 36–39, 47–48
Agnes of Prague, 51–53
Albert of Pisa, 121–24, 127, 129–30, 132
Alexander IV, Pope, 7, 11, 17, 46–48
  See also Rainaldo, Cardinal
Althusser, Louis, 59–60
Amata, Sister, 24
Ambazac, 88
Ambrose of Milan, 39, 151, 169
Ammannati, Giulia, 176
Andrew, Brother, 70–71
Angarde (prioress of Fontevraud), 76
Angelico of Spoleto, 21
Angelo, Brother, 25
Angeluccia, Sister, 21
Anselm of Laon, 79
Anthony of Padua, 129
Arendt, Hannah, 59–60
Argenteuil, 79, 83
Arnulf, Brother, 126
Assisi
  commune of, 26
  social classes in, 23–30
Astralabe (son of Peter Abelard and Heloise), 79
Augustine of Hippo, 48, 168
Augustinian Rule. *See* Rule of St. Augustine

Baldwin of Brandenburg, Brother, 120
Balvina, Sister, 24, 28, 41
Bartholomew of Spoleto, Bishop, 7
Bartoli Langeli, Attilio, 160, 162–64, 177, 182
Baudri of Dol, 74

Beatrice (Clare of Assisi's sister), 14, 23–24
Becker, Alfons, 192
Benedetta (abbess of San Damiano), 21, 25
Benedictine Rule. *See* Rule of St. Benedict
Benedict of Aniane, 65, 67, 198
Benedict of Nursia, Saint, 15, 19, 65, 67, 72, 84, 86, 151, 202
  See also Rule of St. Benedict
Benvenuta of Lady Diambra, 25, 27
Benvenuta of Perugia, Sister, 8–9, 13–14, 24, 36–37, 39
Beranger (father of Peter Abelard), 83
Bernardino (Clare of Assisi's great-grandfather), 25
Bernardo, Brother, 14
Bernard of Clairvaux, 79, 113
Bertrand, Brother, 104
Bloch, Marc, 189
Bona of Guelfuccio, 24–25, 27–28, 37
Bonaventure (Franciscan minister general), 117
Boniface VIII, Pope, 157
Bruno of Cologne, 19
Bynum, Caroline, 197

Caesaria of Arles, 17
Caesarius of Arles, 17
Caesarius of Speyer, 120–21
Camaldoli, 19, 93
Capitaneo of Collemedio, 24
Cecilia, Sister, 14, 21, 24
Charlemagne, 157
Charles the Simple, King, 46
Charles V, Emperor, 47
Christian paradox, 3, 54–61, 73–74, 201
Cicero, 168
Cîteaux, 19, 65, 93
Clare of Assisi, Saint, 114, 169, 197–98, 202
  as abbess, 12, 36–38, 65
  birth of, 7

225

226 INDEX

Clare of Assisi, Saint (*continued*)
  canonization process of, 7–13, 21
  death of, 7, 23, 25
  enters religion life, 8–9, 14, 27, 42–43
  exile in Perugia, 26
  form of life of, 17–18, 20–21, 47–48, 50, 180
  humility of, 7, 11
  letters to Agnes of Prague, 51–53
  social status of, 11, 23–24, 27
  virginity of, 37, 39
  vision of the breast, 41, 169
  washes feet, 7–9, 12–13
Clement VII, Pope, 47
Cluny, 32, 34, 36–37, 65, 101
Constance of Hungary, 51
Constantine, Emperor, 53
converts
  at Fontevraud, 75–77, 93, 107, 135
  in the Dominican Order, 105–6, 109, 131, 135
  at Grandmont, 93–102, 135
  at the Paraclete, 82–83, 135
  old style vs. new style, 19
Cristiana of Bernardo of Suppo, Sister, 42
Cristiano of Parisse, 24
Cristina, Sister, 24
Cusato, Michael, 181
Cyprian of Carthage, 151

Damasus, Pope, 54–55
Debord, Guy, 201
Diambra, Lady, 27
Dominic, Saint, 103–10, 114, 116, 127, 135–36, 138, 202
  attempts to resign, 108, 110, 136
  canonization process of, 103–5, 107–8
Dominican Constitutions, 105, 108–10
Duby, Georges, 189, 202
Dudo of Saint-Quentin, 46

Elias of Cortona, 10, 123–28, 131–32, 135–36, 167
Ermengarde (abbess of the Paraclete), 79
Eusebius of Caesarea, 53
Eustochium, 85

Favarone (Clare of Assisi's father), 23–25, 27, 37
Filippa, Sister, 8–10, 13–14, 24, 36–39, 41
Filippo, Brother, 14
Fleury, 65
Florentina of Seville, 17

Fontevraud, 19, 42, 70–78, 87, 93, 100, 136
  Peter Abelard refers to, 80–82
  statutes of, 75, 82, 85–86
Foucault, Michel, 1–2, 148–59, 172–73, 183–85, 188, 196–201
Francesca, Sister, 24
Franciscan Rule. *See Regula bullata*; *Regula non bullata*
Francis of Assisi, Saint, 14, 111–19, 124, 127–28, 130, 133, 135, 138–39, 189–95, 202
  armed as knight, 26
  autograph note to Brother Leo, 160–87, 199–200
  in Clare of Assisi's vision, 41
  cuts Clare's hair, 43
  as deacon, 123, 132
  death of, 10
  education of, 165
  in Giles of Assisi's vision, 125
  in John of Bannister's vision, 125
  literacy of, 163–64
  maternal government of, 167–72, 196–98
  receives tonsure, 116–17
  resignation of, 136, 186
  writes *Canticle of Brother Sun*, 22, 24
  writes Form of living for Clare, 15, 17, 49
Frederick II, Emperor, 39, 44, 51–52
Fulbert (canon of Paris, Heloise's uncle), 79
Fulbert of Chartres, 192–93
Fulk of Toulouse, 103–4
Fulk V of Anjou, 77

Gauchet, Marcel, 137, 200
Genet, Jean, 2, 178
Geoffrey of Mayenne, 71, 101
Geoffrey of Vendôme, 101
Gilbert (bishop of Paris), 81
Gilbert of Sempringham, 19, 91
Giles of Assisi, Brother, 125, 130–31
Giorgio of Ugone of Tebalduccio, 25
Giovanni of San Paolo, Cardinal, 116–17
Giovanni of Ventura of Assisi, 25, 27
Girard, René, 178
Gogol, Nikolai, 150, 157
governmentality, 3, 146–48, 151, 153, 194, 196, 199–201
Grande Chartreuse, 19, 93
Grandmont, 88–102, 105, 112–14, 127–28, 136, 138
  election of priors, 97–102
Gratian, 94, 192

INDEX

Gregorian reform, 47, 72–74, 93, 100, 102, 157, 198–99
Gregory I the Great, Pope, 35–36, 48, 65, 68, 89, 150–51, 157, 174
Gregory VII, Pope, 47, 72–73, 88
Gregory IX, Pope, 10, 15, 43–44, 46, 124, 126, 129, 194
  Decretales of, 116
  letters to Agnes of Prague, 52–53
  See also Hugolino, Cardinal
Gregory of Nazianzus, 153
Gualterio Cacciaguerra of Spello, 21, 24
Guelfuccio of Assisi, 8, 23–24, 27
Guida, Marco, 11
Guido II (bishop of Assisi), 24
Guiduccia (wife of Hugolino of Pietro Girardone), 27
Guyotjeannin, Olivier, 194

Haymo of Faversham, 122, 124, 129
Hector, 45
Heloise of the Paraclete, 20, 79–87
Henry III, King of England, 51
Henry VI, Emperor, 26
Henry of Treviso, 122, 130
Heresende of Montsoreau, 75–76
Hirsau, 19, 93
Honorius III, Pope, 15, 101, 103, 105, 111, 191, 194
Hugh Lacerta, 88, 94
Hugolino, Cardinal, 15–17, 65, 194
  See also Gregory IX, Pope
Hugolino of Pietro Girardone, 25, 27

Iliad, the, 45
Illuminata of Pisa, Sister, 48
Innocent III, Pope, 46, 103–4, 111, 116, 185, 191
Innocent IV, Pope, 16–17, 46–48, 131
Isabelle of France, 33

Jan Hus, 155
Jerome, Saint, 55, 83, 85–86, 137, 151, 179
Joachim of Fiore, 156
John, Brother (author of *The Beginning of the Order*), 116, 194
John, King of England, 192
John Cassian, 151
John Chrysostom, 151
John of Bannister, Brother, 125, 130–31
John of Spain, Brother, 103–8, 110
John Parenti, 123–24, 129, 132
Johnson, Timothy J., 38

John the Simple, Brother, 118, 133
John Wyclif, 155
John XXII, Pope, 98
Jonas of Orléans, 198
Jordan, William Chester, 137
Jordan of Giano, 120–24, 127–28, 191
Jordan of Saxony, 104–5

Kantorowicz, Ernst, 47

Lactantius, 53
Lawrence the Englishman, Brother, 104
Leander of Seville, 17
Le Goff, Jacques, 137, 197
Leo, Brother, 118, 133, 160–87, 195, 198
  corrects Francis's autograph note, 166, 175, 182
Leonardo of Ghislerio, 8, 24
Letter of Philibert. *See* Fulbert of Chartres
Louis IX of France, Saint, 33, 137, 158
Louis the Pious, Emperor, 65, 198–99
Lucy (Peter Abelard's mother), 82

Maire Vigueur, Jean-Claude, 192–93
mandatum, 32–34, 36, 38
Mannes (Dominic's brother), 104
Marbode of Rennes, 71, 101
Martha and Mary (Biblical story), 46, 75, 78, 91, 96–97, 111, 127, 134–36
Martino of Coccorano, 24, 28, 41
Marx, Karl, 60
Mary Magdalene, 35–36, 38, 82
Mathilda of Anjou, 77
Matthew "the abbot," 104
Melville, Gert, 134
Menestò, Enrico, 160
Michael of Spain, Brother, 104
Milo of Benevento, 88
Montesquieu, 66
Muret (hermitage of), 88, 94–102, 112, 128

Newman, Barbara, 202
Nicholas of the Rhine, 121, 129
Nietzsche, Friedrich, 201
Norbert of Xanten, 19

Odier, Brother, 104
Odilon of Cluny, 32, 34
Odo of Cheriton, 168–69
Odysseus, 45
Odyssey, the, 45
Offreducio (Clare of Assisi's grandfather), 25

INDEX

Oportulo of Bernardo of Assisi (*podestà* of Assisi), 8, 16, 24
Ortolana (Clare of Assisi's mother), 23–24, 27
Ottokar I of Bohemia, 51

Pacifica of Guelfuccio, Sister, 8–9, 12–14, 23–25, 27–28, 36
Paolazzi, Carlo, 163, 171–72, 182
Paraclete, the, 20, 79–87, 136
paradox. *See* Christian paradox
pastoral power, 146–56, 173, 180, 183–84, 188, 196–98
Patroclus, 45
Penelope, 45
Pepin I of Aquitaine, 198
Peregrine of Bologna, 132
Peter Abelard, 20, 79–87, 89, 91, 93, 136–37, 202
Peter Bernard of Boschiac, 95
Peter Cattani, 123, 129, 132
Peter Lombard, 56
Petronilla of Chemillé, 76–78, 136
Philibert. *See* Fulbert of Chartres
Philip IV, King of France, 157
Pietro of Bernardone (Francis of Assisi's father), 26, 111, 168, 188
Pietro of Damiano of Assisi, 23, 25, 27, 37
Pillius of Medicina (glossator), 192
Plato, 149
Portiuncula, 14, 43, 133, 176
Prémontré, 19, 93
Priam, 45
Prouille, 114

Rainaldo, Cardinal, 17, 49
  See also Alexander IV, Pope
Rainiero of Bernardo of Assisi, 25, 27
Regula bullata, 111, 115–16, 168–69, 185–86, 191
Regula non bullata, 111–12, 115, 168, 180, 191
Riccerio, Brother, 189–90
Richard of Cornwall, 125, 131
Richard of Ingworth, 122
Ricoeur, Paul, 1
Robert of Arbrissel, 42, 70–78, 81–87, 89, 91, 100–101, 112, 135–36, 139, 202
  attacked by Roscelin of Compiègne, 81–82
  referred to by Peter Abelard, 81–82
Robert of Molesmes, 19
Rollo (jarl of the Normans), 46

Romulus Augustulus, Emperor, 59
Roscelin of Compiègne, 79, 81
Rudolf of Faenza, Brother, 107–8
Rufino, Brother, 25
Rule for Hermitages, 111, 127, 133, 168, 186, 189
Rule of Fructuarius, 68
Rule of Grandmont, 90–91, 94–100, 105–6, 135, 200
Rule of St. Augustine, 20, 71, 105
Rule of St. Benedict, 15, 20, 32, 36, 65–69, 71–72, 74, 78, 91, 98–99, 116, 134, 150, 198
Rule of the Master, 65

Saint-Denis, 79
Saint-Gildas de Rhuys, 79
Saint-Romain (Toulouse), 104, 106
Salimbene of Adam, 39, 125–28
San Damiano, 7, 9, 114
  serving sisters of, 14–22, 48–49
  social status and, 23–30
San Paolo delle Abbadesse, 14, 43
San Rufino (cathedral of), 23, 25
Sant'Angelo di Panzo, 14
Sartre, Jean-Paul, 2
Sempringham, 19, 93, 134
Simon of Montfort, 103–4
Smaragdus of Saint-Mihiel, 198
Spoleto note. *See* Francis of Assisi: autograph note to Brother Leo
Stephen of Liciac, 88, 94
Stephen of Muret, 88–89, 94–96, 101, 105, 132, 191, 202
Stirnemann, Patricia, 79

Theodosius, Emperor, 53
Thomas of Celano, 7, 10
  education of, 10–11, 40
  as Clare of Assisi's hagiographer, 7–13, 20, 28, 38–40, 43–44, 47, 49
  as Francis of Assisi's hagiographer, 10, 116–18, 130, 177, 183, 185, 189–90
Thomas of Eccleston, 121–25, 127, 130–31
Todeschini, Giacomo, 118
Toubert, Pierre, 193

Urban III, Pope, 100

Vallombrosa, 19, 93
Vauchez, André, 26, 188
Vitalis of Aversa, 44

Weber, Max, 134
Wenceslas of Bohemia, 51–52
William Ætheling, 77
William Durand, 46
William of Aquitaine, 192–93
William of Auvergne, 79
William of Champeaux, 79

William of Hirsau, 107
William of Saint-Thierry, 79
William of Treignac, 100

Yves of Chartres, 192

Zink, Michel, 202